CANADIANS & THE IRS

What You Need to Know About Uncle Sam

ANGELA PRETEAU

WINNIPEG, MANITOBA, CANADA

KNOWLEDGE BUREAU
NEWSBOOKS

Angela Preteau

CANADIANS & THE IRS
What You Need to Know About Uncle Sam

Library and Archives Canada Cataloguing in Publication

Preteau, Angela, 1968-, author
        Canadians & the IRS : what you need to know about
Uncle Sam / Angela Preteau.

Includes index.
ISBN 978-1-927495-17-9 (pbk.)

1. Canadians--United States--Finance, Personal.
2. Canadians--Taxation--United States. 3. Canadians--
Legal status, laws, etc.--United States. 4. United States.
Internal Revenue Service. I. Title. II. Title: Canadians
and the IRS.

HG181.P74 2013   332.024008911073   C2013-907590-9

Published by:
Knowledge Bureau, Inc.
187 St. Mary's Road, Winnipeg, Manitoba, Canada, R2H 1J2
204-953-4769
Email: reception@knowledgebureau.com

Publisher: Evelyn Jacks
Editors: Greer Jacks, Larry Frostiak, and Karen Milner
Cover Design and Layout: Evelyn Jacks and Carly Thompson
Page Design and Layout: Karen Armstrong Graphic Design

MIX
Paper from
responsible sources
FSC® C016245

Table of Contents

Acknowledgements

I would like to dedicate this book to my husband Dean and my son Tanner. My husband is the inspiration behind my desire to learn about U.S. taxes and become a U.S. CPA because he is a dual citizen of Canada and the U.S. Without my family's love and support I would not have had the time to write this book; thank you and I love you!

I would also like to thank Larry Frostiak for his continued support, encouragement and guidance throughout my professional career and assistance in the editing of this book.

Introduction

If you are amongst the millions of people living in Canada who are trying to understand what the U.S. tax filing rules are, what they mean and how they could affect you, **you need to read this book**!

Canada-U.S. tax filings are a real issue for both Canadian residents with investments or property in the south and for U.S. citizens who live in Canada. The sensational media coverage about U.S. and Canadian government crackdowns on international tax cheats has caused *anxiety, bordering on hysteria for some,* especially with regard to the big penalties for missing U.S. filing requirements.

Numerous people have come to see me in utter panic about these "new U.S. filing requirements." Many have lived in Canada for 30 or 40 plus years and have never filed in the U.S.; some didn't even realize they were U.S. citizens. The questions I am repeatedly asked are:

1. Do I have to file U.S. taxes?
2. Will I owe taxes in the U.S.?
3. Is the IRS going to take my life savings?

What I can tell you is…please, relax. Frankly, much of this is unnecessary panic and anguish.

With this book at your side, I am going to take you through the rights and obligations of Canadians and what they need to know about Uncle Sam. And, you'll find the information easy to digest and understand, so that you can stay on the right side of tax laws.

For instance, 3 facts you absolutely *need to know* are these:

1. U.S. citizens living in Canada may be required to file a U.S. income tax return to report their worldwide income, but in most cases they won't owe U.S. income tax.

2. If you are physically present in the U.S. for more than 183 days over a 3 year period, you can be deemed a U.S. resident for tax purposes and therefore, required to file a U.S. tax return to report your worldwide income. But there is a reprieve: if you meet the closer connection exception.

3. Canadians owning U.S. situs assets can be subject to U.S. estate tax, but they are also entitled to a proportionate share of the U.S. lifetime estate tax exemption.

Also, did you know…?

•   You might be a U.S. citizen by naturalization *if you have a U.S. citizen parent, therefore subjecting you to U.S. tax filing rules.*

•   Employment income by a non-resident under $10,000 that is earned in either Canada or the U.S. can be *tax exempt* in that non-resident country under the income tax treaty.

•   The U.S. limits the ability of certain professionals to incorporate which can result in *severe double taxation* if proper planning is not used.

Remember; even if you consider yourself a Canadian, the U.S. rules may apply to you and may significantly impact your tax and overall financial situation. If you were born in the U.S. or born to U.S. parents, you will likely be considered to be a U.S. citizen and subject to all the U.S. tax laws and foreign reporting requirements even if you don't live in the U.S. or have never lived or worked in the U.S.

You should also know that Canada and the U.S. do not tax all income in the same manner, so in some situations, *tax can result on one side of the border but not on the other*.

If any of these facts concern you, you need more information to understand your responsibilities and tax filing obligations. In this book, you'll learn how to keep more of your hard-earned money if you are a Canadian with income or assets in the U.S. or a U.S. citizen living in Canada. For example:

Chapter 1 Tax Filing Requirements discusses how you are taxed, depending on your status and/or citizenship in both Canada and the U.S. U.S. tax is based on citizenship and Canadian tax is based on residency, so the filing requirements can be slightly different in both countries. You'll learn what you need to know about residency, residential ties and how you can be a deemed resident of one country even if you are physically living in the other country. Most important, find out what the filing deadlines are in both Canada and the U.S. and what forms to file depending on your status.

Chapter 2 Reporting Income & Assets provides you with the real facts about the differences in the Canadian and U.S. tax systems. What are those common tax discrepancies that we all need to be aware of to stop tax erosion? Even Grandma needs to know how her gambling winnings in the U.S. will be taxed! In fact, gambling winnings are taxed differently in both countries and just because these are not taxed in Canada doesn't mean that tax is not applicable in the U.S. Another important tax discrepancy involves family businesses and homes: the U.S. does not have a lifetime capital gains exemption and they have a cap on the capital gains sheltered for a principal residence disposition.

Chapter 3 Reporting Foreign Holdings is really important because it sets the record straight on foreign asset reporting – a hot topic these days in both Canada and the U.S. Find out the filing requirements for Canadians holdings including U.S. investments over a certain threshold. Find out about the filing requirements that exist for U.S. citizens and residents with foreign accounts and investments held outside the U.S. Keep in mind that you can be living in the U.S. and have these filings requirements or living outside the U.S. and have these filing requirements as well. Canadians have foreign asset reporting requirements, too.

Chapter 4 Snowbirds and Uncle Sam focuses on the tax life of a Snowbird. Exactly what do you need to know about Uncle Sam if you winter down south? The amount of time you spend in the U.S. and how to calculate the number of days under the U.S. substantial presence test is very important, so you don't get caught in an unfavourable tax position.

Chapter 5 Non-residents owning U.S. real estate asks, what exactly do Canadians need to know about owning U.S. real estate? In this chapter, learn how different ownership options lead to different tax consequences. Then you'll know what forms are required to be filed, if any. More and more Canadians are purchasing U.S. real estate for personal and/or rental use so this is a very important topic to understand *before* the purchase is made.

Chapter 6 Investing in the U.S. and U.S. source income asks these questions; will your Canadian pensions be taxed in the U.S., and will your U.S. pension be taxed in Canada? One of the big differences that everyone needs to be aware of is that an early withdrawal of a U.S. pension almost always results in a 10% early withdrawal penalty on top of the regular income tax. Withholding taxes applicable on U.S. investment income earned by Canadians and potential filing requirements in the U.S. are also discussed.

Chapter 7 Married to a U.S. citizen and moving between countries. Married to an American? What are the tax implications of marrying someone from across the border and moving between countries? Canada can impose a departure tax when leaving Canada but the U.S. only applies an exit tax when renouncing one's citizenship or long-term residency status. Filing a joint tax return with a U.S. citizen spouse isn't necessarily a good idea because it exposes the non-U.S. citizen to all the U.S. tax laws.

Chapter 8 Going to school or working temporarily in the U.S. Did your child win a scholarship to a prestigious U. S. School? What are the tax implications? This chapter details the tax treatment of foreign students attending college in the U.S. and also explains the tax treatment and options available when working in the U.S. on a temporary basis. You can be a non-resident of Canada and a resident of the U.S. while physically working in the U.S. or you can still be a Canadian resident and non-resident of the U.S. while physically working in the U.S., your circumstance will generally determine the tax treatment.

Chapter 9 U.S. Inheritances When is the inheritance from your U. S. based parents taxable and in which country? When you inherit property from a decedent, you generally inherit it at the fair market value on the date of death, which means that you only pay tax on the appreciation of the property after it is actually sold. A common statement made by many people is that inheritances are taxed in the U.S. but not in Canada and this is not entirely true.

Chapter 10 Doing business in the U.S. Is your online company taking off in the U.S.? What are your tax filing obligations when you start earning business income in the U.S.? The U.S. has a number of different business structures available when conducting your affairs in the U.S., whether your business is rental property or operating a viable small business. Canada treats many of these structures differently than the U.S. and if you are not careful, the end result can be double taxation.

Chapter 11 I'm Canadian but could I be an American too. Can you be a U. S. citizen for tax filing purposes and not know it? The arms of Uncle Sam indeed have a long reach! This is a statement we hear more often than we'd like but it's true. Did you know that you could be a citizen of the U.S. without even being born there? Citizenship in the U.S. means tax obligations and because it is a criminal offense not to file your taxes or abide by the numerous reporting requirements, it is IMPORTANT for you to know your status and what it means for you.

Chapter 12 U.S. gift & estate tax for a non-resident Do gift and estate tax only apply to U.S. citizens and residents? No, in fact, they can apply to non-residents as well but Canadians only need to worry about this in certain circumstances. Owning U.S. assets could subject you to these rules in this chapter, we will shed some light on what it all means.

I wrote this book to help you answer all of these questions and because I hope to help you make more informed decisions if any of the situations discussed in this book apply to you....I hope you enjoy it.

Angela Preteau.

CHAPTER 1

Tax Filing Requirements

HOT OFF THE PRESS! "Harper Government cracks down on off-shore tax evasion with launch of paid informants program… strengthens foreign income reporting requirements… and proposes the mandatory reporting to the CRA of international electronic funds transfers over $10,000, which will help identify international non-compliance."

CRA NEWS RELEASE, JANUARY 14, 2014

Cross border taxation has become alarming for many taxpayers who live in Canada. Whether you are a Canadian with property in the United States (U. S.), or a U. S. citizen living in Canada, there is a lot you need to know about Uncle Sam to manage your tax risk.

So who's at risk? If you can answer yes to any of these questions, it's possible you are:

- Do you own real estate in the U.S.?
- Do you have a bank account or prepaid credit cards south of the border?
- Are you a U.S. citizen living in Canada?

Do you know when to file a tax return in either or both countries? If you are not sure – **and millions in your situation are not** – you'll want to read this chapter. It explains some of the more common areas of taxation that have similarities and differences in the rules between Canada and the U. S. so that you can have a good basic understanding of the tax filing obligations that come with both citizenship and residency.

Citizen or Resident?

One of the most important ways that the U.S. and Canadian tax systems differ is in their very basic tax filing obligations. Consider this:

Tax Filing Obligations in the United States. Unlike most countries, the U.S. bases its tax system on *citizenship*.

No matter where U.S. citizens live in the world, they must abide by the U.S. tax laws and could possibly be subject to tax in the United States of America on their worldwide income.

This may also be true in certain situations (if you hold a green card for example) and if you are a U.S. resident *but not a citizen*. A U.S. resident, including a permanent resident, aka green card holder, is required to abide by the same tax rules as a U.S. citizen, and even non-residents can also be subject to the tax laws of the U.S. if they have U.S. source income (i.e., income that comes from an investment originating in the U.S.).

Tax Filing Obligations in Canada. The Canadian tax system is based on *residency*, which means, unless you are a non-resident who has Canadian source income of some kind, you will only be subject to income tax in Canada if you are a Canadian resident.

 Canadians are required to report worldwide income in Canadian funds.

Keep in mind that there are different types of "residents." For instance, there are factual residents and deemed residents; knowing which one you are, is important. We'll expand on this a bit later.

Taxable Income. Various types of income are taxed differently within Canada and the United States as well. For example:

- Gambling/lottery winnings are taxable in the U.S. but not taxable in Canada;
- Capital dividends are tax exempt in Canada but fully taxable in the U.S.;
- Taxable capital gains are taxed at marginal rates in Canada on only 50% of the gain whereas they are subject to set rates in the U.S. depending on the longevity of the gain on 100% of the gain;
- Canada allows every individual access to what is called a capital gains exemption but there is no such thing in the U.S.; and
- Tax rates for corporations are generally more favourable in Canada than in the U.S. if you operate an active business.

All of these items will be discussed in more detail later. But for now, let's drill down on the definition of residency; frankly, it's often quite difficult to determine.

Residency

Residency is a key factor in any tax environment and can be determined by many factors but it is mainly determined by the following:

- physical presence (i.e., number of days in a country);
- residential ties to a country; and
- a person's intentions.

Keep in mind that for tax purposes you can only be considered a resident of one place at a time and also, *citizenship and residency are two entirely different concepts* and can completely change a person's situation when it comes to income tax filing obligations. Where an individual could be a resident of both Canada and the U.S., residency status will be determined in accordance with the tax treaty the countries have with one another,.

 Tax Treaties. At the time of writing, Canada had 92 tax treaties with various countries around the world. These are also known as tax conventions or agreements. The purpose of the agreements is the avoidance of double taxation.

Here are some of the factors that are taken into account in determining the country of residency:

- where the permanent home is available; and/or
- the country where personal and economic relations are closer (centre of vital interests); and/or
- the country in which a habitual abode exists (i.e., the place where the most time is habitually spent); or
- the country of citizenship; and/or
- if it can't be determined otherwise, the competent authorities of the countries in question settle the question by mutual agreement.

Residential Ties

You might imagine that no two circumstances of residency are ever quite the same. That's why all of the circumstances must be reviewed for every situation to get an accurate picture of one's residency status. Residential ties can still deem you to be a resident of a particular country even though you may feel you are no longer a resident. And that means you'll need to file a tax return in that country.

The determination of residency is very important because it means the difference between a person being subject to income tax on "worldwide income" versus only being taxed on the income sourced in that particular country or state.

 Canadian residents are taxed on their worldwide income; whereas non-residents are only taxed on their Canadian-sourced income.

Taxes payable by a Canadian resident are to be paid on the taxable income for each year for each Canadian considered to be a resident *at any time* during the year.

Residential Ties to Canada. These factors can bind you to Canada for tax filing purposes even if you reside in the U.S. or another country:

- a home in Canada;
- a spouse or common-law partner or dependants in Canada;
- personal property in Canada, such as a car or furniture;
- social ties in Canada;
- economic ties in Canada;
- a Canadian driver's licence;
- Canadian bank accounts or credit cards; and
- health insurance with a Canadian province or territory.

Non-residents of Canada are only subject to Canadian income tax for a taxation year if they:

a) were employed in Canada;
b) carried on a business in Canada; or
c) disposed of a taxable Canadian property.

 The same is true for U.S. residents and non-residents; however: U.S. citizens are taxed on worldwide income no matter where they are actually physically resident.

Residential ties that you maintain or establish in another country may also be relevant in establishing residency status for tax purposes. Let me explain.

Deemed Residency. Both Canada and the U.S. have "physical presence" tests that can determine a person's residency status. In Canada, if you are present in the country for 183 days or more in one year, you can be "deemed" or considered to be a Canadian resident for that tax year. However, in the U.S. the test is 183 or more in the current year or 183 days or more over a 3-year period. These tests will be discussed further in chapter 4.

Real Life: Canadian working temporarily in U.S.

Jo-Anne is a Canadian resident who worked in Canada for 11 months of the year and 1 month in the state of California. Jo-Anne will be required to file a Canadian income tax return and pay tax on her worldwide income. She will also be required to file a 1040NR non-resident U.S. federal tax return and a non-resident California state tax return to claim and pay any required tax on her U.S. source income. The tax paid in the U.S. can be used as a foreign tax credit on Jo-Anne's Canadian tax return in accordance with Article XXIV of the Canada-U.S. Tax Convention.

Real Life: U.S. Resident working in Canada

Frank is a resident of North Dakota and earns an annual salary of $60,000 but recently his job took him to Canada for a couple of months where he earned an additional $15,000 in wages. Frank will be required to file a U.S. federal 1040 return and a North Dakota resident return and pay tax on his worldwide income.

He will also be required to file a non-resident Canadian tax return and pay income tax on the $15,000 earned in Canada. A foreign tax credit will be claimed on his U.S. 1040 return for the taxes paid in Canada; however, *a credit is not available for his state return*. (The Canada-U.S. Tax Treaty is only a federal tax treaty). This means that he will not receive a credit in North Dakota for any taxes paid in Canada and therefore will be double taxed.

U.S. Citizenship

Are you a U.S. citizen?

Many Canadians say no when asked this question simply because they don't know who is considered to be a U.S. citizen. This will be discussed in more detail in chapter 9 but we will summarize it below.

Generally you are a U.S. citizen if:

* you were born in the U.S.;

* you were born outside of the U.S. to U.S. citizen parents;

* you were born outside of the U.S. to one U.S. citizen parent and that parent meets a physical presence test in the U.S.; or

* you hold a U.S. green card (you are not an actual citizen for immigration purposes in this instance but for tax purposes, green card holders are treated the same as citizens no matter if the green card is active or not).

Real Life: Dual Citizens

1. Marsha was born in 1949 to two Canadian parents; however, she was born in Utah while her father was working there on a temporary work visa. Marsha is a U.S. citizen (dual citizen actually).

2. Phelix was born 6 weeks early in Hawaii while his Canadian parents were vacationing there but was only in the U.S. for 3 days before traveling back to Canada and has lived in Canada ever since. Phelix is a U.S. citizen (dual citizen actually).

3. Veronica was born in Vancouver, BC, in 1979. Her mother is a U.S. citizen who moved to Canada at the age of 25. She met Veronica's father, a Canadian citizen, 2 years later and was married 4 years later. Veronica is a U.S. citizen (dual citizen actually).

4. Michael is what we call a border baby; he was born in a U.S. hospital located on the other side of the border from where his family lived because that was the closest hospital and his provincial health coverage allowed that to occur; he has never lived or worked in the U.S. Michael is a U.S. citizen (dual citizen actually).

Income Tax Return Deadlines

Canadian filing deadlines

Employment status	Deadline
Employee or retired individual	April 30th of the following tax year
Self-employed individual	June 15th of the following tax year

In all cases, any taxes owing are due no later than April 30th to avoid an interest charge. Filing extensions do not exist in Canada.

Canadian residents are required to file a regular T1 individual income tax return. A non-resident of Canada files the same T1 individual income tax return but declares non-resident status and the taxpayer's particular situation will determine the type of information to be reported on that return. The type of income to be reported is very important because only certain credits are allowed to non-residents of Canada depending on their particular situation.

There is no monetary threshold in Canada that determines if you have to file an individual income tax return, only specific situations; however, we will not discuss these requirements in this book. You can refer to the Canada Revenue website for further information (www.cra.gc.ca).

U.S. filing deadlines

Residency status	Deadline
U.S. resident or non-resident earning U.S. employment income	April 15th of the following tax year
U.S. citizen living outside the U.S. not earning U.S. employment income	Automatic 2 month extension to June 15th of the following tax year

A taxpayer can apply for a 6-month extension of time to file if the extension request is submitted by their original due date. In all cases, taxes owing are due by April 15th and no extension is offered. U.S. residents are also required to file a state tax return for the state they were resident in during that year, and potentially other states as well, depending on their particular situation for the year. Every state in the U.S. has their own due dates and rules for filing extensions, so you will want to be sure to research what is required in each particular situation.

U.S. citizens are required to file a federal 1040 U.S. income tax return each year no matter where they live. Renouncing one's citizenship is the only way to get out of the annual filing requirements applicable to a U.S. citizen.

What form to use?

Type of taxpayer	Form #
U.S. citizen and/or U.S. resident	1040 Individual income tax return
Non-resident and non-citizen of the U.S.	1040NR Non-resident individual income tax return

This is very important since different tax credits and exemptions apply to U.S. citizens and non-residents and each return has different filing requirements. For example, non-residents only report U.S. source income on their 1040NR return, whereas U.S. citizens report income on a worldwide basis.

Filing status and filing threshold

The following is a listing of the various filing statuses that exist in the U.S. and the monetary filing thresholds (i.e., worldwide income thresholds) one must meet in their particular filing status in order to have to file; the meaning of each filing status will be defined in the definitions section at the back of the book. The following thresholds apply to 2014 and all are indexed for inflation.

Filing Status	Age	Filing threshold
Single	Under 65	$ 10,150
	65 or older	$ 11,650
Married filing jointly	Under 65 (both spouses)	$ 20,300
	65 or older (one spouse)	$ 21,500
	65 or older (both spouses)	$ 22,700
Married filing separately	Any age	$ 3,950
Head of household	Under 65	$ 13,050
	65 or older	$ 14,550
Qualifying widow(er) with dependent child	Under 65	$ 16,350
	65 or older	$ 17,550

Figure out what your filing status is to determine what your income tax filing threshold is and whether or not you are required to file a tax return for a particular year.

 Always remember, the income thresholds are based on gross income, not taxable income!

Tax Filing Requirements: What You Need to Know

Canadian Residents with Foreign Holdings

• A form T1135 must be filed each year to report foreign investments with a cost base of more than $100,000; penalties can be severe if this form is filed after April 30th of the following tax year (i.e., if filed late).

• Income received on these investments is fully taxable in Canada (i.e., your worldwide income is taxed in Canada).

• Depending on the type of foreign income, a tax return may also be required in the foreign country but not always.

Canadians Living in the U. S.

• Even though you are physically present in the U.S., residential ties to Canada could still deem you to be a Canadian resident for tax purposes.

• If you are considered a U.S. resident, you must abide by all the U.S. income tax and reporting requirements.

• Worldwide income is taxable in your country of residence.

U.S. Citizens Living in Canada

• You must abide by all the U.S. income tax and reporting requirements no matter where you live in the world (i.e., you are required to file U.S. returns each year as long as you maintain your U.S. citizenship status).

• Foreign tax credits are available in both countries on income tax paid in the other country on the same income.

• Worldwide income is reportable and potentially taxable in both Canada and the U.S.;

• Your filing status determines your requirement to file.

• Not all income is taxed the same on both sides of the border so make sure you know the rules ahead of time so you can plan accordingly.

WHAT YOU NEED TO KNOW ABOUT UNCLE SAM:

A taxpayer's particular circumstances are what determine where and when a tax return is required to be filed and in what country.

Canadian tax is based on residency; whereas U.S. tax is based on citizenship. This means that if you are a U.S. citizen you must abide by the U.S. tax laws no matter where you live in the world; however, you will generally only be required to file and pay Canadian income tax if you are resident in Canada. Non-residents of both countries are only to file and pay tax in the non-resident country if they earn income there.

Residency is key in determining what type of return one needs to file in a given year and also where you will be required to file that return. Your personal situation can deem you to be a resident of another country (whether you think you are or not), which would require additional tax filings and potentially double taxation. Filing the right tax forms is very important to ensure you are claiming the appropriate tax credits for your particular situation. Tax filing deadlines are different in both countries. Knowing the rules is important!

Not all income is taxed in the same manner in both countries so you need to be aware of the rules in order to not get caught off guard and not to pay more tax than you need to. Situations where this can arise are more common than you might think as many Canadians travel to the U.S. to gamble, purchase U.S. real property and even conduct regular business.

CHAPTER 2

Reporting Income & Assets

Jane works in a cross-border town on the border between Canada and the U.S.

John and Malena just purchased a winter home in Tuscon.

Jason, a Canadian resident, just sold his U.S. based Small Business Corporation.

What do Jane, John and Malena, and Jason all have in common? They may have tax filing obligations in both Canada and the U.S. Failure to file, unfortunately, could come with steep penalties. Here's what they need to know.

What's Taxable in Canada vs. the U.S.

There are many different types of income that an individual can earn and be required to pay tax on; however, we are only going to focus on a select few that have slightly different tax rules in Canada and the United States, such as:

- gambling/lottery winnings
- employment/earned income
- rental income
- taxable capital gains
- lifetime capital gains exemption
- corporate vs. individual income tax
- capital dividends

Let's take a moment now to understand some of the different tax rules relating to common income sources that might cause concern.

Gambling/lottery winnings

 Canada does not tax gambling or lottery winnings; however, the United States does.

Many people have the misconception that gambling winnings are only taxable in the U.S. if you are a U.S. citizen or resident, and that is simply not true. Gambling/lottery winnings from the U.S. are fully taxable to anyone and must be reported on a U.S. tax return. There is no requirement to file a U.S. tax return unless withholding taxes have not been taken on the income or too much has been taken. If the required withholdings are taken, one does not have to file a return; however, if a tax refund is desired because the withholding tax is too high, one must file in order to claim it. Gambling income includes, but is not limited to, winnings from lotteries, raffles, horse races, casinos, cash winnings and also the fair market value of prizes such as cars and trips.

Recovering Taxes on Gambling Winnings. A 25% withholding tax is applicable on winnings over a certain dollar amount and the only way to recover the tax is to file a tax return to claim the refund. This process is different for a U.S. non-resident and a U.S. citizen/resident.

U.S. Residents. The only way to recover the tax is to deduct gambling losses for the year against the winnings for that year but you can only deduct enough losses to cover the winnings, nothing more. A U.S. citizen/resident can only deduct the losses as part of their "itemized deductions" but the problem is that most people in this situation do not itemize their deductions. Instead they take the "standard deduction" amount on the tax return, because it results in a higher deduction.

 This means that the taxes withheld on the gambling winnings cannot be recovered in most cases.

U.S. non-residents. Canadians gambling in the U.S. would deduct gambling losses on form 1040NR; however, these are not deducted as an itemized deduction but on a separate section of the return specifically for gambling activity.

 The personal exemption cannot be deducted against gambling/lottery winnings by non-residents.

It is important to keep an accurate diary or similar record of your gambling winnings and losses in case the IRS asks for proof of your losses to support your claim. To deduct your losses, you must be able to provide receipts, tickets, statements or other records that show the amount of both your winnings and losses.

Real Life: *Canadian (non-U.S. citizen) hitting it big in the U.S.*

Johnny is a Canadian resident, (non-U.S. citizen) who likes to frequent the casinos in Las Vegas. While in Vegas he was a lucky man and won $10,000 playing blackjack. In accordance with the U.S. tax laws, the casino withheld $2,500 and issued a W-2G slip to Johnny for use in filing his tax return. Johnny's losses for the year total $8,000, which means that he can only claim the $8,000 of losses against his $10,000 of winnings, giving him a withholding tax recovery of $2,000. (In this case, he ends up having to pay $500 in tax on his winnings for the year, $2,500 - $2,000.)

U. S. Citizens Living in Canada. If a U.S. citizen is also a Canadian resident and he or she wins a Canadian lottery, the winnings are not taxable in Canada but are fully taxable in the U.S.; therefore, it is always good tax planning to ensure that the Canadian spouse is the one who declares the lottery win if there is a U.S.-citizen spouse in the family.

Employment/Earned income

Foreign earned income exclusion

A U.S. citizen living and working in Canada is required to file a U.S. income tax return on his world-wide income, which means that the Canadian source income is reportable and potentially taxable in the U.S. However, if the taxpayer meets either the physical presence test or the bona fide resident test (defined below), up to $99,200 (2014 limit; $97,600 2013 limit) of earned income can be excluded from taxable income in the year without having to worry if enough income tax has been paid in Canada.

Keep in mind that even though your Canadian earned income may be exempt from income tax in the U.S. under this earned-income regime, U.S. income tax return is still required to be filed.

This exclusion can be very effective for many individuals because Canada and the U.S. apply certain credits and deductions differently (as we'll see in the following example), which can result in less tax payable in Canada than would otherwise be payable in the U.S. This means that there may not be enough foreign tax credits available to offset the income tax on the same income in the U.S. So whenever possible, the earned income exclusion should be claimed each year to reduce any potential U.S. tax that may result upon filing your U.S. 1040 return. This type of exemption is not available in Canada. There are some circumstances that make using the foreign earned income exclusion not to one's benefit but this is usually something that is best determined by your accountant when your tax return is being prepared and only comes into play when your earned income is above a certain level. If this is the case, full foreign tax credits would be used instead.

Real Life: *Canadian resident, dual citizen earning Canadian employment income*

Michele is a U.S. citizen and Canadian resident who earned $75,000 in 2013 and contributes $10,000 to her RRSP and meets the bona fide resident test. The RRSP is a deductible contribution on her Canadian return; however, it is not deductible on her U.S. return, which means that she would be required to report and pay tax on the full $75,000. With the deduction of the RRSP contribution, Michele may not pay enough income tax in Canada to fully cover the income tax requirement on her U.S. return if she does not utilize the foreign earned income exclusion.

Physical presence test. A taxpayer will meet the U.S. physical presence test if he or she is physically present in Canada for 330 full days during a period of 12 consecutive months. The 330 qualifying days do not have to be consecutive and the test applies to both U.S. citizens and resident aliens.

Bona Fide Resident Test. A taxpayer will meet the bona fide residence test if he or she is a bona fide resident of Canada for an uninterrupted period that includes an entire tax year. You do not automatically acquire bona fide resident status merely by living in a Canada for one calendar year. The bona fide residence test applies to U.S. citizens and to any U.S. resident alien who is a citizen or national of a country with which the United States has an income tax treaty in effect (i.e., U.S. citizen or long-term resident living in Canada).

Green Card Holders. Green card holders are considered to be long-term U.S. residents no matter where they live as long as they "keep" their green card, active or not (i.e., surrendering the card to severs the ties). This means that they are treated just like U.S. citizens for tax purposes.

Treaty exemption for employment income. The Canada-U.S. Tax Convention exempts the taxation of income from employment earned in the country in which an individual is not a resident if it is under $10,000 and is not present in the U.S. for 183 days or more in any twelve month period. Keep in mind that the $10,000 exemption is per employer.

Real Life: *Canadian resident going to school in the U.S. and earning minimal U.S. employment income*

Angie is a Canadian resident who was also a student at the University of New York where she worked on campus to earn $6,000 in wages over the course of the school year. During the non-school year, Angie returned to Canada to work at a summer job where she earned $12,000 in wages. Angie is required to file a Canadian tax return and report and pay tax on the full $18,000 of income she earned in the year. As a student, Angie is considered an exempt individual for the U.S. substantial presence test, which means she will not meet the 183-day test and, because her income in the U.S. is under $10,000, she is not required to pay income tax in the U.S. on the employment income she earned there.

However, remember that the treaty is applicable to federal taxes only so she will still need to determine if a New York State return is required for the income she earned. Also, if there were any taxes withheld from her income earned, Angie will want to file a U.S. 1040NR return to claim back the tax as a refund because it would otherwise be denied as a foreign tax credit on her Canadian return. This is because the treaty exempts her U.S. income for U.S. tax-filing purposes and the Canadian government is not required to give a tax refund for money that need not be taxed in the other contracting state.

Rental income

Rental income is virtually treated the same in both countries in terms of what is taxable as income and what is deductible as an expense; however a difference arises in respect of depreciation.

In Canada, depreciation can only be deducted to bring rental income to zero; however, in the U.S. depreciation is mandatory, even if a loss is created or increased by the deduction. Because depreciation is mandatory in the U.S., even if no taxable income is generated in a tax year, or any real rental activity is present in a tax year, a U.S. tax return should still be filed to record the depreciation applicable to the rental property for that year.

The other difference relating to rental income earned in Canada or the U.S. relates to withholding taxes applicable on the gross rental income. A withholding tax rate of 25% in Canada and 30% in the U.S. is applied to the gross rental income earned by a non-resident; however, in the U.S. a non-resident can elect to treat their rental income as effectively connected income in the U.S. which allows them to avoid the withholding tax all together. Making the election requires the non-resident to file a U.S. tax return to report the net rental income and pay any required income tax at that time. This topic will be discussed further in a later chapter.

Taxable capital gains

In Canada, capital gains are only 50% taxable at graduated rates.

 In the U.S. capital gains are 100% taxable and the tax rate depends on whether the gain is long-term or short-term.

Short-term capital gains result when the property is held for less than a 12-month period and **long-term capital gains** result when the property is held for more than a 12-month period. Property can mean real estate, other physical assets or investment property (i.e., securities).

In the U.S., short-term capital gains are taxed at the taxpayer's regular income tax rates whereas long-term capital gains are normally taxed at a flat 15% tax rate.

There is an exception, however, which was introduced in 2013. A flat rate of 20% is used in situations where an individual's taxable capital gain would have otherwise been subject to the highest marginal rate of income tax if the flat rate rule didn't exist. The highest marginal rate of tax is slightly different depending on your filing status.

Some capital gains are taxed at different rates if they are from the disposition of specific property.

Lifetime capital gains exemption

The lifetime capital gains exemption is a Canadian tax concept that does not exist in the United States. Income tax in the U.S. can result when this exemption is claimed in Canada because it is not available in the U.S. and sometimes this tax can be very significant.

 This will come as a shock to U.S. citizens residing in Canada who sell shares of a qualifying small business corporation.

For example, if a Canadian resident shareholder claims the $800,000 capital gains exemption (indexed for inflation after 2014) on his $800,000 capital gain, he does not pay the regular rate of income tax in Canada but instead would be subject to a refundable alternative minimum tax.

However, if the taxpayer is a U. S. citizen living in Canada, a 20% flat rate would apply, resulting in taxes of $160,000!

Obviously, this is not an insignificant amount! Planning is required.

Corporate vs. individual income tax

Individuals in Canada are subject to much higher personal income tax rates than corporations reporting active business income (i.e., eligible for the $500,000 small business limit). This explains why many Canadian residents incorporate their businesses and retain excess income in the corporation.

However, in the U.S., individuals are taxed at lower personal income tax rates than their corporate counterparts and the U.S. actually goes a step further to apply penalties on excess revenues held in a corporation as well as limiting the ability of certain professionals from using a corporation.

Personal Services Income. Doctors, architects, lawyers, and accountants, to name a few, cannot earn business income within a corporation in the U.S. unless it is a large business with other professionals in addition to the U.S. shareholder.

This income is considered to be personal services income, which is taxable to the individual if profits remain in the company after corporate taxes are paid (in other words, the U.S. "looks through" the company and taxes the individual shareholders on the profits remaining for the applicable tax year).

If a U.S. citizen, Canadian resident own shares in a Canadian Controlled Private Corporation (CCPC) operating a medical practice, any profits left in the company at the end of the tax year will be taxable in the U.S. to the U.S. shareholder in the form of a dividend (i.e., the U.S. looks through the company and apportions the remaining profits as taxable dividends to the U.S. shareholder). This income is based on the percentage of ownership in the company by the U.S. shareholder.

Unfortunately there is no offsetting foreign tax credit if the same type of income is not reported in Canada (i.e., no dividend income in Canada but dividend income in the U.S.). For this reason, Canadian tax planning will need to change slightly when U.S. citizens are involved. ***Double Taxation and the Dollars Can be Huge!***

Capital dividends

Capital dividends are Canadian tax-free dividends made up of the tax-free portion of investment income reported within a corporation (i.e., the non-taxable portion of a capital gain, life insurance proceeds, etc.). Capital dividends are received tax-free to a Canadian resident shareholder; however, this is not the case if the shareholder is also a U.S. citizen. Recall this person is required to file a U.S. tax return.

Capital dividends are fully taxable in the U.S. which means that a Canadian resident/ U.S. citizen shareholder receiving a capital dividend may end up paying income tax in the U.S. on that dividend and not having a foreign tax credit available from Canada to offset the tax.

 This tax rule usually surprises a lot of people who are business owners in Canada.

Reporting Income & Assets: What You Need to Know

Canadian Residents with Foreign Holdings

- Rental income is taxable in the U.S. as well as Canada; depreciation is mandatory in the U.S.

- You are not required to file a U.S. non-resident return if the property withholding taxes have been taken but if you want to claim a refund you must file a 1040NR return.

U.S. Citizens Living in Canada

- Not all income types are taxed the same on both sides of the border so know the rules first before entering into what you may think is a "tax-free" transaction.

- Filings for citizens and non-residents on the same type of income is not always the same either due to the different credits and exemptions available to each different class of taxpayer.

WHAT YOU NEED TO KNOW ABOUT UNCLE SAM:

There are many different types of income sources taxpayers may be required to report on their tax return; the important thing to remember is that everything is not taxed in the same manner on both sides of the border. The main differences between income taxability are important to U.S. citizens and U.S. long-term residents living in Canada because they must report worldwide income on both sides of the border.

The most alarming differences are with regard to the taxation of Canadian capital dividends and Canadian capital gains that are eligible for the lifetime capital gains exemption. Both of these income streams can result in tax-free distributions from a Canadian perspective; however, they are both fully taxable income streams in the eyes of the U.S. tax system.

Non-residents of Canada and the U.S. are generally only required to file a non-resident income tax return in situations where the proper amount of withholding tax has not been taken on the income, a refund is desired or income tax is owed.

U.S. citizens and long-term residents can earn the same type of U.S. source income as a U.S. non-resident and end up with very different tax results, i.e., gambling winnings. A U.S. non-resident may have gambling winnings and losses and be able to recover some or all of the withholding tax but a U.S. citizen or green card holder may have the same situation but will not be able to recover the tax because of how the income and losses are reported on the different tax returns.

CHAPTER 3

Reporting Foreign Holdings

FATCA STARTS JULY 1, 2014! "The Foreign Account Tax Compliance Act became U.S. law in March 2010 but will take effect around the world on July 1, 2014. The goal of the law is to find offshore accounts held by U.S. taxpayers…banks from around the world will be asked to sift through their accounts to look for clients with U.S. connections, then share that information with the U.S. Internal Revenue Service."
AMBER HILDEBRAND, CBC NEWS, JANUARY 13, 2014

Governments around the world are comparing notes…they want to know if you hold assets offshore and they are asking you – under threat of heavy penalties – to file forms to let them know. This is true of Canadians who have bank accounts and real estate in the U.S. and elsewhere, as well as U.S. citizens living outside of the U.S. In this chapter we will tell you what forms will need to be filed, the penalties for failure to file, and how to avoid them.

Reporting Foreign Holdings for Canadian purposes. Canada has minimal filing requirements for individual taxpayers who own foreign investments or have foreign bank accounts outside of Canada. Also there is only a requirement to disclose investments held outside Canada that have a cost base over $100,000, excluding real estate held for personal purposes.

Form T1135 Foreign Income Verification. Starting in 2013, the T1135 form is being revised to clarify the filing requirements and include more detailed information for each specified foreign property; the compliance fees relating to properly preparing this form can be quite high depending on the particular taxpayer. Penalties for failure to file this form are usually $25 per day for up to 100 days (maximum $2,500), but can be as high as $500 per month for up to 24 months ($12,000 maximum) if the failure is intentional or due to gross negligence.

The reassessment period for a particular tax year is also extended to 6 years instead of 3 starting in 2013 if the taxpayer fails to properly file the T1135 and report the income from the foreign property. As you can see, these penalties can be substantial; $12,000 per tax year when the form is over 24 months late for up to 6 years of forms, that's $72,000!

Reporting Foreign Holdings for U.S. purposes. The U.S. on the other hand, has a number of reports which individual taxpayers must file in respect of their foreign holdings.

 The U.S. 1040 personal income tax return is just one of the annual filing requirements for U.S. citizens and residents.

Depending on the particular situation, a taxpayer may be required to file the following forms for a given tax year:

- Form 8891 (Information Return for Beneficiaries of Certain Canadian Registered Retirement Plans)
- TDF 90-22.1 (Foreign Bank Account Report)
- Form 8938 (Statement of Specified Foreign Financial Assets)
- Form 5471 (Information Return of U.S. Persons with Respect to Certain Foreign Corporations)
- Form 3520 (Annual Return to Report Transactions With Foreign Trusts and Receipt of Certain Foreign Gifts)
- Form 8621 (Information Return by a Shareholder of a Passive Foreign Investment Company or Qualified Electing Fund)

 Late filing penalties of $10,000 per year, per form are applicable to all of the forms mentioned above (except form 8891).

However, penalties can be much higher and more severe if certain circumstances exist (i.e., intention to hide information). See Appendix I at the back of the book for a chart providing a snapshot of the filing requirements.

FATCA (Foreign Account Tax Compliance Act)

Canada and the U.S. signed an intergovernmental agreement (IGA) on February 5, 2014 under the longstanding Canada-U.S. Tax Convention. Under this agreement, Canadian financial institutions will not have to report the FATCA disclosure information directly to the IRS; instead they will report the information to the CRA. The CRA will then exchange the information with the IRS through the existing provisions of the Tax Convention, which is in accordance with Canada's privacy laws.

Also under this IGA, certain accounts are exempt from the FATCA reporting requirement and as such are not reportable. These accounts include RRSPs, RRIFs, RDSPs, TFSAs and others.

The Foreign Account Tax Compliance Act (FATCA) will affect most types of financial institutions that receive U.S. income, hold U.S. investments and have U.S. taxpayers as members.

The foreign reporting required for individuals under this regime was already enforced starting in the 2011 tax year when the IRS required the filing of form 8938 for applicable taxpayers.

 As of July 1, 2014, foreign entities will be required to report certain types of information to the I.R.S. about U.S. citizens holding financial accounts with them.

FATCA also requires foreign financial institutions to enter into an agreement with the IRS to identify their U.S. account holders and to disclose the account names, TINs (social security numbers), addresses, and the account balances, receipts, and withdrawals during the year. Foreign institutions that do not comply will be subject to a 30% withholding penalty.

FFIs can include, naming a few:

- Banks and any other entity that is a depository institution;
- Mutual funds and any other entity considered a custodial institution;
- Investment entities such as hedge funds and private equity funds; and
- Insurance companies that have cash value products or annuities.

Foreign entities that are not considered financial institutions will also be affected if they receive U.S. income or hold U.S. assets; these entities would be considered Non-Financial Foreign Entities or NFFE's. Every entity that is not an FFI is considered an NFFE.

If the NFFE derives more than 50% of its gross income from passive sources (i.e., investment income is passive source) and has more than 50% of passive assets (i.e., assets not used in an active business), any withholdable payments by the withholding agent will be subject to the 30% FATCA withholding, unless the NFFE certifies that it has no substantial U.S. owners or it provides to the withholding agent the name, address and identification number of each substantial U.S. owner.

Some NFFEs will be exempt from the FATCA rules if they are considered excepted NFFEs. An excepted NFFE is an NFFE that is not subject to FATCA requirements. An NFFE is considered excepted if:

- It certifies that it does not have substantial U.S. owners; and
- It is considered as posing low risks of tax evasion.

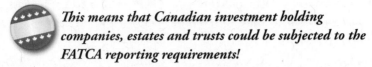 *This means that Canadian investment holding companies, estates and trusts could be subjected to the FATCA reporting requirements!*

Canadian estates, trusts, and investment holding companies can be considered FFIs if more than 50% of their income is passive income and more than 50% of their assets are passive assets and their investments are professionally managed. This test is not just a U.S. income or U.S. asset test.

These reporting requirements are in addition to the requirement for reporting of foreign financial accounts on the TDF 90-22.1 and means that the IRS will now have information they can use to verify what you are reporting to them.

What action is required?

- An FFI must register under FATCA to receive a GIIN (Global Intermediary Identification Number) by April 25, 2014.
- Form W-8BEN-E must be completed by all FFIs and NFFEs.
- An FFI must disclose certain information to the IRS or suffer a 30% withholding tax.

Reporting Foreign Holdings: What You Need To Know

Canadian Residents with Foreign Holdings

- T1135 foreign reporting requirements are becoming more complex in Canada and significant penalties can result if compliance is not met.
- Foreign holdings can include U.S. stocks and U.S. real estate but only if the real estate is used for business purposes (i.e., rental property) and not just a personal vacation home.
- The Canadian foreign holdings threshold is $100,000 in asset cost, not fair market value.
- Status under the new FATCA rules must be determined so any required reporting is taken care of within the necessary deadlines.

U.S. Citizens Living in Canada

- The U.S. has many filing requirements when it comes to foreign reporting so it is good to know what your requirements are each year.

- Holding foreign financial accounts with an aggregate value over $10,000 requires annual reporting using TDF 90-22.1.

- Having foreign financial assets above certain thresholds requires a taxpayer to file Form 8938 to report certain foreign assets. FATCA comes into effect July 1, 2014, which means that the IRS will now have access to more information about you and will have the ability to verify the information you are reporting to them.

- Status under the new FATCA rules must be determined so any required reporting is taken care of within the necessary deadlines.

WHAT YOU NEED TO KNOW ABOUT UNCLE SAM:

Remember that these are only some of the differences between Canadian and U.S. tax law, not all of the differences. If there is ever a question as to how something is treated in one country or the other you should also research it or consult a professional with knowledge in that area of taxation.

CHAPTER 4

Snowbirds and Uncle Sam

Do you spend your winter months "down south" in a warmer climate?
Do you wish you could escape the cold in Florida, Arizona, or some other
warm U.S. location, or do you plan to do this when you retire? If so then
you need to know what being a "snowbird" means for tax purposes.

Case Study

Nancy and Henry have been vacationing in Ft. Lauderdale, Florida, for the past 10 years and plan to continue vacationing there for many years to come. Property values were dropping due to the poor economy so in March of 2012, when the price was right, they jointly bought their vacation home on the coast for $162,000 and have used it for personal vacations only, spending approximately 16 weeks per year there.

Starting in January 2014, they intend to rent their property on a weekly basis to anyone wishing to vacation there on a temporary basis. They plan to charge $1,000 per week to help cover their monthly expenses of approximately $1,150 but they still plan to use the property for 16 weeks of the year.

Henry and Nancy think that the housing market will rise again so they are hoping that in 15 to 20 years they can sell the property for twice what they purchased it for.

Questions & Answers:

Are Nancy and Henry deemed residents under the U.S. substantial presence test?

16 weeks per year equates to approximately 4 months of the year and assuming that every month has not more than 30 days in it, the total number of days Nancy and Henry spend in the U.S. per year is 120 days. They would not be deemed residents under the U.S. substantial presence test because they do not meet the 183-day test ($120 + (120/3) + (120/6) = 180$). If the number of days per year is

actually over 120 (i.e., some months may have 31 days) then Nancy and Henry might meet the test, which means they would need to file Form 8840 and claim closer ties to Canada.

What are their filing requirements in the U.S.?

Prior to 2014 when the property is solely used for personal use, there are no filing requirements unless they meet the 183-day test (i.e., an 8840 Form would then be required). However, once they start renting the property, a 1040NR will need to be filed by each of them to report the income and "business" expenses from the rental property (remember you must exclude personal expenses).

What is the taxable amount of the Schedule D capital gain they will need to report in the U.S. if they sell the property for $350,000?

Total capital gain in the U.S. is $188,000 (350,000 – 162,000) or $94,000 each because they own the property jointly.

"Snowbird" Defined

The term "snowbird" refers to a person who is ordinarily resident in Canada but spends part of the year in the U.S.

A person who spends part of the year in the U.S. for vacation purposes or health reasons will generally not be considered to have given up Canadian residence, and therefore will still be treated as a factual resident in Canada.

Depending on the amount of time spent in the U.S. by snowbirds, they can be deemed to be residents of the U.S. under the substantial presence test; this is referred to as dual residency.

For this reason, most snowbirds will be required to file a form 8840 claiming closer ties to Canada for each tax year.

United States Substantial Presence Test

In the United States, the substantial presence test determines residency; in order to be considered a U.S. resident, you must pass both the 31-day and 183-day tests.

The 31-day test:

Were you present in the United States for 31 days, at any time, during the current year?

The 183-day test:

> A. Current year days in United States x 1 =_____days
>
> B. First preceding year days in United States x 1/3 =_____days
>
> C. Second preceding year days in United States x 1/6 =_____days
>
> D. Total Days in United States =_____days (add lines A, B, and C)
>
> If line D equals or exceeds 183 days, you have passed the183-day test.

Exceptions: Do not count days of presence in the U.S. when:

- you are a commuter from a residence in Canada or Mexico;
- you are in the U.S. less than 24 hours in transit;
- you are unable to leave the U.S. due to a medical condition that developed in the U.S.;
- you are an *exempt individual* (defined below);
- you are a regular member of the crew of a foreign vessel traveling between the U.S. and a foreign country or a possession of the U.S. (unless you are otherwise engaged in conducting a trade or business in the U.S.).

Exempt Individual defined:

- Foreign Government Related Individual
  - Employee of foreign government
  - Employee of international organization
  - Usually on A or G visa;
- Teacher, Professor, Trainee, Researcher on J or Q visa
  - Does *not* include students on J or Q visas.
  - Does include any alien on a J or Q visa who is not a student (physicians, *au pairs*, summer camp workers, etc.).
  - Must wait 2 years before counting 183 days; however if the J or Q alien has been present in the U.S. during any part of 2 of the prior 6 calendar years in F, J, M, or Q status, then he is not an exempt individual for the current year, and he must count days in the current year toward the substantial presence test.
  - Classification as an Exempt Individual applies also to spouse and child on J-2 or Q-3 visa;
- Student on F, J, M or Q visa
  - Must wait 5 calendar years before counting 183 days.

- ◦ The 5 calendar years need not be consecutive; and once a cumulative total of 5 calendar years is reached during the student's lifetime after 1984 he may never be an Exempt Individual as a student ever again.
- ◦ Classification as an Exempt Individual applies also to spouse and child on F-2, J-2, M-2, or Q-3 visa.
- Professional athlete temporarily present in United States to compete in a *charitable* sports event (note the very clear purpose specified in this case; this exemption does not apply to professional athletes playing regularly in the U.S.).

 Even if you are deemed a resident of the United States because you meet the Substantial Presence Test, there are some exceptions that allow you not to be treated as a U.S. resident for income tax purposes.

There are different exceptions depending on the person's situation so you first need to determine which situation applies to the particular taxpayer.

Closer Connection Exception for Foreign Students Only

Foreign students in the U.S. are treated a bit differently when it comes to time spent in the U.S. under the substantial presence test and because of this there are different tests that need to be met in order for the student to claim closer ties to Canada. As a student, to determine if you have closer ties to Canada, answer the following questions:

- Do you intend to reside permanently in the United States?
- Have you taken any steps to change your U.S. immigration status toward permanent residency?
- Have you substantially complied with the United States immigration laws for your student non-immigrant status while in the United States?
- While in the United States, have you maintained a closer connection with a foreign country other than with the United States (i.e., Canada)?

If you answered "no" to the first two questions above, and "yes" to the last two questions, then you have a basis to claim you are still a non-resident alien, even though you have passed the substantial presence test. To claim the exception for students on an income tax return, a student should attach Form 8843, Statement for Exempt Individuals and Individuals with a Medical Condition, to the form 1040NR.

Closer Connection Exception for All Aliens

The basic rule for deemed residency in the U.S. is to determine if you meet the substantial presence test. All foreign individuals, with the exception of students, have the ability to "get out" of the deemed residency rules if they can claim closer ties to Canada. To determine if you have closer ties to Canada, answer the following questions:

• Were you present in the U.S. fewer than 183 days in the current year?

• Is your tax home/primary place of work in a foreign country (i.e., Canada)?

• Do you maintain a closer connection to that country than to the United States (refer to chapter 1 for residential ties that can give you a closer connection)?

• During your current year in the United States, have you taken any steps to change your United States immigration status to permanent residency, or have you taken any steps to adjust your immigration status in the United States?

If you answered "yes" to the first three questions above and "no" to the last question, then you have a basis to claim that you are still a non-resident alien, even though you have passed the substantial presence test. Form 8840, Closer Connection Exception Statement for Aliens, should be attached to your 1040NR individual income tax return to claim this exception. If you are not required to file a tax return, file Form 8840 by itself with the IRS.

Even if you answered "no" to the first question above, you may still be able to claim closer ties to Canada; however, you must claim closer ties under the Canada-U.S. Tax Treaty. To make this claim, you should attach Form 8833, Treaty-Based Return Position Disclosure, to your non-resident U.S. 1040NR return.

 You will need a U.S. ITIN to properly file these forms with the IRS (discussed later in this chapter).

Filing a 1040NR & Obtaining an ITIN

If you are a non-resident of the U.S. and you don't already have a U.S. Individual Taxpayer Identification Number (ITIN), and you are required to claim closer connections to Canada using the treaty exemption (i.e., form 8833), you will need to apply for one in order to file the U.S. non-resident 1040NR return.

Day count

When traveling to and from the U.S. by vehicle, the U.S. border guards will swipe your passport as you enter the country; however, the Canadian border guards don't always swipe your passport when you come back to Canada. Without your passport being swiped on your re-entry to Canada, no one can really confirm how many days you spent outside the country. That is all about to change.

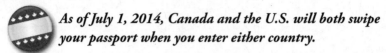 *As of July 1, 2014, Canada and the U.S. will both swipe your passport when you enter either country.*

This means that both governments will now have information that will tell them how many days a person is absent from Canada and how many days a person is present in the U.S. This will be of particular interest to those affected by the U.S. substantial presence test, which means you better keep track of the number days you spend in the U.S. and file the necessary forms required each year.

U.S. Individual Taxpayer Identification Numbers (ITINs)

In order to receive a U.S. ITIN, you have to qualify under one of the options listed on the W-7 tax form. One of those options is the requirement for a non-U.S. taxpayer to claim a treaty exemption (i.e., claim that the income earned in the U.S. is exempt from tax in the U.S. under the treaty). In order to get your application processed, you need to prove that you meet the filing requirement so if this is the basis on which you are applying for an ITIN, you need to submit your completed 1040NR return and form 8833, with your W-7 ITIN application.

The process for applying for an ITIN and filing the 1040NR return in the situation described above is as follows:

- Complete a W-7 ITIN application form and attach a certified copy of your Canadian passport. (Note: your Canadian passport can only be certified by the issuing agent – i.e., a Canadian passport office.)
- Complete a 1040NR return and form 8833, leaving blank any areas that ask for an identifier number.
- Attach the 1040NR package to the W-7 application form and submit all to the ITIN administration office (address will be in the W-7 instructions).

Once you have been issued a U.S. ITIN, the number will be entered on your 1040NR and all other applicable forms and the return will be forwarded to the correct IRS office for processing. There is a reliance on the ITIN office to complete their processing correctly; however, I have seen taxpayers receive letters indicating that an ITIN is required to process their return. In an instance like this, you would need to resubmit the forms to the appropriate IRS office with the ITIN included in the appropriate places on the forms (this situation is not common, but it does happen).

Canada's Physical Presence Test

Canada also has a physical presence test for non-residents. However, the calculations are slightly different than in the U.S. You are a deemed resident of Canada for tax purposes if you fall into one of the following situations:

- You lived outside Canada during the tax year, and you are a government employee, a member of the Canadian Forces including their overseas school staff, or working under a Canadian International Development Agency (CIDA) program. This could also apply to the family members of an individual who is in one of these situations.

- You sojourned in Canada for 183 days or more (the 183-day rule) in the tax year; do not have significant residential ties with Canada; and are not considered a resident of another country under the terms of a tax treaty between Canada and that country.

Note: If you are considered a resident of a country with which Canada has a tax treaty, you may be considered a deemed non-resident of Canada for tax purposes. This can create unwanted tax consequences in Canada if you are subject to the deemed disposition rules and you didn't plan for it. Know the rules and how they apply to your situation so you aren't "caught with your pants down" as they say.

When you calculate the number of days you stayed in Canada during the tax year for the physical presence test, include each day or part of a day that you stayed in Canada. These include:

- the days you attended a Canadian university or college;
- the days you worked in Canada; and
- the days you spent on vacation in Canada, including on weekend trips.

If you lived in the United States and commuted to work in Canada, do not include commuting days in the calculation.

Provincial & State Residency

Being considered a resident of a particular country generally means that you will also be considered a resident of a particular province or state. The only time this may not actually be the case is when an individual is deemed a resident because they have met the physical presence test.

 A Canadian resident will pay provincial tax in the province they are resident in at December 31st of each particular year.

However, if they work in a couple of different provinces throughout the year, they will still only pay provincial tax in the province they are "resident in" at December 31st.

Real Life: Canadian resident in Manitoba

If Paul lives in Manitoba, he will not only be considered a resident of Canada but also a provincial resident of Manitoba, which means that he will be subject to Manitoba provincial tax rules in addition to the Canadian federal tax rules. Paul is subject to the specific tax rules of that particular province but he is also eligible for all the federal and provincial tax credits and benefits eligible to their residents.

Now if we assume Paul lives in Manitoba and works in Manitoba for 6 months of the year but also works in Alberta for 6 months of the year, he will receive a T4 slip from Manitoba as well as a T4 slip from Alberta, but if he is resident in Manitoba on December 31st, he will file a Canadian income tax return as a resident of Manitoba and pay federal and Manitoba taxes on both the Manitoba and Alberta income earned.

The United States works a bit differently when it comes to state taxation.

 Every state in the U.S. has its own tax laws and they are all slightly different.

Some states require you to pay tax on worldwide income only if you are a resident of that particular state but some states can deem you to be a resident based on the amount of time spent in the state and because of this can tax you on your worldwide income for the period in which you are deemed a resident. The main difference between provincial and state taxation is that in Canada, you pay tax only in your official province of residence; whereas, in the U.S., you can pay tax in every state. How you are actually taxed at the state level in the U.S. all depends on the nature of your interaction with a particular state in a given year. Some states only consider you a resident if your intention is to make that state your home, while others consider you a resident based on the number of days spent there in the year.

Real Life:*U.S. resident earning income in more than one state*

If Jason lives in Minnesota and ordinarily works in Minnesota, he will pay Minnesota state tax on his worldwide income each year. Now let's assume that he travels to Texas 10 times a year to perform some of his regular work duties and receives a tax slip showing he has taxable income from Texas as well as Minnesota. This means that he pays tax on his worldwide income in Minnesota (i.e., on both his Minnesota- and Texas-sourced income) but he is also subject to Texas tax rules, which means that he will have to pay tax in the state of Texas on his Texas-sourced income as well.

Real Life:*Snowbird meeting the U.S. substantial presence test*

Martin lives in Manitoba but likes to spend his winters in Arizona. He usually stays in Arizona from February 1 to April 10 and then returns to Arizona from November 1 to January 6. He has no U.S.-source income but rents a condo while he is in Arizona.

Because Martin is in the U.S. for approximately 136 days each year, he meets the substantial presence test over a 3-year period so he must file IRS Form 8840 (closer connection form), or risk being taxed as a deemed resident of the U.S. on his worldwide income (not a desired result).

Martin was unaware of the 6-month provincial health coverage regulation but is happy he hasn't stayed in the U.S. for a period of 6 months or longer (discussed in more detail below).

U.S. Visitors

If you are visiting the U.S. from Canada, you are "deemed" to be travelling into the U.S. on a visitor's visa even if you don't have the paperwork to prove it. But if you want to stay longer than six months, you will have to apply for the real thing. This is important information for snowbirds as many of them spend a significant amount of time in the U.S., which causes some to worry they will pass the six-month mark. If you are a snowbird and know that you might be cutting the six-month test close in a particular year, you should apply for an actual visitor's visa well in advance so you don't have to interrupt your stay in the U.S. and come home to Canada in order to avoid any hassles at the border during that stay or subsequent visits. **Keep in mind that the 183-day test is a tax test and the six-month test above is an immigration test, two separate tests.**

According to www.workpermit.com, "business travelers may enter the United States using a B1, or 'Visitor for Business' Visa. In practice these visas are invariably issued as jointly with B2, or 'Visitor for Pleasure' (i.e., tourist) visa. This practice means that, if a candidate has an old tourist visa, it may be valid for a planned business trip. Additionally, most citizens of Canada and Bermuda traveling to the U.S. as a visitor don't need a visa.

While in the U.S. as a business visitor, an individual may:

- Conduct negotiations
- Solicit sales or investment
- Discuss planned investment or purchases
- Make investments or purchases
- Attend Meetings and participate in them fully
- Interview and hire staff
- Conduct research.

The following activities *require a working visa*, and may not be carried out by business visitors:

- Running a business
- "Gainful employment" (i.e., to get a job)
- Receiving payment from an organization within the U.S.
- Participating as a professional in entertainment or sporting events.

Those entering on visitor visas will generally be granted 6 months admission (the maximum allowable is one year) on entry. It may be possible to obtain a six-month extension to the visitor visa as long as the candidate will be maintaining visitor status, and there are good reasons to do so.

A summary of the visa types and uses are as follows:

Visa Types	Visa Description	What Can You Do?
B1	Visitor in U.S. on business; includes athletes (competing for prize money only)	• Conduct negotiations • Solicit sales or investment • Discuss planned investment or purchases • Make investments or purchases • Attend meetings and participate in them fully • Interview and hire staff • Conduct research

B2	Visitor in U.S. for pleasure or medical reasons	• Tourism • Vacation (holiday) • Visit with friends or relatives • Medical treatment • Participate in social events hosted by fraternal, social, or service organizations • Amateur participation in musical, sports, or similar events or contests, if not being paid for participating • Enroll in a short recreational course of study, not for credit toward a degree (for example, a two-day cooking class while on vacation)
F or M	Non-resident U.S. student	• Attend college or university • Work for the college or university only
K-3	Spouse to a U.S. citizen	• Can live in the U.S. while immigrant visa application is in process; not permitted to work
H, L, O, P, Q and R visas	Temporary employment visas	• Can work for a U.S. employer (must be sponsored by that employer)
TN	NAFTA visa (professional worker)	• Run a business • "Gainful employment" • Receive payment from an organization within the U.S.

Provincial Health Coverage

Before you travel to the U.S. for an extended period of time, you should verify your particular province's health-coverage rules and regulations to ensure you will still be covered while travelling abroad.

According to www.travelinsurancefile.com, "all provinces, except Ontario and Newfoundland, require you to actually live in your home province for at least six months plus a day (183 days in most years) in order to be considered a permanent resident of that province, and therefore qualify for provincial health insurance (Medicare) benefits. Ontario allows you to be out of the country for 212 days (seven months) and Newfoundland for eight months without risking loss of your provincial health care benefits." There is talk that these time periods will be increased in each province.

When you leave your province of residence, for any reason, your medical coverage doesn't usually follow you so it is generally a good idea to purchase supplementary health-care coverage before you leave Canada.

Getting Sick in the U.S.

It is state law in every U.S. state that you cannot be turned away from an emergency medical facility because of your inability to pay for emergency treatment. If you have supplementary insurance coverage, you need to call their emergency assistance line shortly after being admitted to the hospital. If you don't have supplementary coverage, you need to contact your provincial Medicare office as soon as possible. If your stay in the U.S. is going to be extended over six months due to medical reasons, you may need to apply for a B-2 visitor's visa.

Remember, if you are required to stay in the U.S. for medical reasons (provided you got sick while in the U.S.), those days are exempt from being counted under the substantial presence test for determining U.S. residency in a given year.

Owning Vacation Property in the U.S.

In today's society, many snowbirds go a step further and instead of just vacationing in the U.S., they actually purchase a vacation home in the state they like to visit.

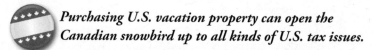 *Purchasing U.S. vacation property can open the Canadian snowbird up to all kinds of U.S. tax issues.*

The main issue with owning this type of property is an ongoing one and relates to U.S. estate tax. U.S. estate tax is calculated on the market value of the property of the deceased whereas in Canada only the gain on the deemed disposition at death is taxed. As a result, if you hold U.S. real estate when you die the portion of your estate that is situated in the U.S. may be subject to a tax rate of 40%, depending on the estate tax rules in the year of death and if the Fair Market Value (FMV) is over the applicable estate exemption allowed in that year ($5,340,000 for 2014). Another issue is the creation of U.S.-sourced income if the individual decides to turn their vacation home into a rental property. This topic will be discussed in more detail in the next chapter.

US Estate and Gift Tax

Estate Tax

Canadians who die owning U.S. real estate or other U.S. situs assets must file a U.S. estate tax return if the total value of their gross assets situated in the U.S. on the date of death exceeds $60,000; however, the Canada-U.S. Tax Convention allows Canadians access to a proportionate share of the U.S. estate tax exemption to reduce the effect of U.S. estate tax (i.e., U.S. property/assets divided by worldwide estate value multiplied by the U.S. estate tax exemption amount). Let's look at an example to see how this all works in practice.

Real Life: Canadian owning U.S. real estate at death

Maggie was a Canadian citizen and resident who bought her vacation home in Palm Springs for $125,000, 15 years before she passed away. During that time, she enjoyed spending 4 months of the year in Palm Springs with her family and was planning to sell her property at some point before she passed away. However, Maggie suffered a sudden heart attack in April 2013 before being able to do so. The value of the property on the date of her death was $250,000, which means that Maggie would need to file a U.S. estate tax return because the value of her property is over $60,000; however, she would not have to pay U.S. estate tax if the total value of her worldwide estate was under $5,250,000 (2013 estate exemption amount).

Gift Tax

 U.S. gift tax is virtually U.S. estate tax during a person's lifetime.

Gift tax is a transfer tax applied to the transfer of property where the person making the gift receives less than fair value in return; tax is born by the person making the gift. Most individuals think that U.S. gift tax is only applicable to U.S. citizens and residents; however, that is not the case. Non-residents of the U.S. can still be subject to the U.S. gift tax rules on their U.S. situs property, (same as U.S. estate tax). A gift made to any individual with regard to a U.S. situs asset may be subject to U.S. gift tax rules no matter if the person receiving the gift is a resident or non-resident of the U.S., which is why it is important for everyone to know the rules and how they might be affected.

U.S. gift and estate taxes will be discussed in more detail in chapter 12.

Snowbirds: What You Need To Know

- The number of days you spend in the U.S. in the current year and the 2 preceding years can deem you to be a U.S. resident for tax purposes but you can claim closer ties to Canada to get out of being taxed as a U.S. resident if your situation actually gives you closer ties.

- Non-residents owning U.S. situs property (i.e., property located in the U.S.) can still be subject to U.S. gift and estate tax on that U.S. property but the tax treaty allows for a prorated portion of the U.S. exemptions for some relief (i.e., lifetime exemption in 2014 is $5,340,000).

- Earning rental income in the U.S. requires the filing of a U.S. non-resident tax return, which also requires an ITIN.

- As of July 1, 2014, the Canadian border guards will be required to scan your passport upon re-entry into Canada so the government will now have a better idea of the number of days you have spent in the U.S.

WHAT YOU NEED TO KNOW ABOUT UNCLE SAM:

Enjoying the warmer weather down south is fine, but make sure you keep track of how many days you are spending across the border or you could get caught by the U.S. deemed residency rules. Having to file a U.S. tax return to claim worldwide income may be an issue for some taxpayers, especially when not all income is taxed the same in both countries and the U.S. have a lot more foreign reporting requirements to follow.

Many snowbirds own their vacation properties in the U.S. and some even go as far as renting them. If the property is held for personal use only, then there are no U.S. tax filings required until the property is sold; however, if the property is rented, a U.S. tax return is required for each year the property is used in this fashion.

Canadians owing U.S. situs assets can still be subject to U.S. gift and estate tax but only on those U.S. situs assets. The Canada-U.S. Tax Convention does allow non-residents of the U.S. to access a prorated portion of the U.S. estate tax exemption ($5,340,000 in 2014), which in many cases means that even though an estate tax return may need to be filed, estate tax isn't always payable. You need to be aware of how owning these kinds of assets can affect you in your particular situation and find out if there is anything you can do to properly handle or structure the ownership of these assets in order to avoid paying these taxes, or at least to minimize their impact.

U.S. gift and estate tax can be managed in many cases, but the proper ownership structure is sometimes key to effective tax management. This will be discussed more in chapter 12.

CHAPTER 5

Non-Residents Owning
U.S. Real Estate

Case Study

Jerry is a Canadian resident and citizen who recently purchased a condo in Phoenix, Arizona, on July 15, 2013, for $125,000. Jerry's plan has always been to rent it out on a short-term basis for the entire year, with the exception of 3 weeks in the month of August, when he will use it personally. After a few minor repairs, Jerry had the condo ready for renters by August 1, 2013; however, he didn't actually have anyone interested to rent the condo until January 2014.

Questions & Answers:

What is Jerry's filing requirement in the U.S. for 2013?
Because Jerry's intention is to rent the property, even though he doesn't have any renters until 2014, he must report the purchase of the condo and take depreciation for the 2013 tax year; therefore, he must file a 1040NR return.

Does it make a difference if Jerry plans to use the condo solely for personal purposes instead of renting it?
If he uses the property solely for personal use then he has no filing requirement in the U.S. until he sells it.

In what country(s) does Jerry need to report his rental income and expenses?
The U.S. rental income and expenses must be reported in both the U.S. and Canada. In the U.S. because the property is located in the U.S., and in Canada because Jerry is a Canadian resident and is subject to tax on a worldwide income basis.

U.S. Real Property Interests

Since the recent economic downturn in the U.S., it has become more common for Canadians to purchase U.S. real estate. Some purchase property for business or investment purposes and some purchase simply for personal use.

 No matter what the reason, eventually there will be some sort of income tax filing that is required.

Owning U.S. situs assets, i.e., U.S. real estate is a U.S. situs asset, can cause a non-resident and non-citizen of the U.S. to have taxable U.S. income at some point in time and be subject to U.S. gift and estate tax if one is not careful. Knowing the tax implications of owning U.S. property can significantly make buying and selling decisions easier as well as help to simplify questions around how to own such property to reduce compliance requirements and potential taxation later down the road.

A U.S. real property interest is defined as any interest in real property (including a mine, well, or other natural deposit) located in the U.S. Real property includes land and un-severed timber, crops and minerals.

Every individual who has or who will eventually have a taxable transaction to report in the U.S. will need a U.S. identification number. If you are a non-resident and non U.S. citizen you will need an ITIN. An ITIN is similar to a U.S. social security number in its look; however, it does not allow a person to live or work in the U.S. but instead is only a filer number so the IRS can identify you in their system.

Generally you do not need a U.S. ITIN when purchasing U.S. property interests; however, if the seller is applying for a reduced amount of withholding tax using form 8288-B, discussed in more detail later in the chapter, both the buyer and the seller need ITINs. As mentioned in Chapter 4, an ITIN is applied for using form W-7.

Individual Taxpayer Identification Number (ITIN)

The IRS is very cautious when it comes to issuing U.S. tax filer numbers; they want to be sure they are issuing numbers only to those who actually need them. To obtain an Individual Taxpayer Identification Number, an individual must meet one of the options available to apply for an ITIN. The options available are as follows:

a. non-resident alien required to get ITIN to claim tax treaty benefit

b. non-resident alien filing a U.S. tax return

c. U.S. resident alien (based on days present in the U.S.) filing a U.S tax return

d. dependant of U.S. citizen/resident alien

e. spouse of U.S. citizen/resident alien

f. non-resident alien student, professor, or researcher filing a U.S. tax return or claiming an exception

g. dependant/spouse of a non-resident alien holding a U.S. visa

h. Other (must meet one of 5 exceptions)

- *Exception 1: passive income – third party withholding or tax treaty benefits.* You may apply for an ITIN if you receive partnership income, interest income, annuity income, rental income, or other passive income subject to third party withholding.

- *Exception 2: other income.* You may apply if you are claiming the benefits of a U.S. income tax treaty with a foreign country and you receive wages, salary, compensation and honoraria payments, scholarships, fellowships and grants or gambling income; or you receive taxable scholarship, fellowship or grant income but are not claiming the treaty benefits.

- *Exception 3: mortgage interest - third party reporting.* You may apply if you have a home mortgage loan on real property you own in the U.S. that is subject to third party reporting of mortgage interest.

- *Exception 4: dispositions by a foreign person of US. real property interest – third party withholding.* May apply if you are a foreign person selling or buying U.S. real property to or from another foreign person (generally withholding tax applies).

- *Exception 5: Treasury decision (TD) 9363.* May apply for an ITIN if you have an IRS reporting requirement under a specific section of the treasury decision and are submitting form W-7 with form 13350.

More information regarding these exceptions and what supporting documentation is required to be submitted with the ITIN application can be found in the instructions to form W-7 on the IRS website, www.irs.gov.

The process of applying for a U.S. ITIN was previously discussed in chapter 4 so please refer to that chapter for a refresher of the rules.

FIRPTA and Capital Gains on the Sale of U.S. Real Estate

 When a U.S. property is sold it triggers a taxable event no matter what your residency status is.

When U.S. real property is sold by anyone, a taxable event takes place which requires the person to calculate whether a capital gain or capital loss exists and if a capital gain exists then income taxes may be due on that disposition. When a foreign person sells U.S. real property, the disposition of that property is subject to the Foreign Investment in Real Property Tax Act of 1980 (FIRPTA) income tax withholding. That is, anyone purchasing U.S. real property interests from foreign persons is required to withhold 10% of the purchase price; foreign persons can be individuals or corporations (there are special rules for foreign corporations holding and selling U.S. real estate, more on that a little later in the chapter). The withholding tax is simply a prepayment of the income tax that may result on the disposition of the property but is not in addition to regular income tax. The withholding tax is applicable even if a loss results from the disposition; however, you can request a reduced amount of withholding tax in a situation like that (see below for further details).

 The FIRPTA withholding tax amount is 10% of the gross proceeds for an individual disposing of the property.

Generally, the buyer (the transferee) must deduct and withhold a tax equal to 10% of the total amount realized by the foreign person on the disposition (i.e., gross sales proceeds). The amount realized is generally the total amount paid for the property. In most cases, the buyer is the withholding agent. It is incumbent upon the buyer to find out if the seller is a foreign person. If the seller is a foreign person and the buyer fails to withhold, the buyer may be held liable for the tax.

 If the seller (transferor) is a foreign person and the buyer fails to withhold, the buyer may be held personally liable for the tax. It doesn't matter where the buyer is resident or what the buyer's citizenship status is.

If you are a Canadian selling U.S. real estate, then not only will your total proceeds from the sale of the property be subject to the FIRPTA withholding tax, but you may also have to pay capital gains tax in the U.S. and/or Canada. The point is that you need to have your head up about U.S. real estate investments; know what you're getting into and plan accordingly in order to minimize the cross-border tax hit (i.e., other potential taxes exist relating to U.S. property but that is discussed later in this chapter). Let's work through an example to see how a Canadian selling a U.S. property might be affected by these tax rules.

Real Life: FIRPTA withholding on sale of U.S. property by a Canadian

To keep this example simple, assume that Jesse owns a property in Tennessee and it has solely been for personal use. He bought the property in 2009 and paid $110,000 USD. He did some renovations in 2011 and added a new deck for $10,000 but then in 2014 he received an offer to sell the property for $200,000 so he took it. The buyer is also from Canada and plans to use the property as a vacation home. Jesse received a cheque for $180,000 in June of 2014, net of a 10% withholding tax, subject to FIRPTA, on the gross sale proceeds.

Jesse will have to file a 1040NR return to report the capital gain of $80,000. The same capital gain will have to be reported on his Canadian return, except the amounts will have to be converted to Canadian dollars at the applicable exchange rates on the dates the property was purchased, renovations were made and the date the property was sold.

In the U.S., because Jesse held the property for more than 1 year, the gain is considered a long-term capital gain for tax purposes which means that 100% of the gain is taxed at 15% (or possibly 20% if he meets the income test); however, $20,000 was already withheld on the initial sale so he should expect a refund of $8,000 when he files his 1040NR return ($80,000 @ 15% = $12,000 of tax, minus $20,000 of withholdings).

In Canada, Jesse will pay tax on 50% of the Canadian dollar capital gain at his applicable exchange rate but he will be able to claim a foreign tax credit for the $12,000 of tax already paid in the U.S.

The FIRPTA tax withheld on the purchase of U.S. real property from a foreign person is reported and paid using Form 8288. Form 8288 also serves as the transmittal form for copies A and B of Form 8288-A, Statement of Withholding on Dispositions by Foreign Persons of U.S. Real Property Interests.

The form must be filed and the amount withheld (or lesser amount as determined by the IRS) must be reported and paid within 20 days following the day on which a copy of the withholding certificate or notice of denial is mailed by the IRS.

The withholding agent must prepare a Form 8288–A for each person from whom tax has been withheld. This serves as the tax slip to be attached to the U.S. return when it is filed so the seller can claim the withholding tax against the final tax payable on the return.

As briefly mentioned earlier in the chapter, if the seller wishes to apply for a reduced amount of withholding tax to be taken on the disposition, form 8288-B must be completed. This is referred to as applying for a withholding certificate from the IRS. If the principal purpose of applying for a withholding certificate is to delay paying the tax withheld to the IRS, the transferee will be subject to interest and penalties.

Keep in mind that in order for the reduced amount of withholding tax to be taken, the withholding certificate must be received prior to the closing date of the sale or the buyer is required to withhold the 10%. One reason a reduced amount of withholding may be requested is if the net tax owing on the disposition will be less than the 10% tax taken on the gross proceeds (i.e., if the tax on the capital gain will be less than 10% of gross proceeds, a reduced amount of withholding tax may be requested so more money is kept in your pocket now rather than waiting for the refund later).

Real Life: *Sale of U.S. real property by a Canadian receiving a withholding certificate*

On March 2, 2014, Sven, a Canadian citizen, agreed to sell his Phoenix home to another Canadian resident who is going to be using it as a vacation property. Sale price was $385,000 and original cost was $205,000.

Because the capital gain realized on the sale is only $180,000, Sven wanted to apply for withholding tax to be taken only on the net gain rather than the gross proceeds so he completed form 8288-B and hopes to have the approved withholding certificate in his hands prior to the sale closing date of June 30, 2014.

Provided the withholding certificate is approved and received by Sven prior to the close of the sale, the withholding tax required will only be $18,000 ($180,000*10%) instead of $38,500 ($385,000*10%).

For cases in which a U.S. business entity such as a corporation or partnership disposes of a U.S. real property interest, the business entity itself is the withholding agent. If the property sold (transferred) was owned jointly by U.S. and foreign persons, the amount realized is allocated between the transferors based on the capital contribution of each transferor.

A foreign corporation that distributes a U.S. real property interest to its shareholders must withhold a tax equal to 35% of the gain it recognizes on the distribution.

Exceptions to FIRPTA Withholding

There are some exceptions to FIRPTA withholdings. Below is a list of some of the more common exceptions where FIRTA withholdings are generally not required:

1. The buyer (transferee) acquires the property for use as a home and the amount paid for the property (generally the sales price) is not more than $300,000. In this case, the buyer or a member of the buyer's family must be planning to live at the property for at least 50% of the time the property is used by any person during each of the first 2 years after the property is purchased. When counting the number of days the property is used, do not count the days the property will be vacant.

Real Life: Sale of U.S. real property by a Canadian

In October 2013, Steven, a Canadian citizen, sold his Florida home to another Canadian resident who was going to be moving to the U.S. in February 2014 to work in Florida. Sale price was $285,000 and original cost was $185,000.

Because the buyer is going to be living in the Florida home and the sale price is under $300,000, no withholding taxes are required under FIRPTA.

2. The seller (transferor) provides the buyer with a certification stating, under penalties of perjury, that the transferor is not a foreign person and containing the transferor's name, U.S. taxpayer identification number, and home address (or office address, in the case of an entity).
3. The buyer receives a withholding certificate from the Internal Revenue Service that excuses withholding.
4. The amount the seller realizes on the transfer of a U.S. real property interest is zero.
5. The property is acquired by the United States, a U.S. state or possession, a political subdivision thereof, or the District of Columbia.

There are more exceptions than this but this book only discusses the more common exceptions. Refer to the IRS website for a detailed list of FIRPTA withholding tax exceptions (www.irs.gov).

Gift Tax

U.S. gift tax is a tax on the transfer of property from one individual to another while receiving nothing, or less than full value, in return. Gift tax is basically estate tax applied while a person is alive.

 Trusts and corporations are not subject to gift tax.

The gift tax applies to any property, so if you give property (including money), or the use of or income from property, without expecting something of equal value or more in return, you are giving a gift. If you sell something at less than its full value or if you make an interest-free or reduced-interest loan, you may be making a gift as well.

 Even though gift tax is a U.S. tax, it is applicable to all U.S. property, no matter who owns it.

For example, if a non-resident owns U.S. property, he or she must be aware of the potential U.S. gift tax on that property. The annual gift tax exemption amount is $14,000 per person; however, an exemption of $145,000 ($143,000 in 2013) is allowed by a donor to a spouse who is not a U.S. citizen. Gift tax is combined with estate tax when a person dies.

Gift tax rates are graduated and range from 18% to 40% for 2013 and 2014 (35% was the maximum amount for 2012).

Real Life: Canadians gifting U.S. situs assets (i.e., assets physically located in the U.S.)

Rhonda and Randy jointly own a home in Scottsdale, Arizona, where they have vacationed for the last 20 years. Randy's health has been declining so traveling isn't an option anymore and because of this they want to give their property to their children. The Scottsdale home is now worth $180,000.

If they decide to gift their U.S. property to their son and daughter, they will be subject to gift tax on the amount of the gift over the $14,000 annual limit (i.e., each will be deemed to be gifting $45,000 to each of their children and $31,000 would be a taxable gift). We will discuss gift tax dollar amounts in a later chapter.

U.S. Estate Tax

Estate tax is a tax on your right to transfer property at your death. An individual's gross estate consists of everything you own or have an interest in on the date of death and is generally calculated using fair market value (FMV) on the date of death. However, an alternative valuation date may be used if the value of the estate is less on that date than on the date of death. The alternative valuation day is any day between the date of death and six months after the date of death.

 Every U.S. citizen and resident has access to the estate tax exemption amount of $5,340,000.

This means that a person's estate is not taxable unless it is over this exemption amount. Any amount over the estate exemption is taxed at a rate of 40% (current for 2013 and 2014).

 Most people think that U.S. estate tax is applicable only to U.S. citizens and residents; however, it can be applicable to non-residents of the U.S. as well.

All U.S. property held by an individual, no matter where that individual lives or is a citizen of, can trigger U.S. estate tax. However, the Canada/U.S. Tax Convention allows a Canadian resident the ability to claim a prorated portion of the U.S. estate tax exemption amount, which can help to minimize the total estate tax payable (i.e., the $5,340,000 exemption is multiplied by the ratio of U.S. situs assets over worldwide assets). Let's look at an example to see how this exemption works.

Real Life: Canadian using the prorated estate exemption

Phylecia (a Canadian citizen) died in 2013, leaving behind a fairly large estate worth a total of $2,989,675. Her estate was a mixture of U.S. and Canadian situs assets. Her Canadian assets totaled $2,354,675, while her U.S. assets only totaled $635,000. Phylicia's total estate is below the estate tax exemption of $5,250,000; therefore, she will not be subject to U.S. estate tax. Her percentage of the estate tax exemption is calculated as follows:

- $5,250,000 * 635,000/2,989,675=$1,115,088

- U.S. situs property = $635,000

- Estate exemption available = $1,115,088 (more than the value of the U.S. situs assets)

The *gross estate* includes the value of all property you own partially or outright at the time of death and includes the following:

- life insurance proceeds payable to your estate or, if you owned the policy, to your heirs;
- the value of certain annuities payable to your estate or your heirs; and
- the value of certain property you transferred within 3 years before your death.

the value of certain property you transferred within 3 years before your death.

The allowable deductions in the U.S. used in determining your taxable estate include:

- funeral expenses paid out of your estate;
- debts you owed at the time of death;
- the marital deduction (generally, the value of the property that passes from your estate to your surviving spouse);
- the charitable deduction (generally, the value of the property that passes from your estate to the United States, any state, a political subdivision of a state, the District of Columbia, or to a qualifying charity for exclusively charitable purposes); and
- the state death tax deduction (generally any estate, inheritance, legacy, or succession taxes paid as the result of the decedent's death to any state or the District of Columbia.

There are a few ways to structure the purchase of U.S. situs assets in order to help reduce the estate tax exposure one might be subject to; this will be discussed at the end of this chapter.

Estate and gift tax is discussed in more detail in Chapter 12.

Rental Income

To help cover some of the overhead costs associated with owning a second property, some people make the decision to rent out their vacation home in the months they aren't using it. This results in the individual earning U.S. source income and requires an income tax return to be filed.

 Generally, a 30% withholding tax applies to the gross amount of rent paid to a non-resident of the U.S. on real estate located in the U.S.

However, to avoid this withholding tax deduction, a Canadian can make an election to file a U.S. tax return and pay tax on their net rental income by completing a form W-8ECI (elect to treat the income as effectively connected with a trade or business in the U.S.). This is generally the desired option because the taxpayer can deduct expenses related to the rental property, such as property tax, mortgage interest, maintenance fees, insurance and utilities against the rental income and pay tax only on the net profits received from the rental property.

The main difference between Canada and the U.S. with regard to the deductibility of rental expenses relates to depreciation. In Canada, you are only allowed to deduct depreciation up to the amount of profit reported before depreciation is taken but you cannot create a loss for income tax purposes using depreciation (i.e., you must deduct less than the maximum allowed for depreciation, simply to nil out income). This is not the case in the U.S. In the U.S. depreciation is mandatory on all property/assets used for income-producing purposes, which means that even if the deduction of depreciation creates a loss for income tax purposes in the U.S. you must take the full deduction. In most instances, this generally means that by electing to file a non-resident income tax return and claim the rental income as effectively connected income in the U.S., the non-resident taxpayer pays no income tax at the end of the year and saves having to claim back the 30% withholding tax that would have been taken during the year.

Keep in mind that only the "business portion" of the rental expenses is deductible against the rental income. In other words, if the property is used at all for personal purposes, a prorated portion of the expenses must be excluded to account for the personal use.

 If the property in the U.S. is used for non-active business purposes (i.e., rental property) and the cost of the property is over $100,000, a separate foreign property reporting form is required in Canada - a T1135.

If the property is owned in joint title, both owners will need to apply for ITINs and file separate 1040NR returns (chapter 4 discusses this topic briefly as well). The ITIN application process is the same for sole ownership or joint ownership and is as follows:

- Complete a 1040NR return and related real estate rental forms and schedules (i.e., schedule E, form 4562, or, if you filed W-8ECI, then Schedule C), leaving blank any areas that ask for an identifier number.

- Complete a form W-7, Application for Individual Taxpayer Identification Number (ITIN), and attach a certified copy of your Canadian passport (can only be certified by the Canadian passport office) along with the completed 1040NR return and related schedules

- Submit entire package to the ITIN application office for processing

If you complete form W-8ECI, the net rental income and expenses are accounted for on schedule C instead of Schedule E because you are treating them as being effectively connected with a trade or business in the U.S., which means the statement of business income and expenses should now be used. Keep in mind that a state return may be required as well, depending on where your vacation home is located.

If you decide not to use your vacation home as a rental property and simply use it for personal use, no income tax filings are required until the property is sold and an ITIN may not be needed until then either.

If you use the property for rental purposes but also use it personally during the year, you will not be restricted with regard to deductible rental expenses as long as the personal use doesn't exceed the greater of 14 days or 10% of the number of days rented by fair value renters.

Real Life: Canadian owning U.S. rental property

Alysha and her husband Anthony love to vacation in Florida, so in 2013 they decided to purchase jointly a vacation home just outside Miami where they stay 30 days of the year. The expenses to maintain their home in Canada as well as the property in Florida were getting a little overwhelming for them so at the beginning of 2014 they decided to rent out their Florida home on a short-term basis in the months that they don't use it.

Most of their renters stay 1 to 2 weeks at a time and are tourists to the Miami area. Alysha and Anthony receive rent of approximately $1,500 per month but incur expenses of approximately $1,300 per month, including management fees of $200 per month (they pay a management company to manage the collection of the rental income and take care of the property while they are away).

Alysha and Anthony will each need to apply for an ITIN and file separate 1040NR returns claiming 50% of the rental income and expenses each, as well as 50% of the depreciation allowed. They will also need to exclude approximately 8% of the total expenses for the year as that is the personal use percentage (30/365).

The same is true for their Canadian tax returns. Alysha and Anthony will each report 50% of all income and expenses, but the amount of depreciation available to them may be limited depending on the amount of profit before depreciation.

Ownership Structures for Canadian Residents Owning U.S. Property

There are a few options for Canadians when it comes to purchasing U.S. property interests. The U.S. property can be purchased in a Canadian holding company if it is used for rental purposes, it can be purchased by a trust, or it can be purchased directly by the individual(s).

 Purchasing the property directly by the individual is the simplest purchase option.

One can purchase the property with multiple individuals or by oneself. By purchasing the property jointly, you multiply the estate tax exemption opportunities which means that U.S. estate tax is less likely to apply if you still own the property when you die (i.e., the estate tax exemption is available to each individual and the FMV of the property is split between each joint interest). Multiple owners may use a partnership to purchase the property as well but if a partnership is used, you need to remember that partnerships have their own reporting rules and filing requirements, even though the income is taxed in the hands of the partners in the end.

 Purchasing the property in a Canadian holding company will avoid U.S. estate tax because estate tax is a tax only applicable to individuals.

When using a corporation to purchase any kind of property, you need to be sure you put only business property in the company because the Canadian tax rules will penalize the individual shareholder of the corporation for putting personal-use property inside a corporation; the penalty is not desirable. The same is true for U.S. companies holding personal property.

 Using a trust to hold U.S. property can be a beneficial ownership structure but there are a few things that need to be considered before this type of structure is utilized.

The first is that the property needs to be purchased directly by the trust. The U.S. have what is called "grantor trust rules" which means that if an individual purchases a U.S. property and then wants to roll it into the trust, the grantor trust rules will ignore the trust as being the owner and still treat the individual to be the owner for U.S. estate tax purposes and for income tax purposes; this is not the desired result.

If the property is purchased directly by the trust, U.S. estate tax is avoided because trusts are treated as separate entities and not as individuals and the U.S. grantor trust rules will not apply because an individual never owned the property at any given time. Also keep in mind that a trust has a 21-year rule in Canada which means that after 21 years the trust is deemed to dispose of the property and immediately re-acquire it, resulting in capital gains issues. Further, remember that inter vivos trusts (i.e., trusts created while a person is still alive) in Canada are taxed at high rates so the taxes paid each year may be higher than the taxes on the property if it was owned personally.

According to the IRS website, "Foreign trusts to which a U.S. taxpayer has transferred property are treated as grantor trusts as long as the trust has at least one U.S. beneficiary. The income the trust earns is taxable to the grantor under the grantor trust rules. Grantor trusts are not recognized as separate taxable entities, because under the terms of the trust, the grantor retains one or more powers and remains the owner of the trust income. In such a case, the trust income is taxed to the grantor, whether or not the income is distributed to another party." This means that the use of some Canadian trusts will be less attractive and not as useful to some individuals because the income and the property that the trust owns may still be deemed to be earned and owned by the U.S. person who created the trust in the beginning because of the U.S. grantor trust rules. The trust may work for Canadian tax planning purposes but may not for U.S. purposes if it falls under the U.S. grantor trust rules.

Separate state tax rules may apply to all the above situations so you need to research the particular state rules before making any decisions. Using a U.S. trust may be a better option in certain states to help avoid probate fees in that state.

Real Life: *Canadian transferring a U.S. property into a trust*

Sam was vacationing in Las Vegas last summer and came across a nice house that was for sale at a price he couldn't pass up. He bought the property personally because he wanted to make sure he didn't miss out on this property. Sam's intention was always to have the property held in a trust so it could be available for his family's use and tax implications could be reduced if anything happened to him, so he thought it would be a simple transaction to just roll the property into the trust the way we normally would if the property was in Canada.

The problem is that under the U.S. grantor trust rules, when an individual transfers property into a trust, that property is still deemed to be "owned" by the transferor; therefore, any income earned from that property is still attributed to the transferor, and the property is still considered owned by the transferor for estate tax purposes. That is, the property is still considered part of the transferor's estate and is taxed accordingly. These rules effectively negate all the advantages of using a trust.

Non-Residents Owing U.S. Rest Estate: What You Need to Know

- U.S. gift and estate tax is applicable to all U.S. situs assets, which mean that non-residents can be subjected to this tax as well.
- FIRPTA withholding taxes apply to the disposition of U.S. real property by a foreign person unless certain exceptions exist; the withholding tax rate is 10% of gross proceeds.
- On capital gains, 100% of the gain is taxed in the U.S. whereas only 50% is taxable in Canada; however, the U.S. tax paid can be used as a credit against the Canadian tax payable.
- U.S. real property can be purchased individually, in a trust or within a corporation; however, each structure has its advantages and disadvantages.

WHAT YOU NEED TO KNOW ABOUT UNCLE SAM:

Many Canadians are purchasing U.S. real estate for personal and/or for rental use. No matter what the reason, tax could result in either case. The disposition of U.S. real estate is a taxable transaction in the U.S. as well as Canada, but the gains are taxed differently on both sides of the border.

One hundred percent of a capital gain is taxed in the U.S. whereas only 50% is taxed in Canada; and in Canada the gain is taxed at a person's marginal tax rate, whereas in the U.S. long-term gains are taxed at set rates and short-term gains are taxed at marginal rates. Tax paid on U.S. real property can be used as a foreign tax credit in Canada against the tax owing on that same income.

U.S. gift and estate tax can be applicable to a non-resident's U.S. situs assets but there may be a way to structure the purchase of such assets to help mitigate these taxes. Every situation is different so there is no universal answer for everyone. ***Know the rules and plan ahead prior to purchasing your U.S. property so you aren't left owing any extra U.S. tax!***

CHAPTER 6

Investing in the U.S.
& U.S. Source Income

Case Study

Peter is a 56-year-old Canadian citizen who lives and works in Calgary, Alberta. Over the years he has invested a substantial amount of money and has managed to build an investment portfolio worth over $1 Million. Peter invests in both Canadian and U.S. stocks and bonds and earns a significant amount of investment income each year through dividends, interest and capital gains. He has also contributed $250,000 to his RRSPs over the years.

In 2013, Peter earned $3,600 in dividends and $363 of interest from his U.S. stocks and bonds. He also earned $3,650 in dividends from his Canadian stocks. A 30% withholding tax was taken on the U.S. dividends and interest payments.

Questions & Answers:

Is Peter required to file a U.S. tax return in 2013?
Technically, yes, because the gross income amount is over the filing threshold (see chapter 1 for thresholds) but because withholding tax has been taken on his U.S. source income he doesn't really have to; however, it would be in his best interest to file a return because too much withholding tax was taken (i.e., he will get a refund).

What amount of income tax will Peter be required to pay on his U.S. income?
15% on his U.S. dividends and 0% on his U.S. interest for U.S. purposes and whatever marginal rate he is subjected to in Canada on the dividends and interest.

What should Peter do to make sure the correct amount of withholding tax is taken on his U.S. source income?

Peter should complete a W-8BEN Form and give it to the payor of his U.S. dividends and interest so they are aware of what the appropriate withholding tax rates are under the treaty.

Residents of Canada and the U.S. both have many investment options available to them. Some of these investments assist individuals with saving for retirement, reducing income tax, and saving for their children's education; however, these investments are not treated the same way on both sides of the border for tax purposes.

Canadian Retirement Plans

RRSPs & RRIFs

An RRSP (Registered Retirement Savings Plan) is a Canadian retirement savings plan that you can establish for yourself or your spouse or a common-law partner. Deductible RRSP contributions can be used to reduce your tax in Canada. Any income you earn in the RRSP is exempt from Canadian tax as long as the funds remain in the plan; however, withdrawals from the RRSP are subject to tax and are reportable on the Canadian T1 return.

A RRIF (Registered Retirement Income Fund) is a Canadian plan that you can establish with a financial institution and register with the Canada Revenue Agency (CRA). A RRIF is established when you transfer property to the institution from an RRSP, RPP (Registered Pension Plan), or from another RRIF; the institution is then required to move periodic annuity payments to you. Establishing a RRIF can be done at any time, but must be done no later than the year the annuitant turns 71. Once a RRIF is established, there cannot be any more contributions made to the plan and the plan cannot be terminated except through death. You can have more than one RRIF and you can have self-directed RRIFs as well

Although the above retirement plans are tax deferred plans in Canada, this is not automatically the case for U.S. purposes.

 For U.S. purposes, these are foreign pension plans, which means that a tax deduction is not available for contributions made to the plan and they are not automatically treated as tax-deferred plans either (i.e., you could potentially be taxed on the income earned each year within the plan).

The Canada-U.S. Tax Convention allows an election to be made in the U.S. to have these plans treated as tax-deferred retirement plans in the same manner that they are treated in Canada. The election is made using Form 8891.

A Registered Pension Plan or RPP is another type of tax-deferred pension plan in Canada that is often set up through one's employer and is not managed by the employee. This retirement plan is more comparable to U.S. pension plans, which does allow it to receive automatic tax-deferred treatment under the tax treaty. Deductions to this type of plan are allowed in the U.S. under the treaty and these plans receive special exemptions from foreign trust rules as well.

Real Life: Dual citizen with a Canadian RRSP

Thomas is a dual citizen of Canada and the U.S.; however, he lives and works in Canada. He earns an annual salary of $75,000 and contributes $12,000 to his RRSPs each year.

In Canada he would pay tax only on the net income of $63,000; however, in the U.S. he would not get a deduction from his income for the $12,000 RRSP contribution and he would be required to complete Form 8891 to elect to have his RRSP treated as tax deferred for U.S. purposes the same as it is in Canada. Without this election, Thomas runs the risk of the IRS taxing him on the income earned within the RRSP account even though he is not drawing the money out.

Because there is no U.S. deduction allowed for the contributions to the RRSP, when the RRSPs are drawn upon, Thomas will be subject to tax in the U.S. only on the income portion of the withdrawals; however, he will be taxed on 100% of the withdrawals in Canada.

 RRSPs and RRIFs are considered foreign trusts for U.S. tax purposes; however, the Canada-U.S. Tax Convention specifically exempts them from the separate reporting requirements relating to foreign trusts.

U.S. Retirement Plans - 401(K), 403(B) & IRAs

401(k) Retirement Plans

A U.S. 401(k) plan is a qualified, tax-deferred compensation plan in which an employee can elect to have the employer contribute a portion of his or her cash wages to the plan before taxes. Generally, these deferred wages are not subject to income tax withholding at the time of deferral, and they are not reflected in your taxable income on the 1040 return; however, they are included as wages subject to social security, Medicare, and federal unemployment taxes. The amount that an employee may elect to defer to a 401(k) plan is limited by the Internal Revenue Code and the terms of the plan.

Distributions from a 401(k) plan may qualify for optional lump-sum distribution treatment or rollover treatment as long as they meet specific requirements. A rollover occurs when you withdraw cash or other assets from one eligible retirement plan and contribute all or part of it *within 60 days* to another eligible retirement plan. This transaction is not taxable but it is reportable on your Federal Tax Return as long as it is rolled into another U.S. retirement plan. Most distributions from an eligible retirement plan can be rolled over, but there are exceptions. Any taxable amount of a distribution that is not rolled over must be included in income in the year of the distribution and if you are under age 59 1/2 at the time of the distribution, any taxable portion not rolled over may be subject to a 10% additional tax on early distributions unless an exception applies.

 Distributions received before age 59 1/2 are subject to an early distribution penalty of 10% additional tax unless an exception applies.

This additional tax is in addition to regular income tax and is calculated and due when your income tax payment is due (i.e., April 15th of the following year). A regular 20% withholding tax applies to all 401(k) distributions, unless a reduced rate is applicable under an income tax treaty.

 If a distribution is paid to you, you have 60 days from the date you receive it to roll it over to another eligible retirement plan on a tax deferred basis.

403(b) Retirement Plans

A U.S. 403(b) plan, also known as a tax-sheltered annuity plan, is a retirement plan for certain employees of public schools, employees of certain tax-exempt organizations and certain ministers. A 403(b) plan allows employees to contribute some of their salary to the plan but the employer may also contribute to the plan.

A 403(b) plan may allow employees to take money out of the plan when they:

- reach age 59½;
- have a severance from employment;
- become disabled;

- die; or
- encounter a financial hardship.

Eligible distributions may be rolled over to another plan or an IRA (IRA's are discussed below).

 The employee will have to pay taxes on any amount of the distribution that was not from after-tax contributions and may have to pay an additional 10% early distribution tax unless an exception to this tax applies.

IRAs (Individual Retirement Arrangement)

A U.S. individual retirement arrangement, or IRA, is a personal savings plan that allows you to set aside money for retirement, while offering you tax advantages; similar to Canadian RRSPs. You can set up different kinds of IRAs with a variety of organizations, such as a bank or other financial institution, a mutual fund, or a life insurance company.

You may be able to deduct some or all of your contributions to a traditional IRA and you may also be eligible for a tax credit equal to a percentage of your contribution. Amounts in your traditional IRA, including earnings, generally are not taxed until distributed to you. IRAs cannot be owned jointly; however, any amounts remaining in your IRA upon your death will be paid to your beneficiary or beneficiaries.

To contribute to a traditional IRA, you must be under age 70½ at the end of the tax year and you, and/or your spouse if you file a joint return, must have taxable compensation, such as wages, salaries, commissions, tips, bonuses, or net income from self-employment.

Distributions from a traditional IRA are fully or partially taxable in the year of distribution. If you made only deductible contributions, distributions are fully taxable.

 Distributions made prior to age 59 1/2 may be subject to a 10% additional tax. You also may owe an excise tax if you do not begin to withdraw minimum distributions by April 1st of the year after you reach age 70 1/2.

A Roth IRA is a form of retirement savings plan that is generally created with after tax dollars. A Roth IRA differs from a traditional IRA in several ways:

1. A Roth IRA does not permit a deduction at the time of contribution.

2. Regardless of your age, you may be able to establish and make non-deductible contributions to a Roth IRA, and you do not report Roth contributions on your tax return.

3. To be a Roth IRA, the account or annuity must be designated as a Roth IRA when established.

4. Like a traditional IRA, a Roth IRA can be set up but there is a limitation on the amount that can be contributed for each year and there is a deadline for each contribution.

> *You do not include in your gross income qualified distributions or distributions that are a return of your regular contributions from your Roth IRA(s). A 10% early withdrawal penalty will only apply to a taxable Roth IRA distribution; however, taxable Roth IRA distributions are not common.*

401(k) & IRA Rollover to an RRSP

Depending on age and the rules governing the U.S. plan, a Canadian resident taxpayer can collapse their U.S. plan and transfer lump-sum superannuation or pension benefits under the ITA on plan assets that are individual contributions (i.e., not contributions made by an employer or government entity).

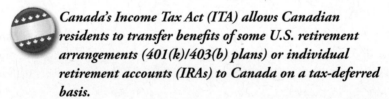

> *Canada's Income Tax Act (ITA) allows Canadian residents to transfer benefits of some U.S. retirement arrangements (401(k)/403(b) plans) or individual retirement accounts (IRAs) to Canada on a tax-deferred basis.*

A rollover from a U.S. 401(k) is only eligible if the amount received from the 401(k) plan is a lump-sum payment, is attributable to services rendered by the individual (or his or her spouse or common-law partner) during the period in which the individual was a Canadian non-resident, and the amount transferred to an RRSP must be specifically designated as a transfer on the personal income tax return for the year of transfer (see contribution limit rules below).

If a withdrawal from an IRA qualifies as an "eligible amount" and is rolled into an individual's RRSP within 60 days after the end of the year, a tax deductible contribution is received. As with transfers from a 401(k) plan discussed above, the amount contributed to an RRSP from an IRA must also be designated on the personal income tax return.

To be an "eligible amount," the amount must be included in income, received as a lump-sum payment and not as part of a series of periodic payments, and derived from contributions made to the plan by either the individual or the individual's spouse or partner, not his or her employer.

> *Although the analysis of the tax treatment of Roth IRAs in Canada is complex, the general consensus is that the receipt of funds from a Roth IRA will not be taxable in Canada. As a result, there would be no benefit to transferring a Roth IRA to an RRSP, even if permitted.*

Under Canadian and U.S. tax rules, funds withdrawn from a foreign retirement plan such as a 401(k) or IRA are taxable as income in the year the plan is collapsed in the U.S. The withdrawal amount must be included as income in the Canadian tax return, but a deduction for the amount transferred to an RRSP can offset the income inclusion (if contributed within 60 days after the end of the year).

> *Upon collapse of the U.S. plan, the U.S. administrator will withhold 15% tax for non-resident aliens.*

Normally the withholding tax is 20% for U.S. residents, but the tax treaty reduces this withholding to 15%.

> *In the U.S., the rollover of your 401(k), 403(b) or IRA withdrawal will be subject to the 10% penalty tax mentioned above if you are under the age of 59 1/2 and the withdrawal will also be taxable.*

The tax treaty limits the tax to 15% for non-residents of the U.S. which means you would have 85% of the withdrawal to put into the RRSP instead of the usual 80%, unless you make up the 15% out of your own pocket (i.e., have extra cash sitting around which allows you to contribute an amount equal to the 15% into your RRSP). This means, however, that the 15% is now subject to income tax in Canada if no additional contribution is made because 100% of the foreign pension was withdrawn but only 85% of the cash is available to roll into an RRSP which leaves 15% as net taxable income because it wasn't rolled into the plan.

Your RRSP contribution limits do not apply if you are only transferring individual contributions; however, if you are transferring employer contributions as well, unused RRSP contribution room can be used to offset the required income inclusion.

Real Life: 401(k) rollover to an RRSP

Larry is 45 years old and was working in the U.S. on a temporary work visa for 3 years and has accumulated $35,000 in a U.S. 401(k). He plans to move back to Canada and wishes to transfer his 401(k) into his existing Canadian RRSP.

When Larry withdraws his funds from the 401(k), $5,250 will be withheld from the distribution, leaving only $29,750 available to be contributed to his RRSP. The full $35,000 will be shown as taxable income in Canada; however, he will receive an offsetting deduction for the $29,750 that is being rolled into the RRSP. Assume his tax rate is 40%, the $5,250 not rolled into the RRSP would generate tax of $2,100 but because he already paid some tax in the U.S. on this amount, he can use the $5,250 in U.S. tax as a foreign tax credit to offset the taxes owing in Canada. He can carry forward any unused foreign tax credit for a period not greater than 7 years (i.e., $3,150 carried forward).

IMPORTANT NOTE: The foreign tax credit carried forward can only be used to offset other foreign income so if you are not going to have foreign income within the following 7 years, proper planning should be done to maximize the use of the credits so double taxation can be eliminated. A planning option would be to not roll as much into the RRSP so you leave more income to be taxed in Canada which will use a higher amount of the foreign tax credit up. If you have no foreign income over the next 7 years the taxes paid in the U.S. are lost and when you draw the RRSP out at a future date, tax will be due in Canada which means double tax will occur (i.e., lose tax credit now and pay more Canadian tax overall plus pay tax later vs. use full credit now to reduce Canadian tax now plus pay later).

RESPs & TFSAs

A Canadian Registered Education Savings Plan (RESP) is a contract between an individual (the subscriber) and a person or organization (the promoter) where the subscriber names one or more beneficiaries and makes contributions to the plan for them and the promoter agrees to pay educational assistance payments (EAPs) to the beneficiaries.

The subscriber generally makes contributions to the RESP but they cannot deduct the contributions from their income on their tax return. The promoter usually pays the contributions, and the income earned on those contributions, to the beneficiaries; income earned is paid as educational assistance payments (EAPs) and is fully taxable to the beneficiary. The contribution portion of the withdrawal is tax-free to the beneficiary because the contributor has already paid tax on these funds.

If the contributions are not paid out to the beneficiary, the promoter usually pays them to the subscriber at the end of the contract. Subscribers do not have to include the contributions in their income when they get them back. Beneficiaries have to include the EAPs in their income for the year in which they receive them; however, they do not have to include the contributions they receive in their income.

These plans are eligible to receive a government grant which is referred to as a Canada Education Savings Grants (CESG); however, if the beneficiary does not pursue post-secondary education, the CESG must be returned to the government.

The Tax-Free Savings Account (TFSA) allows Canadians, age 18 and over, to set money aside tax-free throughout their lifetime. Each calendar year, you can contribute up to $5,500 ($5,000 from 2009 to 2012), any unused TFSA contribution room from the previous year, and the amount you withdrew the year before. Contributions to a TFSA are not deductible for income tax purposes. Any amount contributed as well as any income earned in the account (for example, investment income and capital gains) is tax-free when it is withdrawn.

The types of investments permitted in a TFSA are the same as those permitted in an RRSP. RESPs and TFSAs can be great investment tools in Canada for helping save money for your children's education or to save for a "rainy day" but they are not treated as favourably in the U.S. for U.S. citizens living abroad.

 For U.S. tax purposes, RESPs and TFSAs are considered foreign trusts and, under the U.S. tax laws, foreign trusts are subject to separate reporting requirements and taxation rules.

For example, U.S. citizens and residents who have these types of accounts are required to include the accrued income within the accounts in their taxable income on the U.S. returns in the applicable years as well as complete a 3520 and 3520-A Foreign Trust reporting form to report contributions to and deemed dispositions from these accounts in any given year. Refer to chapter 8 for further details on the filing requirements relating to these forms.

The compliance fees relating to these foreign trust forms can be substantial and can far outweigh the benefits of having these types of accounts.

Because of this, many U.S. citizens who reside in Canada are closing these accounts and waiting until they renounce their U.S. citizenship to reopen them; therefore, TFSA contribution room is not lost. They are also making sure that these types of accounts are held only by their Canadian spouses.

Because TFSAs are a fairly new concept (introduced in 2009), they are not specifically exempt in the Canada-U.S. Tax Convention with regard to the foreign trust rules.

Real Life: Dual citizen with TFSA

Alex is a dual citizen residing in Canada who earns $75,000 per year. He opened a TFSA account in 2009 and has contributed the maximum amount to the account every year since. In 2013, he earned $250 of dividend income from the investments within his TFSA.

In Canada, he does not have to report anything with regard to the dividend income earned or the investment as a whole; however, in the U.S. the $250 of dividends is taxable to him on his 1040 return and he is required to complete a 3520 and 3520-A to report the investment as a whole.

Canadian Mutual Funds and Like Investments

Wikipedia defines a mutual fund as "a 'pooled' investment fund, consisting of a portfolio of publicly–traded securities, including: cash, stocks, bonds, and also other funds. Unlike most other types of investment funds, mutual funds can be 'open-ended,' which means as more people invest, the fund issues new units or shares. A mutual fund may invest mainly in government bonds, stocks from large companies or stocks from certain countries. Some funds may invest in a mix of stocks and bonds, or other mutual funds."

Canadian mutual funds are considered Passive Foreign Investment Companies (PFICs) for U.S. tax purposes, which mean that separate reporting requirements and tax treatment exists for these types of investments.

For example, any distributions from these types of investments are to be treated as dividend income for U.S. tax purposes, no matter if the distribution is actually in the form of a capital gain or interest or dividend. The dividend income is reported on the individual's 1040 return plus a separate 8621 form is required, which can result in further income being taxable in the year.

Wikipedia defines an exchange-traded fund (ETF) as "an investment fund traded on stock exchanges, much like stocks. An ETF holds assets such as stocks, commodities, or bonds, and trades close to its net asset value over the course of the trading day. Most ETFs track an index, such as the S&P 500 or MSCI EAFE. An ETF combines the valuation feature of a mutual fund or unit investment trust, which can be bought or sold at the end of each trading day for its net asset value, with the tradability feature of a closed-end fund, which trades throughout the trading day at prices that may be more or less than its net asset value."

Wikipedia also defines a real estate investment trust or REIT as "a security that trades like a stock on the major exchanges. A REIT invests in real estate directly, either through properties or mortgages. REITs receive special tax considerations and typically offer investors high yields, as well as a highly liquid method of investing in real estate. The REIT structure was designed to provide a real estate investment structure similar to the structure that mutual funds provide for portfolio investments."

 All of these investments are treated as PFICs for U.S. tax purposes as well and are subject to the foreign trust reporting rules described above, which means that separate reporting requirements and tax treatment exists for these types of investments.

Remember that the major issue with the U.S. tax treatment surrounding these types of accounts is that **double taxation** can result and the compliance fees relating to these types of foreign reporting requirements can be extremely expensive.

Non-Registered Portfolio Investments

Residents of Canada and residents of the U.S. can invest in publicly traded securities of companies from either country without restriction. As previously discussed, Canada taxes on residency, whereas the U.S. taxes on citizenship and residency. This means that if you live in Canada you report and pay income tax on your worldwide income and if you live in the U.S. you report and pay income tax on your worldwide income. However, if you are a citizen of the U.S., you also must report and pay income tax on your worldwide income for U.S. purposes no matter where in the world you live.

Under the Canada-U.S. Tax Convention, gains from the sale of portfolio investments are taxable only in the taxpayer's country of residence (i.e., capital gains from non-registered portfolio investments are considered to have been earned outside a country's tax system when you don't physically reside in that country). This basically means that gains on these types of investments are considered "sourced" in the taxpayer's country of residence for income tax purposes. However, this isn't necessarily true for U.S. citizens.

 In order for U.S. portfolio investments to be treated as "sourced" in Canada for U.S. citizens living in Canada, the taxpayer needs to have paid a minimum of 10% in income tax on these same gains in Canada.

 Keep in mind that U.S. stocks are considered U.S. situs assets for U.S. estate tax purposes, which means that a non-resident of the U.S. holding U.S. securities in a non-registered portfolio can potentially be subject to U.S. estate tax on his or her death.

However, U.S. securities held inside a Canadian mutual fund or within a Canadian corporation are not seen as U.S. situs assets and are therefore not subject to U.S. estate tax.

Real Life: Dual citizen with U.S. security gains

Chantelle is a dual citizen living and working in St. John's, Newfoundland. She has a non-registered investment portfolio that is a blend of Canadian and U.S. securities; the U.S. portion consists of stocks that are traded on the NASDAQ stock exchange. Currently Chantelle has unrealized gains of $65,000 in her portfolio account, $30,000 of which come from investments in U.S. securities.

Because of the treaty rules surrounding gains realized on the disposition of these securities, Chantelle can treat the full $65,000 of unrealized gains as Canadian source income for U.S. tax purposes, provided that she pays at least $6,500 in Canadian income tax in the year of disposition. This is a reasonable expectation, as most individual tax rates in Canada are higher than the individual tax rates in the U.S. No individual Canadian tax rates are currently below 10%.

What this means for U.S. tax purposes is that when Chantelle files her U.S. 1040 return to report her worldwide income, she can claim a foreign tax credit in the U.S. on the disposition of these U.S. securities which will likely mean the she will not owe U.S. income tax in that year, since she will have already paid the tax required in Canada. This is a desired result for many taxpayers, especially since few actually are aware of their filing requirements for U.S. tax purposes. If Chantelle was not able to claim a foreign tax credit on this income for U.S. tax purposes, the tax on these gains would first be calculated in the U.S. and a payment of the tax would be due by April 15th of the year following the disposition. A foreign tax credit would then have to be claimed on her Canadian return for the tax paid in the U.S. This doesn't mean double taxation but rather just means that now you have to file a U.S. return to calculate and pay your tax by a much earlier deadline and then claim a credit on your Canadian return; usually an undesired hassle.

If taxes are due in the U.S. and not paid on time and/or the return is not filed on time, the taxpayer faces potential penalties for non-compliance.

 Remember: all of these types of investments held outside the U.S. are required to be reported on the TDF 90-22.1 Foreign Bank Account Reporting form or new form FinCEN 114.

Many individuals will receive annual income from their non-registered portfolio investments in the form of dividends and interest and this can come from both Canadian and U.S. sources.

Withholding Tax

The purpose of withholding taxes is to ensure the applicable government agency receives all the tax revenue it is entitled to on income earned within its country when the individual earning the income is a non-resident and not necessarily required to file an income tax return (i.e., they cannot be certain a tax return will be filed in order for the proper tax amount to be paid). If a non-resident earns income from another country (i.e., not the country in which they are resident) and the appropriate withholding taxes are taken, no income tax returns are required to be filed; however, it may be in the taxpayer's best interest to file a return if the actual tax they may be subject to is less than the withholding tax amount. For example, withholding tax taken on rental income is on the gross rent amount; however, taxes payable will only be calculated on the net income after deducting rental expenses so too much tax would be withheld in this case.

An individual's residency status for tax purposes can determine how much withholding tax can apply on the income received from a non-resident country. For example, the withholding tax rate in Canada for payments made to a non-resident is 25%; however, the withholding tax rate in the U.S. for payments made to a non-resident is 30%. The Canada-U.S. Tax Convention (i.e., the tax treaty) dictates reduced rates of withholding taxes on various types of income earned by a non-resident of either country. If a reduced rate of withholding is not dictated in the treaty then the standard rates generally apply. Some of the more common income types and the applicable withholding taxes or other special tax rules under the treaty are:

- Article X – Dividends

  "…the tax so charged shall not exceed:

  (a) 5 percent of the gross amount of the dividends if the beneficial owner is a company which owns at least 10 percent of the voting stock of the company paying the dividends; or

  (b) 15 per cent of the gross amount of the dividends in all other cases."

- Article XI – Interest

  Interest arising in a Contracting State and beneficially owned by a resident of the other Contracting State may be taxed only in that other State" (i.e., 0% withholding tax)

- Article XII – Royalties

  "Royalties may also be taxed in the Contracting State in which they arise, and according to the laws of that State; but if a resident of the other Contracting

State is the beneficial owner of such royalties, the tax so charged shall not exceed 10 per cent of the gross amount of the royalties." This is the general rule but royalties arising from certain products are only taxable in the beneficial owner's state of residence.

- Article XIII – Gains

  Gains are only taxable in the country of residence with the exception of gains on the disposition of real property situated in the other country. Real property gains have their own withholding tax rules (i.e., FIRPTA in the U.S.).

- Article XVIII – Pension and Annuities

  - "Pensions may also be taxed in the Contracting State in which they arise and according to the laws of that State; but if a resident of the other Contracting State is the beneficial owner of a periodic pension payment, the tax so charged shall not exceed 15 per cent of the gross amount of such payment; and

  - annuities may also be taxed in the Contracting State in which they arise and according to the laws of that State; but if a resident of the other Contracting State is the beneficial owner of an annuity payment, the tax so charged shall not exceed 15 per cent of the portion of such payment that would not be excluded from taxable income in the first-mentioned State if the beneficial owner were a resident thereof."

  This means that if the owner of the pension payments lives in another country then the payor country can only take 15% tax on the pension payments.

  - Benefits under the social security legislation in a Contracting State paid to a resident of the other Contracting State shall be taxable only in that other State. If U.S. social security is received by a Canadian resident, Canada has agreed to allow for a 15% deduction/exemption from income in the same manner that the U.S. would if it was earned by a U.S. resident. If any amount of this income is not taxable in the payor country it will not be taxable in the resident country either.

Real Life: Canadian earning U.S. investment income

Tasha is a Canadian citizen living and working in Canada. She has an investment portfolio that consists of Canadian and U.S. stocks, some of which pay her an annual dividend. In 2013 she was paid a dividend of $560 from her stock in Microsoft and a total of $168 (i.e., 30%) was withheld in U.S. federal taxes.

Tasha will want to ensure she files a U.S. tax return to claim the reduced amount of tax on the dividend in accordance with the treaty (i.e., maximum 15% rate) and receive a refund from the IRS.

To prevent too much withholding tax from being withheld from her dividends in the future, Tasha could complete a W8-BEN form and give that to her investment broker to ensure only the treaty rate is withheld (i.e., 15%).

To ensure the appropriate amount of withholding tax is taken on U.S. income earned by non-residents, an individual should complete a W-8BEN, Certificate of Foreign Status of Beneficial Owner for United States Tax Withholding, and submit this form to the withholding agent or payor if you are a foreign person and you are the beneficial owner of an amount subject to withholding. This form will notify the payor that you are eligible for special treaty rates on a particular type of income and what withholding tax rate they are required to apply to each payment.

Even U.S. citizens can have issues when it comes to withholding taxes if they live outside the United States. Although U.S. citizens are required to file income tax returns each year no matter where they live and earn income, when they live outside the United States they are considered non-residents by many payor companies, with the result that withholding taxes may be taken on payments they receive from U.S. sources. This just means that a prepayment of the tax is taken up front and any applicable refunds will not be available until their U.S. return is filed. In these instances, a U.S. citizen can complete a W-9 Form, Request for Taxpayer Identification Number and Certification, and give it to the payer to notify them that they are a U.S. person and not subject to withholding taxes or at least a reduced rate of withholding tax. This also allows the payor to prepare the necessary tax forms for the IRS to report the payments made.

Investing in the U.S. and U.S. Source Income: What You Need To Know

Canadians with U.S. investments

- U.S. pensions can be rolled into a Canadian RRSP on a tax-free basis in Canada in some cases but it always triggers a taxable event in the U.S.

- Canadian mutual funds and like investments are not treated favourably for U.S. tax purposes; double taxation can result.

- A flat rate of Canadian withholding tax is taken on U.S. source investment income; however, a reduced rate may be available under the tax treaty.

- As a non-resident & non-citizen of the U.S., you do not have to file a U.S. non-resident return to report U.S. investment income if the proper amount of withholding tax is taken.

WHAT YOU NEED TO KNOW ABOUT UNCLE SAM:

Many individuals ask me about transferring their U.S. pension into their Canadian RRSP; however, they don't realize that this type of transfer triggers tax in the U.S. and in some cases can result in an additional 10% early withdrawal penalty. The tax-free side of these transactions are only on the Canadian tax side and that is only if you meet certain requirements.

Both Canada and the U.S. have flat withholding tax rates applicable to payments made to non-residents of either country; however, the tax treaty between the two countries allows for reduced rates of withholding tax on various types of income. As long as the correct amount of withholding tax is taken in either country, a non-resident doesn't really need to file a tax return in the payor country. However, if too much tax is withheld, then it is in the taxpayer's best interest to file a non-resident return and claim the refund.

CHAPTER 7

Married to a U.S. Citizen & Moving Between Countries

Case Study

While vacationing in Florida 6 years ago, Sandy met Ian, who is now her husband. Sandy is a Canadian citizen and resident; Ian is a U.S. citizen and, at the time they met, he was also a U.S. resident. After they got married, Ian decided to move to Canada with Sandy and has now lived there for the past 3 years.

Ian and Sandy both work full-time for Canadian employers but because of Ian's U.S. citizenship status, he is still required to file a U.S. tax return and report his worldwide income to the IRS. Ian and Sandy have a 2-year-old son who was born in the U.S. and another child on the way who they hope will be born in Canada.

Questions & Answers:

Should Ian be filing his taxes jointly with Sandy in the U.S.?
No, not unless Sandy wants to be treated as a U.S. person and subject to all the U.S. tax laws.

Are the children U.S. citizens?
Yes. Their son is a citizen because he was born in the U.S. and their unborn child will be a U.S. citizen by naturalization because Ian meets the appropriate tests which transfer his citizenship status onto his children automatically.

If Sandy and Ian decide to move to the U.S. in the future, what does Sandy need to do?
Sandy would need to apply for an appropriate U.S. visa and they would both need to sever their ties with Canada in order to stop the tax clock there (i.e., they do not want to be taxable in Canada once they move).

Marrying a U.S. Citizen and Living in Canada

If a U.S. individual marries a Canadian resident citizen and wants to live with them in Canada, what is involved in making this happen? Many people ask if marrying a Canadian citizen automatically gives them Canadian citizenship and the answer is no. The individual must first apply for permanent residency status and then once that is granted, they can apply for Canadian citizenship but they must meet all the same tests as anyone else applying for Canadian citizenship.

According to Citizenship and Immigration Canada, "to apply for Canadian citizenship as an adult, you must:

- be a permanent resident;
- be 18 years of age or older;
- have lived in Canada for at least 1,095 days in the four years before the date you sign your application (time spent residing in Canada prior to acquiring permanent residence counts as a half day of residence);
- have an adequate knowledge of either English or French;
- have an adequate knowledge of Canada and the responsibilities and privileges of citizenship;
- not be under a removal order (in other words, the Government of Canada has not ordered you to leave the country);
- not be a security risk;
- not be criminally prohibited; and
- attend a ceremony and take the oath of citizenship.

Effective October 25, 2012, sponsored spouses or partners must now live together in a legitimate relationship with their sponsor for two years from the day they receive permanent residence status in Canada. If you are a spouse or partner being sponsored to come to Canada, this applies to you if:

- You are being sponsored by a permanent resident or Canadian citizen
- You have been in a relationship for two years or less with your sponsor
- You have no children in common
- Your application was received on or after October 25, 2012

If you are a Canadian citizen or a permanent resident of Canada, you can sponsor your spouse, conjugal or common-law partner, dependent child (including adopted child) or other eligible relative to become a permanent resident under the Family Class (FC).

If your family member is a permanent resident, they can live, study and work in Canada."

Leaving the U.S.

For tax purposes it is fairly inconsequential if a U.S. person wants to leave the U.S. to move to Canada and maintain their U.S. citizenship or long-term residency status. If the individual is moving to Canada then there are a few things that take place on the Canadian side for tax purposes that make a big impact on the person's overall tax results on both sides of the border.

The U.S. does not have deemed disposition rules like Canada does; however, Canada will (with some exceptions), give the emigrant a bump up in cost base for all assets owned at the time of the move.

The cost bump means that Canada will only tax the income that is earned while a resident of Canada. The cost bump is part of Canada's deemed disposition rules, discussed further in the section title 'Leaving Canada' below.

 Canada considers an emigrant to have sold each property for its fair market value immediately before emigrating and then immediately buying it back for the same fair market value (i.e., cost base for each property is stepped up to the market value immediately prior to entering Canada).

The cost bump, however, does not apply to taxable Canadian property already owned by the emigrant, which means the original cost of the property is still the cost base after emigrating to Canada. The cost bump is important because this means that Canada will only tax the gains that are accrued after moving to Canada, which means that less income will actually be taxable to the individual while resident in Canada.

 One big issue is that double taxation can arise for the emigrant in the year of actual disposition.

Because there is no deemed disposition in the U.S. on departure, for any assets, the cost of the assets remains at their original cost when the individual first bought them. In Canada; however, gains realized after the time that the individual became resident in Canada would be seen as Canadian sourced income, in accordance with the Canada U.S. Tax treaty, which means that Canada would be able to tax these gains as Canadian sourced income rather than foreign income. Because these assets were owned by the emigrant prior to leaving the U.S., the U.S. also has the right to tax the gains as U.S. sourced which means that neither Canada or the U.S. will allow a foreign tax credit claim for any of the tax paid in either country on the same income. This is known as double taxation.

To avoid this issue, it is good practice to physically sell the assets prior to leaving the U.S. and then buy them back once you become a Canadian resident

Real Life: *U.S. citizen moving to Canada*

Phylecia is a U.S. citizen who moved to Canada 2 months ago from Boston. Before she moved, she had an investment portfolio with a cost base of $35,000 and a fair value of $105,000, a car with a cost base of $40,000 and a fair value of $25,000 and a cabin in Blue Lake, Ontario with a cost base of $75,000 and fair value of $132,000.

Phylecia will not have any immediate tax consequences or adjustments to her assets for U.S. tax purposes but for Canadian tax purposes, her investment portfolio will receive a bump in basis to $105,000, her car will maintain the same cost base because the fair value is less than original cost and her cottage will keep its original cost as well because it is taxable Canadian property.

Assume she sells her entire portfolio investments for a $$110,000. In Canada she would realize a net gain of $5,000 but in the U.S. she would realize a net gain of $75,000. Canada will consider the $5,000 gain to be Canadian sourced and will not allow a foreign tax credit for any tax paid in the U.S. on the same gain. The U.S. will consider the $75,000 gain to be U.S. sourced because all the assets were purchased while she was a U.S. resident, which means that they too will not allow a foreign tax credit for any tax paid in Canada on the same income. The overall result is that Phylecia will be double taxed on the $5,000 gain realized in Canada.

Filing U.S. Taxes

Even though a U.S. citizen moves out of the U.S., it doesn't mean that they get to stop worrying about U.S. tax requirements. As previously mentioned, U.S. citizens are taxed on their worldwide income no matter where they live in the world. However, non-residents and non-citizens of the U.S. do not have filing requirements unless they have U.S. source income.

 Many individuals wonder if their non-U.S.-citizen spouse has to file a U.S. tax return with them and the answer is no.

Some professionals will advise an individual to file a joint return with their non-U.S.-citizen spouse; however, this is not always a good idea. When a joint return

is filed, the U.S. individual is electing to treat their non-citizen spouse as a U.S. person for tax purposes from that day forward until they elect not to. What this means is that the non-citizen spouse is now subject to all the U.S. tax rules and regulations in the same manner as the U.S. citizen; making their Canadian income potentially subject to income tax in the U.S. as well, and making their Canadian assets subject to U.S. gift and estate tax as well as all the financial reporting requirements.

 A common error that often occurs in filing a joint U.S. return is claiming the non-citizen spouse as a dependant without also reporting the spouse's worldwide income.

The result is that the U.S. citizen incorrectly claims an increased personal exemption and standard deduction and incorrectly calculates a tax that is lower than it ought to be. Most individuals don't realize that filing a joint return subjects their non-U.S.-citizen spouse to all the same U.S. tax laws, which is generally not a good outcome.

U.S. Expatriation

Some individuals who immigrate to Canada consider renouncing their U.S. citizenship or relinquishing their long-term residency status so they can stop the U.S. tax clock from ticking. All expatriates must determine whether or not they will be subject to the *alternative expatriation tax*.

According to RIA Federal Tax Handbook 2012, "under a mark-to-market deemed sale rule, property of certain U.S. citizens who relinquish their U.S. citizenship and certain long-term residents who terminate their U.S. residency after June 16, 2008, will be treated as having been sold on the day before the expatriation date for its fair market value (FMV)." This tax is only applicable to those expatriates who meet certain tests immediately before renouncing, discussed below.

The "mark-to-market" tax is imposed on the net unrealized gain in the property as if the property had been sold for its FMV on the day before the expatriation or residency termination. This is the same concept as Canada's deemed disposition rules on death. There is some relief however; the net gain on the deemed sale is reduced by an inflation adjusted amount that is $636,000 in 2011, $651,000 in 2012, $663,000 in 2013 and $680,000 in 2014. Subsequent gains or losses that are realized are adjusted for the gains and losses reported under the deemed sale rules, without regard to the exemption.

Real Life: Renouncing U.S. citizenship and being subject to "exit tax"

Phil renounced on January 2, 2014. Immediately prior to renouncing, his net worth was $2,455,000, which means that he is deemed to dispose of his assets immediately prior to renouncing and pay any exit tax.

His cost base was $1,868,000, which mean that he has a net taxable gain of $587,000; however, he is able to reduce his gain by $680,000 in 2014, which mean that he doesn't pay any exit tax.

If Phil actually sells his assets for $3,000,000 2 years after renouncing, he would realize a capital gain of only $545,000 for U.S. purposes because the gain of $587,000 that was realized on the deemed disposition of his assets is used to reduce his actual gain in the year of real disposition (i.e., this avoids double taxation). *Keep in mind that this gain adjustment only matters for U.S. situs assets that would still be subject to U.S. tax in the year of disposition.*

For Canadian tax purposes, his cost base would be the fair value of $2,455,000 anyway, which means that he would realize a gain of $545,000 for Canadian purposes as well.

A taxpayer may elect to defer payment of tax attributable to property that is deemed to be sold. The election is made on a property-by-property basis and interest is charged for the period the tax is deferred. The deferred tax is generally due at the same time the return is due for the tax year in which the property is actually sold. The benefit of being able to defer the tax is that if you don't have to pay it until you actually sell the property, you will actually have the cash at that point to pay the tax whereas you may not have the cash in the year of deemed disposition.

The alternative expatriate income tax, or exit tax as it is often referred to, applies to U.S. citizens and long-term residents who relinquish their citizenship or terminate residency and meet the average annual net income tax test, net worth test, or the failure to certify test described below:

1. The individual's average annual net income tax for the period of five tax years ending before the date of residency termination is greater than an inflation adjusted amount that is $155,000 for 2013 ($151,000 for 2012; $147,000 for 2011);

2. The individual's net worth as of the date in (1) is $2,000,000 or more.

Or

3. The individual: (i) fails to certify under penalty of perjury that all U.S. filing requirements have been met for the five preceding tax years, or (ii) fails to submit evidence of his compliance as IRS may require. The certification is made on Form 8854.

> *Keep in mind that this "exit tax" is an entirely separate tax from the regular U.S. income tax.*

An exception exists for the above tests but this topic will be discussed at more length in the final chapter, when we discuss "Renouncing U.S. Citizenship."

> *If a person leaves the U.S. but maintains their citizenship, there is no deemed disposition on any assets and they are still required to file income tax returns and other tax reports each year on worldwide income (and are also still subject to the U.S. gift & estate tax).*

Green Cards

> *Applying for a green card means applying for permanent residence status in the U.S.*

For tax purposes you are considered a U.S. resident as soon as you apply for a green card. The green card serves as proof that its holder, a lawful permanent resident (LPR), has been officially granted immigration benefits, which include permission to reside and take employment in the United States. The holder must maintain permanent resident status, and can be removed from the United States if certain conditions of this status are not met.

A person may have technically abandoned their status if he or she moves to another country to live there permanently, stays outside the U.S. for more than 365 days (without getting a re-entry permit before leaving), or does not file an income tax return; however, until you officially surrender your green card, you could still be considered a permanent resident for tax purposes.

> *Failure to renew the green card does not result in the loss of U.S. tax status.*

Marrying a U.S. Citizen and Living in the U.S.

Leaving Canada

Some individuals who marry a U.S. citizen choose to move to the U.S. to live with them. To claim to be a non-resident of Canada for tax purposes, the taxpayer must claim that he or she is a resident in another country. Canada's tax treaties provide that, if an individual is resident in both countries, the individual is considered resident in only one or the other for tax purposes.

The Canada-U.S. Tax Convention states that "when an individual is a resident of both "Contracting States" (i.e., this can mean two countries or two states), then his status shall be determined as follows:

1.   He shall be deemed to be a resident of the Contracting State in which he has a permanent home available to him, if he has a permanent home available to him in both States or in neither State, he shall be deemed to be a resident of the Contracting State with which his personal and economic relations are closer (centre of vital interests);

2.   If the Contracting State in which he has his centre of vital interest cannot be determined, he shall be deemed to be a resident of the Contracting State in which he has an habitual abode;

3.   If he has an habitual abode in both States or in neither State, he shall be deemed to be a resident of the Contracting State or which he is a citizen; and

4.   If he is a citizen of both States or of neither of them, the competent authorities of the Contracting States shall settle the question by mutual agreement."

When Do You Become a Non-Resident?

According to the Canada Revenue Agency website (www.cra.gc.ca), "when you leave Canada to settle in another country, you usually become a non-resident of Canada for income tax purposes on the latest of the following dates:

•   the date you leave Canada;

•   the date your spouse or common-law partner and dependents leave Canada; or

•   the date you become a resident of the country to which you are immigrating.

If you lived in another country before living in Canada and you are leaving Canada to re-establish a residence in the other country, you usually become a non-resident on the date you leave Canada. This applies even if your spouse or common-law partner temporarily stays in Canada to dispose of your home."

Note: You usually become a deemed non-resident of Canada when your residential ties in the other country are such that, under the tax treaty between Canada and that country, you are considered to be a resident of that country and not of Canada.

Determining the proper date you become a non-resident of Canada is very important because your residency (or non-residency) status determines the time frame in which you must report your worldwide income, the date upon which any deemed disposition of assets will occur, and also your eligibility (if any) to receive:

- the GST/HST credit (goods and services tax/harmonized sales tax);
- Canada child tax benefit payments (and any similar provincial program payments); and
- universal child care benefit payments.

Your Tax Obligations in the Year You Leave Canada

You must file a Canadian tax return if you owe tax or want to receive a refund because you paid too much tax in the tax year.

For the part of the tax year that you are a resident of Canada, you must report your worldwide income (income from all sources, both inside and outside Canada) on your Canadian tax return.

For the part of the tax year that you are not a resident of Canada, you are required to pay Canadian income tax only on your Canadian source income, if you have any.

Canadian Deemed Disposition on Departure

In making a decision to become a non-resident of Canada, you need to consider the tax implications that this kind of move can have. Depending on your particular financial situation, significant tax liabilities can result if one is not careful. Make sure you know the rules so effective planning can be done to mitigate any financial burden that could result.

When an individual departs Canada and becomes a "non-resident," he or she is considered to have disposed of his or her property at its fair market value on the day he or she emigrated from Canada, and to immediately have reacquired it for the same fair market value.

This generally results in the realization of capital gains and losses on the disposition of certain investments (e.g. non-registered securities, property that is not taxable Canadian property, etc.). This means that if you own a vacation property in Florida, you will be deemed to dispose of it for Canadian tax purposes immediately before departure and pay tax on any capital gains that result.

Losses on the deemed dispositions that cannot be applied against capital gains in the current or previous three years will be lost unless the taxpayer subsequently disposes of Taxable Canadian Property, becomes a resident at some time in the future, or makes an election to reduce the proceeds of disposition of Taxable Canadian Properties in the future. Canadian deemed disposition losses can only be deducted against Canadian gains so if no further Canadian income exists, the losses cannot be utilized.

There are some exemptions from the deemed disposition at departure rule, which means that there are some assets you are not deemed to dispose of so you don't pay tax on these items until you actually sell them or earn income from them. They include:

- Canadian real property, Canadian resource property, and timber resource property;
- Canadian business property (including inventory) if the business is carried on through a permanent establishment in Canada;
- Pensions and similar rights, including registered retirement savings plans, registered retirement income funds, registered education savings plans, registered disability savings plans, tax-free savings accounts, and deferred profit-sharing plans;
- Rights to certain benefits under employee profit-sharing plans, employee benefit plans, employee trusts, and salary-deferral arrangements;
- Certain trust interests that were not acquired for consideration (i.e., you didn't pay for the beneficial interest);
- Property you owned when you last became a resident of Canada, or property you inherited after you last became a resident of Canada, if you were a resident of Canada for 60 months or less during the 10-year period before you emigrated;
- Employee security options subject to Canadian tax; and
- Interests in life insurance policies in Canada (other than segregated fund policies).

 With regard to a person's principal residence in Canada, this property falls under the real property exemption; however, you can elect to dispose of the property for income tax purposes so you can claim your principal residence exemption in your year of emigration.

This is a very important election because a non-resident cannot make a Canadian principal residence exemption to shelter the full gain after they have been a non-resident of Canada for more than one year. This is because of the +1 rule in the calculation of the exemption. Generally, this exemption is only available to Canadian residents.

If you did not physically sell or don't want to sell your Canadian principal residence before departing Canada, there is a special rule in the Canada-U.S. Tax Convention that can help reduce future tax on capital gains on the sale of your home while you are a resident in the U.S.

 The treaty allows for a "step-up" (to fair value) in the cost of the asset for tax purposes on the day you enter the U.S. provided you file the appropriate treaty election with the required U.S. tax return for that year.

This step-up applies only to non-citizens and non-green-card holders of the U.S.

Other assets that are deemed to be disposed of at FMV for Canadian tax purposes may also receive a cost base step-up for U.S. tax purposes provided an 8833 Treaty election form is filed with the U.S. tax return required in the year of departure from Canada. If the step-up is not received, you could end up paying tax in the U.S. on appreciated value that was not earned while a resident of the U.S. which results in double taxation.

Filing Your Final Canadian Tax Return

As previously discussed, all Canadian residents must file a Canadian income tax return. In the year you become a non-resident, your final return will be reporting income earned while still a resident of Canada. For example, if you emigrate on June 12, 2014, your return would include income earned from January 1 through to June 12, 2014.

 If the fair market value (FMV) of all the property you owned when you left Canada was more than $25,000, you have to include with your Canadian return a list of all your properties inside and outside Canada.

However, certain properties are excluded from this calculation and should not be included in the list. For more information, and a list of the properties excluded from this calculation, see Form T1161, List of Properties by an Emigrant of Canada on the CRA website (www.cra.gc.ca).

File your return by the filing due date. The penalty for failing to file the T1161 by the due date is $25 per day you are late. There is a minimum penalty of $100, and a maximum penalty of $2,500.

Real Life: Canadian moving to Canada

Jenny plans to move from Canada to the U.S. at the end of July 2013 and holds the following Canadian assets:

- Non-registered portfolio with an ACB of $100,000 and a FMV of $150,000

- RRSPs of $120,000

- A house worth $350,000, ACB of $140,000

- A car worth $6,000, ACB of $20,000

In 2013, Jenny will be deemed to dispose of her non-registered portfolio but not her house, car or RRSPs. In addition to her regular employment income, Jenny will have to pay tax on the portfolio gain of $50,000. She can elect a deemed disposition on her house if she wants and claim the principal residence exemption but she doesn't have to because it would normally be excluded under the real property exemption; however, it would be in her best interest to file the election and claim the exemption otherwise she will pay Canadian tax on the gain when she actually sells the property because the principal residence exemption will no longer be available to her after she becomes a non-resident of Canada. Her car would also be exempt because its FMV is under $10,000 (see form T1161 for more information).

If you emigrate from Canada and hold a tax-free savings account (TFSA), you can keep your TFSA and continue to benefit from the exemption from Canadian tax on investment income and withdrawals but no contribution will be allowed and no contribution room will accrue while you are a non-resident of Canada. Keep in mind that TFSAs are treated differently in the U.S. for tax purposes.

The taxpayer can elect to defer paying the taxes on the deemed dispositions by filing a Form T1244 election by April 30 of the year following emigration. When the amount owing exceeds $14,500, security must be provided to CRA but no penalty or interest is applicable to the amount owing as long as sufficient security has been provided. Departure tax can also be reversed if the taxpayer returns to Canada.

Tax Obligations After You Leave Canada

As a non-resident, you will only pay tax on income you receive from sources within Canada. This applies in the year you leave Canada and for each year afterwards so if you have no income in Canada you do not have to file a return.

Generally, Canadian income received by a non-resident is subject to Part XIII tax (withholding tax) or Part I tax (regular income tax).

Part XIII Tax (Withholding tax)

Part XIII tax is deducted from the types of income listed below. To make sure the correct amount is deducted, it's important to advise Canadian payors of your status and the applicable rates under the treaty; you'll need to advise the payors of the following information:

- you are a non-resident of Canada for tax purposes; and
- your country of residence.

The **most common types of Canadian income subject to Part XIII withholding tax are:**

- dividends;
- rental and royalty payments;
- pension payments;
- old age security pension;
- Canada Pension Plan and Quebec Pension Plan benefits;
- retiring allowances;
- registered retirement savings plan payments;
- registered retirement income fund payments;
- annuity payments; and
- management fees.

A withholding tax rate of 25% (Canada) or 30% (U.S.) applies to all non-resident payments unless a reduced rate under a tax treaty applies."

Treaty rates are as follows (Canada/U.S. treaty):

- Interest   0% rate
- Dividends   15% rate (except preferred shares)

    5% rate for corporations owning >10% voting interest
- Royalties   10% rate
- REITs*   15% (dividends & capital gains)

- Rents   30% rate (U.S.); 25% rate (CAN)
- Pensions   25% rate (unless rec'd as annuity, then 15% rate)

· *REIT (Real Estate Investment Trust)

Note: The interest you receive or that is credited to you is exempt from Canadian withholding tax if the payor is unrelated to you, i.e., an arm's-length payor.

Part I Tax (Regular Income Tax)

Part I tax is usually deducted by the payor from the types of income listed below; however, if you carry on a business in Canada, or sell or dispose of taxable Canadian property, you may also have to pay tax on that type of income.

Even if the payor deducts tax from your income or you pay an amount of tax during the year, it may not be enough. Because of this, you may have to file a Canadian income tax return to calculate your final tax obligation to Canada on:

- income from employment in Canada or from a business carried on in Canada;
- employment income from a Canadian resident for your employment in another country if, under the terms of a tax treaty between Canada and your new country of residence, the income is exempt from tax in your new country of residence;
- certain income from employment outside Canada, if you were a resident of Canada when the duties were performed;
- taxable part of Canadian scholarships, fellowships, bursaries, and research grants;
- taxable capital gains arising from the disposition of Taxable Canadian Property; and
- income from providing services in Canada other than in the course of regular and continuous employment.

Electing to File

There are two situations that may make you want to elect to file a Canadian income tax return for income from which withholding tax was deducted:

- when you receive Canadian rental income or timber royalties; and
- when you receive certain Canadian pension income.

These are separate tax returns for a non-resident so depending on the taxpayer's situation; they may need to file more than one Canadian non-resident return in any given year.

Real Life: Non-resident of Canada electing to file a Canadian return

Mathew lived and worked in Canada for 25 years before he moved to Texas to work for a major corporation as its CEO. Mathew kept his home in Canada but turned it into a rental property after departing the country.

Mathew receives $18,000 per year in rental revenues but incurs expenses of $10,000 per year against that rental income. In accordance with the treaty, the tenant withholds 25% of the gross rental income each year for Part XIII tax.

Mathew would want to elect to file a Canadian tax return in order to claim a refund of the Part XIII tax withheld because the withholding tax is taken on the gross rental income rather than on the net rental profits. Tax is only required to be paid on the net profits at year-end.

Returning to Canada from the U.S. (immigration)

 If you are re-establishing Canadian residency and you had a deemed disposition when you left Canada, you can elect to make an adjustment to the deemed dispositions you reported when you emigrated.

This is an election to "unwind" a previous deemed disposition.

If you research this topic on the CRA website (www.cra.gc.ca), you will find that you can make this election to unwind if you still own some or all of the property you were deemed to dispose of when you emigrated. "If you make this election, the amount of the gain from the deemed disposition that you reported on your return for the year you emigrated can be reduced by the least of:

• the amount of the gain reported on your return for the year you departed;

• the fair market value (FMV) of the property on the date you immigrated;

• any other amount to a maximum of the least of the above-noted amounts.

The election to unwind may result in the reduction or elimination of the tax owing on the gain from the previously reported deemed disposition of property on emigration. If you make this election and had previously elected to defer payment of the tax owing on the income from the deemed disposition, some or all of the security you may have furnished may be returned to you."

This is a good thing because it means that if you still own some of the property that you had when you left Canada you can get refunded for any excess tax you paid on a gain that ended up being too high. Because you still own the property and the fair value is less than it was when you left Canada, they will allow you to only pay tax on the lower gain realized on departure or re-entry into Canada. If you haven't actually sold the property yet to realize an actual gain then this adjustment helps reduce your tax on that income to a more reasonable level.

> ### Real Life: Election to unwind Canadian departure tax on re-entry to Canada
>
> Sam emigrated from Canada in 2008 and paid departure tax on taxable capital gains of $66,000. Sam is now planning to move back to Canada in a couple of weeks and still owns all the assets he had when he left Canada. Some of the market values have dropped in the past few years so the taxable capital gains applicable to the property he paid departure tax on is now only $50,000.
>
> When Sam comes back to Canada he should file the election to unwind the departure tax so he can recover the tax on the $16,000 of decrease in the taxable capital gain reported.

Previously Deferred Tax

 When you immigrate to Canada, you are considered to have disposed of and immediately reacquired most properties you own on the date you immigrate.

If you had previously elected to defer payment of the tax owing on the income from the deemed disposition of property on emigration, you may now have to pay the deferred tax.

Potential U.S. Emigration Issues

 If you obtained a green card while living in the U.S., you will need to surrender your green card when you return to Canada in order to stop the U.S. automatic tax clock.

If you maintain your green card, you will still be considered a resident of the U.S. for federal income tax purposes because obtaining a green card is effectively an application for U.S. citizenship in the eyes of the U.S. tax system. If you keep the green card, the IRS takes the view that you can renew it at any time and should therefore still be treated like a U.S. citizen. Remember, U.S. citizens are treated differently for tax purposes and are subject to all kinds of foreign financial reporting regimes and potentially double taxation as well.

Even if you don't retain your green card, if you move from the U.S. and still retain some U.S. investments, there may still be U.S. filing requirements for income earned on these investments (i.e., U.S. real property). Investment income earned after re-entering Canada will only be taxed in Canada but only for those taxpayers who are no longer U.S. citizens or green card holders.

What Does This Mean for Our Kids?

 If you marry a U.S. citizen and choose to make your home in Canada, your children could be considered U.S. citizens.

If your U.S.-citizen spouse lived in the U.S. for a certain period of time prior to the child's birth, this could deem your child to be a U.S. citizen at birth, even if he or she is not physically born in the U.S. This means that they will be required to abide by all the U.S. tax rules no matter where they live in the world.

Dual Citizenship

Based on the U.S. Department of State regulation on dual citizenship, the United States Supreme Court has stated that dual citizenship is a "status long recognized in the law" and that "a person may have and exercise rights of nationality in two countries and be subject to the responsibilities of both. The mere fact he asserts the rights of one citizenship does not mean that he renounces the other." In the case Schneider v. Rusk 377 U.S. 163 (1964), the US Supreme Court ruled that a naturalized U.S. citizen has the right to return to his native country and to resume his former citizenship, and also to remain a U.S. citizen even if he never returns to the United States. I am pointing this out merely because I want to reiterate the point that just because you don't physically live and work in the U.S., doesn't mean you don't have to abide by their tax laws relating to U.S. citizens.

Retiring in the U.S.

Many of my clients have asked me to explain the tax implication of retiring in the U.S. because they want to escape the harsh Canadian winters and our higher income tax rates. It is not always greener on the other side of the fence so you should be aware of the tax implications this type of move can have on you if you are thinking about retiring in the U.S.

Taxation of Canadian OAS, CPP and U.S. Social Security

 For U.S. income tax purposes, Canadian OAS and CPP payments are treated the same as U.S. Social Security payments.

The Canada/ U.S. Tax Treaty states that social security benefits received from either country will only be taxable in the country in which you are a resident. The treaty goes on to state that U.S. social security payments received by a Canadian resident are eligible for a percentage exemption of the amount received so that the payments are not taxed at a higher amount than they would be if they were taxed in the U.S. This simply means that in Canada, you would receive a deduction equal to 15% of the U.S. social security amount so that not more than 85% of the income is taxed in Canada because this is the maximum amount that would be taxable in the U.S. Similarly, OAS and CPP payments received by a U.S. resident are taxed as if they were received under the U.S. Social Security Act.

Taxation of Canadian Pensions

If an individual chooses to retire in the U.S. and receives a pension from Canada in the form of an RRSP, RRIF or RPP, they will pay less Canadian tax than if they continued to live in Canada. Treaty withholding tax rates would apply to the pension income paid to a Canadian non-resident, which is a 15% rate if received in the form of an annuity or as lump-sum amounts. Federal foreign tax credits are available in the U.S. for the Canadian withholding tax paid on the pension income as well so the individual will not be double taxed; however, it will depend on what state you live in to determine if the total U.S. tax on this income will be more than the foreign tax credit claimed. Remember, the U.S. states do not follow the tax treaty, which means they do not allow foreign tax credits.

Real Life: *Canadian moving to Canada*

Mark receives $10,000 per year from his Canadian pension but only receives $8,500 in cash after the 15% withholding tax deduction is taken. He must claim the full $10,000 as income on his U.S. federal and state return; however, he will be able to deduct the $1,500 of tax paid to Canada against his federal tax on this same income.

Let's assume his U.S. federal tax is $1,000 and his state tax is $350. He can use $1,000 of the $1,500 paid to Canada to reduce the federal tax owing on this same income but he will have to pay the additional $350 state tax as they will not allow a foreign tax credit to reduce this amount. The unused $500 can be carried forward on his federal tax return to be used in a future year if needed.

1040 Filing Requirements

As mentioned previously, U.S. citizens and residents are required to file a U.S. 1040 income tax return each year and report their worldwide income on that return. The difference between U.S. residents and citizens is that if you are a U.S. citizen, you must file a U.S. 1040 income tax return each year no matter where you live in the world. For example, if you are a U.S. citizen, you could live in Australia, China, Canada or Europe and you would still be required to file a U.S. 1040 return and report your worldwide income on that return and potentially pay tax in the U.S. on that worldwide income in addition to filing a tax return in your country of residence. Joint returns may be filed for married taxpayers.

A U.S. 1040 personal income tax return is due by April 15th of the year after the tax year in question; however, you can get an automatic 6-month extension if you file a 4868 request for extension no later than April 15th. Any taxes payable are due by April 15th of the following tax year and the extension of time to file does not extend the tax payment deadline; so if you pay any balance due after the April 15th deadline, you will likely be charged a late payment penalty (plus interest) on the balance owing as well.

Married to a U.s. Citizen and Moving Betweeen Countries: What You Need to Know

Canadians Moving to the U. S.

• Becoming a non-resident of Canada means a deemed disposition of almost all your assets at market values immediately prior to departure; i.e., you must pay tax on capital gains before you leave.

• Step-up in cost base exists for U.S. purposes due to deemed disposition rules, which means you only pay tax in the U.S. on accumulated earnings after you move there.

• As a U.S. resident you must abide by all the U.S. tax filing requirements.

U.S. Citizens Moving to Canada

• U.S. does not have deemed disposition rules so no change in asset values for U.S. tax purposes when you leave the U.S., unless you renounce citizenship or long-term residency.

• Canada will give you a step-up in cost base when you enter the country which means that less income is taxable in Canada; however, this can cause a mismatch of taxes between the two countries because the U.S. doesn't change anything.

WHAT YOU NEED TO KNOW ABOUT UNCLE SAM:

One never knows where they will meet their significant other, but if you happen to marry a U.S. citizen and you are not a U.S. citizen, there are some things you should know. When you marry someone from another country, you will likely have to make the decision on where you will live, in your country or your spouse's. One of the many things to consider when making this decision is the tax implications of a residency change.

If you move from Canada to live in the U.S. and now become a non-resident of Canada, you are deemed to dispose of almost all of your assets at fair market value immediately prior to leaving. This means that on your final tax return you must report and pay tax on any accrued gains earned up to the time to leave the country. You are also deemed to immediately buy them back at that same market value so you receive a step-up in cost basis as well which means that you would only pay tax on any gains realized after moving to the U.S. These rules are not the same if you move from the U.S. to Canada.

Moving from the U.S. to Canada doesn't really have any tax implications unless the person chooses to renounce or relinquish their citizenship or long-term residency status. If this is done, similar deemed disposition rules exist in the U.S. but it is referred to as "exit tax" and is only applicable to individuals who meet certain tests. Canada will give the emigrant a step-up in cost basis immediately prior to moving to Canada, which means that only gains realized after the move to Canada will be taxed in Canada. The problem with this is that if the person is still a U.S. person and has not actually disposed of the property, any gains realized will be taxable in the U.S. as well and due to the different treatment regarding the basis, double taxation can result. Because of this, it is usually recommended that U.S. citizens and long-term residents physically dispose of certain assets prior to departure from the U.S. so income can be better matched between countries.

Becoming a non-resident of a country generally means that you no longer have to file tax returns in that country unless you have income from that country; however, this isn't the case if you are a U.S. citizen. Withholding tax applies to payments made to non-residents of both Canada and the U.S. and if the proper amount of withholding taxes is taken you don't need to file a tax return in most cases; however, you may want to file to claim a refund because withholding taxes are applicable to gross income instead of profits.

CHAPTER 8

Going to School or Working Temporarily in the U.S.

Case Study

Mike has lived and worked in Vancouver for the past 15 years; however, he has recently been contacted by a major manufacturing company in Boston, Massachusetts, to assist in the transition with a corporate takeover. His contract would last approximately 4 years and he would be provided with housing to help in his transition to the U.S. Mike's wife works as a nurse in Vancouver and they have 3 kids, two attending high school in Vancouver this year and one who will be attending college at North Dakota State this fall.

Mike's wife and kids aren't sure they want to move to the U.S. for only 4 years as this would mean his wife would have to quit her job and the kids would have to leave their school.

Questions & Answers:

What are Mike's tax implications if his family chooses not to move to the U.S. with him?

Mike would still be considered a Canadian resident and therefore be subject to tax on his worldwide income in Canada. Because of this, he would likely be treated as a non-resident of the U.S., even though he is living and working there, because he would be in the U.S. only on a temporary basis.

Should Mike get a work visa or a green card to work in the U.S.?

Mike should get a work visa to work in the U.S. because he plans to work there only on a temporary basis. If he obtains a green card, he would be treated as a U.S. person for tax purposes until he officially surrenders the card.

Will Mike be considered a U.S. resident for tax purposes?
No, see answer to first question.

Is Mike's child considered a U.S. resident while attending college in the U.S.?
No, because a student is in the U.S. only on a temporary basis, unless they take steps to change their residency status and intend to live in the U.S. permanently.

Would Mike's younger children have to get visas to attend high school in the U.S. if the family did decide to move there?
Yes.

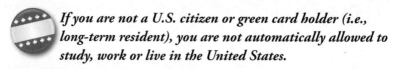

If you are not a U.S. citizen or green card holder (i.e., long-term resident), you are not automatically allowed to study, work or live in the United States.

Non-resident aliens need to apply for special visas in order to be granted such privileges. The application/approval process can take some time (i.e., several months in some cases) so it is best to start the process early enough so you have ample time to receive your required visa prior to your planned entrance into the U.S.

Studying in the U.S.

Many non-residents choose to attend college in the U.S. to further their education rather than staying in their home country; however, an individual cannot do this legally without first obtaining a student visa.

According to the U.S. Department of State website, "generally, a citizen of a foreign country who wishes to enter the United States must first obtain a visa, either a non-immigrant visa for temporary stay, or an immigrant visa for permanent residence. You must have a student visa to study in the United States. Your course of study and the type of school you plan to attend determine whether you need an F-1 visa or an M-1 visa."

To enter the United States to attend:	You need the following visa category:
University or college	F
High School	
Private elementary school	
Seminary	
Conservatory	
Another academic institution, including a language training program	
Vocational or other recognized non-academic institution, other than a language training program	M

Wikipedia defines a J-1 visa as "a non-immigrant visa issued by the United States to exchange visitors participating in programs that promote cultural exchange, especially to obtain medical or business training within the U.S. All applicants must meet eligibility criteria and be sponsored either by a private sector or government program. "

Most students in F-1 or J-1 status do not have specific time limits imposed on their stay in the United States, while aliens in most other non-immigrant statuses do. Aliens in some non-immigrant statuses are allowed to be employed in the United States, while others are not. Non-immigrants allowed to be employed in the United States can usually get a United States social security number.

As dictated on the IRS website, "Foreign Students in F-1 or J-1 status are usually allowed to be employed for no more than 20 hours per week during the academic year, but are allowed to work 40 hours per week during the summer and other vacations. Certain students may be allowed to work off campus with permission from USCIS (United States Citizenship and Immigration Services) or from the Designated School Official (usually the foreign student advisor). Certain students in hardship situations are issued Employment Authorization Documents (EAD) and are allowed to work off campus with no hour limitations. F-1 students are allowed to be employed for a maximum of 12 months in 'practical training' jobs both on and off campus. These are jobs which are related to the student's subject area of study."

U.S. Substantial Presence Test

As mentioned in a previous chapter, non-residents of the U.S. who are in the U.S. for more than 183 days in the current year or 183 days over a 3-year period can be deemed to be U.S. residents for tax purposes and students in the U.S. will generally meet this test each year they attend school; however, non-resident students in the U.S. receive special exemptions under the substantial presence test rules.

The definition of Exempt Individual under the substantial presence test includes:

- Students on an F, J, M or Q visa:
  - They must wait 5 calendar years before counting 183 days;
  - The 5 calendar years need not be consecutive; and once a cumulative total of 5 calendar years is reached during the student's lifetime after 1984 he may never be an exempt individual as a student ever again during his lifetime;
  - The classification of Exempt Individual applies also to a spouse and children on F-2, J-2, M-2, or Q-3 visas.

Once the 5-year period has passed, the student could technically be considered a deemed resident for U.S. tax purposes but even if you are deemed a resident of the United States because you meet the substantial presence test, there are some exceptions that allow you not to be treated this way and they are listed below.

Closer Connection Exception for Foreign Students Only

Answer the following questions:

- Do you intend to reside permanently in the United States?
- Have you taken any steps to change your U.S. immigration status toward permanent residency?
- Have you substantially complied with the United States immigration laws for your student non-immigrant status during your stay in the United States?
- During your stay in the United States, have you maintained a closer connection with Canada than with the United States?

If you answered "NO" to the first two questions, and "YES" to the last two questions, then you have a basis for claiming you are still a non-resident alien, even though you have passed the substantial presence test. To claim the exception for students, a student should attach Form 8843, Statement for Exempt Individuals and Individuals with a Medical Condition to his or her form 1040NR or 1040NR-EZ.

Form 8843 is filed to explain an individual's basis for claiming that he or she is allowed to exclude days of presence in the United States for purposes of the substantial presence test. If the individual is not required to file a 1040NR return in a particular year, form 8843 should be filed on its own by the due date of the 1040NR return. Failure to file form 8843 could result in the individual being denied the exclusion of days and being considered a U.S. resident under the substantial presence test, although I have never seen this applied in real life. If applied this would mean that worldwide income would be taxable in the U.S. unless a closer connection could be claimed under the treaty (see chapter 4 for more details).

Treaty Exemption – Income from Employment

The Canada-U.S. Tax Convention, states that if a resident of another country receives wages, salaries and other remuneration in respect of employment, that income will only be taxable in the resident country unless the employment is exercised in that other country. If the employment is exercised in the other country, that income may be taxed in that other country as well; however, there are some exceptions.

Employment income earned by a resident of another country and exercised in the non-resident country will only be taxable in the recipient's resident country if:

- The compensation does not exceed $10,000 in the currency of the other country; or

- The recipient is present in the non-resident country for less than an aggregate of 183 days in any 12-month period starting or ending in the fiscal year concerned, and the compensation is not paid by, or on behalf of, a person who is a resident of the non-resident country and is not due to a permanent establishment in that other country (i.e., the recipient is in the country less than 183 days over a 1 year period and was not paid by a U.S. employer).

 Note: The $10,000 value is measured against each employment, not the total employment in the other country.

Real Life: Non-resident earning under $10,000 employment income threshold

George is a Canadian citizen and resident who is currently attending college in Boston. During the 2013 school year, he worked part-time on campus and was paid $5,500. He worked for another employer on campus during the 2013 summer break and earned $4,600 for the work that he did during that time. Even though George's total U.S. employment income is over $10,000, because he was paid by two separate employers and each employer paid him less than $10,000, under the provision of Article XV, his U.S. employment income would be exempt from taxation in the U.S.

Keep in mind that this exemption is a federal exemption only. State taxes will likely still apply to this U.S. income.

Real Life: Non-resident student working temporarily in the U.S.

Steven graduated from high school in June of 2013 and now attends college at NYSU (New York State University) on an F-1 visa. His first semester started September 2013 and he will start his third semester in September 2014. Steven decided not to return home to Winnipeg this past summer because he got a job on campus over summer break. Steven is enrolled in a 4-year degree program and plans to move back home once he graduates in the fall of 2017; however, if he receives a good job offer in the U.S., he may consider staying.

U.S. requirements

Steven will have to file a 1040NR return to report his U.S. employment income; however, he may not be taxed on it in the U.S. for federal purposes if the amount is under the $10,000 limit. Steven is an exempt individual under the substantial presence test and will need to make sure he files a form 8843 each year he attends college in the U.S. He will also be required to file a non-resident state return and pay any required tax.

 Even though the income may be exempt, if it is over the personal tax exemption amount allowed to a U.S. non-resident (i.e., $3,950 for 2014 and $3,900 in 2013) a 1040NR tax return is still required to be filed to show the exempt income.

Scholarships & Bursaries

In Canada, a student receiving a scholarship or bursary in a particular tax year is not required to pay tax on that income if he or she is enrolled in a qualified educational institution and qualifies for the tuition deduction amount. This is not the case for U.S. tax purposes.

 A student in the U.S. receiving U.S. scholarships or bursaries in a particular year must report and pay tax on any net scholarship amounts not used to pay for tuition or educational expenses (i.e., books, supplies, etc.).

According to U.S. Publication 970, Tax Benefits for Education, "qualified scholarship and fellowship grants are treated as tax-free amounts if the following conditions are met:

- You are a candidate for a degree at an educational institution that maintains a regular faculty and curriculum and normally has a regularly enrolled body of students in attendance at the place where it carries on its educational activities; and

- Amounts you receive as a scholarship or fellowship grant are used for tuition and fees required for enrollment or attendance at the educational institution, or for fees, books, supplies, and equipment required for courses at the educational institution.

You must include in gross income amounts used for incidental expenses, such as room and board, travel, and optional equipment, and generally amounts received as payments for teaching, research, or other services required as a condition for receiving the scholarship or fellowship grant. Also you must include in income any part of the scholarship or fellowship that represents payments for services."

Claiming the Tuition Deduction on your Canadian Return

In order to claim the tuition and education deduction in Canada when attending a university or college outside of Canada, the student must have the U.S. institution complete a Canadian form TL11A Tuition, Education, and Textbook Amounts Certificate - University Outside Canada. This form is the equivalent of the Canadian form T2202A Tuition, Education and Textbook Amounts Certificate. The TL11A form is needed because the U.S. tuition slip does not indicate the number of months enrolled in full- or part-time education months; it only lists the tuition amount paid in the year.

Real Life: Canadian student in the U.S. with scholarship income

Janelle is a Canadian citizen and resident; however, she will be attending Texas University in the spring of 2014 and will be living on campus while enrolled. Because Janelle had such good grades in high school, she received a number of Canadian bursaries totaling $2,000 and a U.S. scholarship of $10,000 but her total cost of tuition, books and room and board was only $8,000; $2,000 of which was allocated to room and board.

Janelle would qualify for the tuition deduction on her Canadian return if she gets her university to complete a form TL11A, which would mean that she would not have to claim any portion of her scholarships or bursaries as taxable income in Canada; however, because her tuition and books cost only $6,000, Janelle will have to include $4,000 as taxable scholarship income on her U.S. 1040NR return ($4,000 is the amount of income received from her U.S. scholarship net of the cost of tuition and books).

Because Janelle is only a student in the U.S. and would likely still have closer ties to Canada, she would be a non-resident for U.S. tax purposes which means that she can ignore the Canadian bursary amounts for U.S. tax purposes and only be required to include the difference between the U.S. scholarship amount and the U.S. education expenses, excluding room and board, on her U.S. non-resident return.

Temporary Work Visas

Many individuals have the opportunity to work in the U.S. for a U.S. employer or for a U.S. branch of their Canadian employer, or have the opportunity to work for themselves in the U.S.; however, not everyone knows what is required from a legal or taxation point of view for them to actually be able to work in the U.S.

According to the U.S. Department of State, "generally, a citizen of a foreign country who wishes to enter the United States must first obtain a visa, either a non-immigrant visa for temporary stay, or an immigrant visa for permanent residence. Temporary worker visas are for persons who want to enter the United States for employment lasting a fixed period of time, and are not considered permanent or indefinite. Each of these visas requires the prospective employer to first file a petition with U.S. Citizenship and Immigration Services. An approved petition is required to apply for a work visa.

Temporary Visa Categories

Visa category	General description – About an individual in this category:
H-1B: Person in Specialty Occupation	To work in a specialty occupation. Requires a higher education degree or its equivalent. Includes fashion models of distinguished merit and ability and government-to-government research and development, or co-production projects administered by the Department of Defense.
H-2A: Temporary Agricultural Worker	For temporary or seasonal agricultural work. Limited to citizens or nationals of designated countries, with limited exceptions, if determined to be in the United States interest.
H-2B: Temporary Non-Agricultural Worker	For temporary or seasonal non-agricultural work. Limited to citizens or nationals of designated countries, with limited exceptions, if determined to be in the United States interest.
H-3: Trainee or Special Education Visitor	To receive training, other than graduate medical or academic, that is not available in the trainee's home country or practical training programs in the education of children with mental, physical, or emotional disabilities.
L: Intra-Company Transferee	To work at a branch, parent, affiliate, or subsidiary of the current employer in a managerial or executive capacity, or in a position requiring specialized knowledge. Individual must have been employed by the same employer abroad continuously for 1 year within the three preceding years.
O: Individual with Extraordinary Ability or Achievement	For persons with extraordinary ability or achievement in the sciences, arts, education, business, athletics, or extraordinary recognized achievements in the motion picture and television fields, demonstrated by sustained national or international acclaim, to work in their field of expertise. Includes persons providing essential services in support of the above individual.

Labour Certification - Some temporary worker visa categories require your prospective employer to obtain a labour certification or other approval from the Department of Labor on your behalf before filing the Petition for a Non-immigrant Worker, Form I-129, with USCIS. Your prospective employer should review the Instructions for Form I-129 on the USCIS website to determine whether labour certification is required for you.

Petition Approval - Some temporary worker categories are limited in total number of petitions which can be approved on a yearly basis. Before you can apply for a temporary worker visa at a U.S. embassy or consulate, a Petition for a Non-immigrant Worker, Form I-129, must be filed on your behalf by a prospective employer and be approved by the U.S. Citizenship and Immigration Services (USCIS)."

Green Cards

When a non-resident, non-U.S. citizen individual goes to the U.S. to work and live temporarily, after their term is almost up and they are contemplating staying in the U.S. for another term or working for a new employer, many wonder if they should be applying for a U.S. green card rather than renewing their temporary work visa; however, most of the time they don't realize what it means to apply for and obtain a U.S. green card.

 Having a U.S. green card will allow the holder to live and work anywhere in the United States; however, it also subjects that individual to all the U.S. tax laws and regulations that are applicable to other U.S. citizens and permanent residents.

Applying for a green card means applying for permanent residence status in the U.S. which means that you are now subjecting yourself to all the U.S. tax laws applicable to U.S. citizens and residents for as long as you hold your green card.

 For tax purposes, you are considered a U.S. resident as soon as you apply for a green card.

The green card serves as proof that its holder, a lawful permanent resident (LPR), has been officially granted immigration benefits, which include permission to live and work in the United States. The holder must maintain permanent resident status, and can be removed from the United States if certain conditions of this status are not met.

A person may have technically abandoned their status if he or she moves to another country to live there permanently, stays outside the U.S. for more than 365 days (without getting a re-entry permit before leaving), or does not file an income tax return; however, until you officially surrender your green card, you could still be considered a permanent resident for tax purposes, which means you must still abide by all the U.S. filing requirements. Failure to renew the green card does not result in the loss of status.

Filing Requirements While in the U.S.

If you are living, studying and/or working in the U.S. on a temporary basis, you don't necessarily have to file as a U.S. resident for tax purposes; your filing status will depend on your particular situation in the year that you are filing. As stated in chapter 1, residency is the basis for the Canadian tax system but it also dictates how and when a non-resident of either Canada or the U.S. is taxed.

If you temporarily live, study and/or work in the U.S. but still maintain residential ties to Canada, even though you spend more time in the U.S. than in Canada, you may still be considered a non-resident of the U.S. and therefore be required to file a non-resident income tax return (i.e., 1040NR).

Residency

Residency can be determined by many factors but it is mainly determined by the following:

- Physical presence (i.e., number of days in a country);
- Residential ties to a country; and
- A person's intentions.

A taxpayer is ordinarily resident in the place where the individual normally lives and is settled in the routine of his or her life (a factual resident). The Canada-U.S. Tax Convention discusses residency and states that when an individual is considered a resident of both "Contracting States" (i.e., countries or states), then the status shall be determined as follows:

a) shall be deemed to be a resident of the contracting state in which a permanent home is available; if a permanent home is available in both States or in neither State, shall be deemed to be a resident of the Contracting State with which personal and economic relations are closer (centre of vital interests);

b) If the Contracting State in which the centre of vital interests cannot be determined, shall be deemed to be a resident of the Contracting State of an habitual abode (i.e., place where the most time is spent);

c) If an habitual abode is in both States or in neither State, shall be deemed to be a resident of the Contracting State of citizenship; and

d) If a citizen of both States or of neither of them, the competent authorities of the Contracting States shall settle the question by mutual agreement.

Keep in mind that you can only be considered a resident of one place at a time and also, citizenship and residency are two entirely different concepts that can completely change a person's situation when it comes to income tax.

Residential Ties

If you search residency for individuals on the Canada Revenue Agency website (www.cra.gc.ca), you will find it states that "a determination of residence status can only be made after all the factors have been considered. Your circumstances have to be reviewed in their entirety to get an accurate picture of your residence status."

The residential ties you have with Canada are a major factor in determining your residency status. Some residential ties to Canada can include:

- a home in Canada;
- a spouse or common-law partner or dependants in Canada;
- personal property in Canada (i.e., a car or furniture);
- social ties in Canada; and
- economic ties in Canada.

Other residential ties that may also be relevant include:

- a Canadian driver's licence;
- Canadian bank accounts or credit cards; and
- health insurance with a Canadian province or territory.

Residential ties that you maintain or establish in another country may also be relevant to your residency status. It's important to remember that residency isn't usually determined by just one factor so your entire situation must be considered in order to make the right determination.

Real Life: Canadian resident attending university in the U.S.

Megan has been attending university at NDSU (North Dakota State University) on an F-1 visa for the past 4 years and will be graduating with her degree in psychology December 2013. In the summer of 2013 she worked full-time on campus and earned $9,500 in total. Once she graduates, she plans to move back to Regina, Saskatchewan, to start a new job in her field of study.

Megan maintained her bank accounts in Canada and took only the personal items she needed to get by while away at school as she always intended to return to Canada once she completed her degree. She does not own a house in Canada or the U.S. and lived on campus while going to NDSU. Based on the facts, even though Megan spends more time in the U.S. she maintains closer ties to Canada which means that she is considered a Canadian resident for tax purposes.

Filing Requirements

- Each year Megan attends school in the U.S. she will need to file a form 8843, even though she may not be required to file a 1040NR return.

- Megan will need to file a 1040NR return in 2013 to report the $9,500 of employment income that will be exempt from tax in the U.S.
- Megan would claim to be a Canadian resident while she is away at college but would still be required to file a Canadian income tax return and report her worldwide income.

Real Life: Canadian moving to U.S. to work

Jackie is a Canadian citizen and resident. A few months ago she received an amazing job offer from a company operating in Dallas, Texas, and she had to accept. Her new job started July 1, 2013, and she moved to Dallas at the end of June; however, her husband and 2 children won't be moving to Dallas until January 2014.

Jackie's new job does not have a term attached to it, so after a few years, if she likes it, she plans to apply for a green card and live in the U.S. permanently. Her children are 10 and 14 and will be attending school in Dallas as well.

Filing Requirements

- Jackie intends to move to the U.S. on a permanent basis in September 2013; however, her family will not be moving to live with her until January 2014, which means that she will still be deemed to be a Canadian resident in 2013 and required to file a Canadian tax return on a worldwide income basis
- Jackie's residential ties to Canada will deem her to be a non-resident of the U.S. and she will need to file a 1040NR income tax return in 2013.
- Jackie will need a temporary work visa until she applies for a green card; her husband will need a temporary visa and their children will need student visas.
- Jackie will be taxed as a U.S. citizen and resident as soon as she applies for a green card, whether it is approved or not.
- Jackie and her family will file as U.S. residents in 2014.

There can be many different filing requirements depending on what a person's particular situation is, especially when it concerns U.S. filing requirements.

Knowing what tax laws apply in your situation is very important because the onus is always on the taxpayer to know what their requirements are, and ignorance is generally not an accepted excuse for not filing, especially if penalties are applicable.

Going to School or Working Temporarily in The U.S.: What You Need to Know

Canadian residents temporarily in the U.S.

- Going to school in the U.S. doesn't mean you will be treated as a U.S. person for tax purposes.

- If you work temporarily in the U.S. but still maintain closer ties to Canada you can still be a Canadian resident for tax purposes and therefore a non-resident in the U.S. for tax purposes.

- Non-residents of the U.S. are only required to file a U.S. non-resident tax return if they have income in the U.S. and meet the filing threshold.

- U.S. Employment income under $10,000 is exempt from U.S. federal income tax but still may be subject to state taxes.

Canadians changing their U.S. status

- If during the time you are temporarily working in the U.S. you make the decision to apply for a U.S. green card, you are applying for U.S. permanent residency status.

- Residents must abide by all the U.S. tax laws applicable to U.S. citizens.

WHAT YOU NEED TO KNOW ABOUT UNCLE SAM:

If you plan to attend school or work temporarily in the U.S., you may technically be deemed to a U.S. resident for tax purposes. However, in certain circumstances you may actually still be considered a Canadian resident and a U.S. non-resident. This can be beneficial in some cases.

A foreign student in the U.S. on a student visa can work in the U.S. but usually only for the school they are attending because a student visa does not give someone the right to work in the U.S. If the employment income earned is less than $10,000, it will be exempt from federal tax in the U.S. but taxable in Canada. This exemption is for all non-residents of the U.S., not just students.

In order to work in the U.S. you need a temporary work visa and the type of visa required will depend on your professional requirements and the job you are doing. Most work visas are sponsored by the U.S. employer and have an expiry date.

You can physically spend more time in the U.S. than in Canada but still be deemed a resident of Canada instead of the U.S. for tax purposes. There are various residential ties that are used to determine a person's residency status; however, every situation is different. If you are considered to be a U.S. resident, there may be Canadian tax ramifications that you were not counting on (see chapter 7 for more details on deemed dispositions on departure). Applying for a U.S. green card automatically changes your residency status.

All situations can have tax implications so it is best to plan ahead before you get into trouble.

CHAPTER 9

U.S. Inheritances

Case Study:

Cynthia is a Canadian citizen and resident. Cynthia's grandmother, who is a U.S. citizen and resident, is very ill and expected to pass away shortly. Cynthia is a named beneficiary of her grandmother's estate but she is also a direct beneficiary of her grandmother's IRA (Individual Retirement Account).

Her grandmother's estate has a value of approximately $4,350,000, including her IRA of $125,000; however, she understands that the IRA is to be paid directly to her instead of being paid to the estate first and then to her once any estate taxes are paid.

Cynthia's mother, a dual citizen of Canada and the U.S., is the named beneficiary on Cynthia's grandmother's condo in Arizona; it has a current value of $235,000.

Questions & Answers:

Will Cynthia be taxed on the receipt of her grandmother's IRA? Can anything be done to change this and is this something that should be changed?

Yes, Cynthia will be taxed on the IRA both in Canada and the U.S. because it is considered income from a decedent and not just a simple receipt of cash. If the income was first designated to flow through the estate and any residual after tax cash paid out to Cynthia then she would not be subject to tax on the amount received.

Will Cynthia's mother be taxed on the receipt of the U.S. condo?

No, gifts of property are not taxable to the recipient.

Will Cynthia's grandmother's estate be taxable if she died today?

No, because the 2013 estate tax exemption is currently $5,250,000 and her estate is under that value.

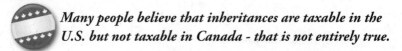 *Many people believe that inheritances are taxable in the U.S. but not taxable in Canada - that is not entirely true.*

Inheritances are not taxable in Canada, and they are not usually taxable in the U.S. either. This of course is referring to the inheritance of property and not of income. In both countries, income generated from inherited property and income is respect of a decedent is always taxable to the beneficiary

Inheritances, Bequests and Devises

Tax-free bequests, devises and inheritances are defined as money and property that passes on the death of a person through a will or without a will.

Gifts and bequests of income, and the income from property that is received as a gift or bequest, are taxable to the recipient, no matter how paid (i.e., pension income, rental profits from an inherited rental property, etc.).

Nontaxable Gifts and Bequests

Under regular IRS code, a beneficiary isn't taxable on any amount received as a gift or bequest of specific property or of a specific sum of money. For example, a gift or bequest of a house, cash or a car isn't taxable. The gift or bequest can actually be paid or credited to the beneficiary all at once or in three or less installments.

Taxable Gifts and Bequests

Under U.S. tax law, property you receive as a gift, bequest, or inheritance is not included in your income. However, if the property you receive produces income such as interest, dividends, or rents, that income is taxable to you when received. If property is given to a trust and the income from it is paid, credited, or distributed to you, that income also is taxable to you when received. If the gift, bequest, or inheritance is income from property (i.e., a direct payout of a U.S. IRA) that income is also taxable to you when received. This is taxable income because the decedent hasn't paid tax on this money and it wasn't designated to first be paid to the estate and then the residual cash paid out to the beneficiary.

Property Acquired from a Decedent

When a U.S. individual dies, his or her estate is either valued at the fair market value on the date of death or at the alternative valuation date (AVD). An executor can make an irrevocable election to use an alternative valuation date to value the decedent's assets rather than use the fair market value on the date of death. The AVD is usually six months after the date of death or the earlier date of sale or actual distribution, but the AVD can only be used if it results in a decrease to both the value of the gross estate and the combined estate and Generation Skipping Tax (GST) tax liability.

> *An executor can only use the AVD if it results in a lower overall tax liability, which is a benefit to the deceased's estate.*

Generally, the basis (i.e., cost base) of property acquired from a decedent through a bequest, inheritance, etc. is equal to the fair market value of the property on the date of the decedent's death if the property hasn't been sold, exchanged, or otherwise disposed of before then.

IRS regulations state that the fair market value of property at the decedent's death or at the AVD, whichever is used, as appraised for federal estate tax purposes is also considered to be the tax cost to the person inheriting the property.

Real Life: *Cost base of inherited property*

Leslie's father passed away last year and in his will he left her the family's vacation home in Palm Springs, California. For U.S. estate tax purposes the property was reported at its fair value of $221,000 on the date of her father's death, even though he only paid $102,350 for the property when he originally bought it 10 years ago.

Leslie will not pay tax on the inheritance of the vacation home and her inherited cost base for the property will be equal to the $221,000 fair value at her father's death.

Income in Respect of a Decedent (after death income)

Income in respect of a decedent (IRD) includes income that the decedent had a right to receive but:

1.   wasn't actually received by a cash basis decedent, or
2.   wasn't accrued by an accrual basis decedent.

This means that any income earned by the decedent but not physically received prior to death would be income in respect of a decedent. IRD can include insurance renewal commissions, a monthly pension paid to a deceased employee's widow, taxable distributions from an Individual Retirement Account or qualified employee plan, a death benefit under a deferred annuity contract, partnership income of a deceased partner or S corporation income of a deceased shareholder.

Who is Taxed on Income from a Decedent?

Income in respect of a decedent (IRD) that is not includible on the decedent's last return because it wasn`t physically received prior to death must be reported when received by:

- The decedent's estate, if the income is to be paid to the decedent's estate;
- The person to whom the income is bequeathed (i.e., to whom it is left in the will), if it isn't to be paid to the decedent's estate; or
- The person who receives the income by bequest, devise or inheritance after distribution by the decedent's estate (i.e., it is flowed through the estate to the direct beneficiary).

Remember, the characteristics of IRD stay the same, as if it had been received by the decedent himself, had he not passed away.

Real Life: Dual citizens inheriting money

Henry and his wife Cecile have lived in Canada for 25 years; however, they are both dual citizens of Canada and the U.S. Cecile's mother passed away 7 months ago and had a U.S. estate worth $2,145,000, on which Cecile was named the sole beneficiary.

Cecile's mother's assets were as follows on the date of her death (FMV chosen for estate tax purposes):

Condo in Miami, Florida	$650,000
Condo is Las Vegas, Nevada	$400,000
IRA	$350,000
Stock portfolio	$275,000
Mesa, Arizona, rental property	$470,000

Cecile was listed as the direct beneficiary of her mother's IRA, which means that it was not paid to her estate and then paid out to Cecile. Because of this, Cecile is receiving a bequest of income, which means that it is fully taxable to her in the year of receipt. The other asset values will become Cecile's inherited basis; any income generated by these assets going forward will be taxable to Cecile in the year the income is earned.

Jason, Jeremy and Julie are all listed beneficiaries of their grandfather's U.S. estate; however, they are all non-U.S. citizens. They will all share in his estate equally and it includes the following assets:

Condo in Denver Colorado	$475,000
House in Nashville Tennessee	$525,000
Rental property in Reno Nevada	$365,000
IRA	$430,000
Roth IRA	$370,000
Stock portfolio	$1,000,000

Their grandfather's will indicates that all assets are to be paid into his estate first and then divided equally between all three of them, after any applicable estate tax is paid. Having the assets bequeathed this way means that all the assets will be distributed to each of them on a tax-free basis because they are simply receiving interest in property or cash (i.e., the IRAs will be cashed out and paid into the estate first, which means that only cash will be distributed to the beneficiaries).

Reporting Requirements

If you are a U.S. person receiving a bequest or inheritance from a foreign/non-U.S. person, you may have to report this information to the IRS using form 3520 - Annual Return to Report Transactions with Foreign Trusts and Receipt of Certain Foreign Gifts. You will have to file this form if you meet the following tests:

- You are a U.S. person who, during the current tax year, received either:
  a) More than $100,000 from a non-resident alien individual or a foreign estate that you treated as gifts or bequests; or
  b) More than $14,723 from foreign corporations or foreign partnerships that you treated as gifts.

In general, Form 3520 is due on the date that your income tax return is due, including extensions. In the case of a Form 3520 filed with respect to a U.S. decedent, Form 3520 is due on the date that Form 706, United States Estate (and Generation-Skipping Transfer) Tax Return, is due (including extensions), or would be due if the estate were required to file a return.

Send Form 3520 to the Internal Revenue Service Center, P.O. Box 409101, Ogden, UT 84409.

Form 3520 must have all required attachments to be considered complete.

Gifts or Bequests from "Covered Expatriates"

 The above rules for gifts, bequests and inheritances are the general rules with regard to these types of situations; however, the rules change if the gift, bequest or inheritance is from a "covered expatriate" and the one receiving the gift, bequest or inheritance is a U.S. person.

The U.S. tax code imposes a tax on each U.S. citizen or resident who receives a "covered gift or bequest" from a "covered expatriate" whose expatriation date was on or after June 17, 2008.

- A covered expatriate is an expatriate who meets the tests to have the alternative tax applied on expatriation from the U.S. (i.e., someone who has renounced their U.S. citizenship or relinquished their U.S. permanent residency status and is subject to the exit tax; refer to chapter 11 for more information).

- A covered gift is any property acquired directly or indirectly from a covered expatriate.

- A covered bequest is any property acquired directly or indirectly by reason of the death of an individual who, immediately before death, was a covered expatriate.

This inheritance tax contrasts with traditional U.S. estate and gift tax because this tax is imposed on the gift recipient, not the gift donor.

A covered gift can include the following:

1. Property directly or indirectly acquired by gift from a covered expatriate; or
2. Property acquired by reason of the death of a covered expatriate.

A covered gift does not include the following:

1. Taxable gifts disclosed on a timely filed gift tax return by the covered expatriate (Form 709);
2. Property included in the gross estate of the covered expatriate disclosed on a timely filed estate tax return (Form 706);
3. Property to which a gift or estate tax charitable or marital deduction would be allowed.

The inheritance tax applies to indirect gifts to U.S. persons, unless they are "taxable gifts."

 Unlike under the regular U.S. gift tax rules, the inheritance tax applies when a covered expatriate pays for the education or medical expenses of a U.S. person.

Under regular gifting rules, a U.S. person is allowed to make gifts under or equal to an annual exclusion amount *per recipient* without the gift being subject to gift tax ($14,000 in 2014 and 2013); however, under the covered expatriate rules, the exclusion amount is for the total value of gifts given that year, not per recipient as in the conventional gift tax regime. Also, if the covered expatriate transfers property to his or her surviving spouse who is a U.S. citizen, the inheritance tax will not apply but if the surviving spouse is not a U.S. citizen, the inheritance tax will apply.

Compare: Inheritance Tax vs. Gift & Estate Tax

The inheritance tax on gifts by a covered expatriate, contrast with the more favourable estate and gift tax treatment of those who are non-resident, non-citizen persons. Under the U.S. tax code, a non-resident, non-citizen person pays no gift or estate tax for transferring property to a U.S. citizen or resident unless the transferred property is situated in the U.S.

A non-resident, non-citizen person has a minimum $60,000 estate tax exemption for bequests of U.S. situs property, but also has access to a larger percentage of the $5.34 million estate tax exemption (2014 exemption) available to regular U.S. citizens and residents under the Canada-U.S. Tax Convention. In contrast, a covered expatriate triggers tax for the recipient on the gift or bequest of property to a U.S. person, regardless of where the property is located, with only a $14,000 per year exception. *Not a $14,000 per person exception!*

A non-resident, non-citizen person can obtain U.S. estate tax deferral, until the death of the surviving spouse, through the use of a Qualified Domestic Trust (QDOT), which is not possible for the covered expatriate subject to the inheritance tax.

 The covered expatriate should make gifts of U.S. property subject to U.S. estate and gift tax and not the inheritance tax, since the estate and gift tax is tax paid by the person making the gift vs. the inheritance tax which is paid by the person receiving the gift.

Tax exclusive means the gift excludes the tax and the tax is paid in addition to the gift by the person making the gift. Tax inclusive means that the tax is included as part of the gift and must be paid after the gift is received by the person who received the gift.

Real Life: *Covered expatriate making a gift to a U.S. person*

A $600,000 gift:

- If a covered expatriate wishes to make a net bequest of $600,000, the bequest of $1M of non-U.S. property would leave a U.S. person with $600,000 after paying the inheritance tax ($400,000 inheritance tax paid by the gift recipient).

- A gift of $600,000 of U.S. property would have a maximum gift tax of $240,000, a tax savings of $160,000 (the donor pays the gift tax, not the recipient).

The point of this example is that in order for a covered expatriate to gift $600,000 (net of taxes to the recipient) to a U.S. person, the gift would need to be made during the covered expatriate's lifetime instead of at death. A lower amount of tax would be paid and it would be paid by the covered expatriate instead of the recipient of the gift/bequest.

Planning for Expatriates

In an article published by Mondaq[1] called United States: Estate Planning For Expatriates Under Chapter 15, various planning strategies are discussed to help reduce the impact of the inheritance tax. The strategies are discussed below.

Non-Citizen/Non-Green Card Holder is Never a Covered Expatriate

 A simple strategy for an individual who is not a U.S. citizen is to simply avoid becoming a covered expatriate; only gifts or bequests from covered expatriates are subject to the inheritance tax.

By avoiding becoming a green card holder, an individual will never be considered a long-term resident who ceases to be a lawful permanent resident and someone who does not have a green card or is not a U.S. citizen cannot be considered a covered expatriate, even if he or she is a former U.S. resident for income tax purposes. Alternatively, an individual who already has a green card could relinquish it prior to becoming a lawful permanent resident of the U.S. to avoid being considered a covered expatriate. Under U.S. law, you could be a covered expatriate if you lived in the U.S. for more than 8 years over the last 15 years (i.e., lawful permanent residency status) prior to expatriation so all the individual needs to do is just relinquish the green card before this test is met.

---

[1] http://www.mondaq.com/unitedstates/x/212828/tax+authorities/Estate+Planning+For+Expatriates+Under+Chapter+15

Real Life: *Individual avoiding "covered expatriate" status while alive*

Francine Smith is a foreign national who had been living in the U.S. for years, but never obtained a green card. Francine decides to return to her home country of Canada, which she establishes as her new domicile. Francine then makes gifts of $20 million of intangible property to family members who are U.S. persons. Because Francine is not a U.S. citizen and never had a green card, she is not a covered expatriate and therefore any gifts she makes are not subject to the inheritance tax. Also, as a non-resident alien, because the gifts are not of real property or tangible property located in the U.S., the transfer is not subject to U.S. gift tax.

Real Life: *Individual avoiding "covered expatriate" status at death*

The facts are the same as in the previous example, except that Francine bequeathed the $20 million of intangible property at death. As above, because Francine is not a covered expatriate, the transfer would not be subject to the inheritance tax. Additionally, as a non-resident alien, because the transfer was not of U.S. situs property, it would not be subject to U.S. estate tax.

Generation-Skipping Transfer Planning

Although the inheritance tax section of the IRS code is designed to capture transfers received from covered expatriates that would otherwise be subject to the U.S. gift and estate tax rules, it does not include tax on a Generation-Skipping Transfer (GST) basis. Prior to the passage of the GST tax, wealthy individuals could transfer wealth to long-term trusts for the benefit of descendants in order to avoid repeated exposure to U.S. gift and estate taxes. By skipping generations, wealthy families were able to keep assets out of the taxable estates of the middle generations. Congress designed the GST tax in order to impose an additional tax at a flat tax rate equal to the highest U.S. estate tax rate on transfers (i.e., 40%) otherwise designed to skip generations, which means that people are now penalized for giving away their wealth to a second-generation individual, or younger. U.S. citizens and residents are potentially subject to GST tax on all transfers but so are non-residents and non-citizens but only if they are transferring U.S. situs assets.

Transfers by non-resident, non-citizens of the U.S. are only subject to the GST tax on direct skip transfers if the transfer is subject to U.S. gift or estate tax (i.e., the transfer must be over the exemption amounts and must be of U.S. situs assets).

For example, if grandpa wanted to give his grandson the $110,000 vacation home in Arizona, the gift would be subject to gift tax because it is over the $14,000 annual limit and it would also be subject to GST because the grandson is a skip person; assuming the grandson's parents are still alive.

Also, a taxable distribution or termination from a trust is subject to the GST tax only to the extent that the initial transfer of property to the trust was subject to U.S. gift or estate tax.

 Therefore, if a covered expatriate makes a transfer to a U.S. person that is not subject to U.S. gift or estate tax, then the GST tax should not apply either.

The ability to bypass generations without being subjected to the GST tax can be a valuable planning strategy for covered expatriates, particularly for wealthy individuals who are elderly or terminally ill.

Real Life: U.S. citizen and GST

Raymond Kim, age 85, is terminally ill. Each of his three children is already very wealthy. He wants to bequeath his entire remaining estate of $54 million to his grandson, who is a U.S. person. Raymond is a U.S. citizen, who has not used his lifetime gift and GST exemption amounts. If Raymond dies in 2014 and we assume a flat combined state and federal estate tax rate of 50% and the GST tax rate is 40%, the total taxes on the transfer would be $43.794 million, leaving only $10.206 million after tax for his grandson.

Real Life: Covered expatriate and GST

The facts are the same as in the previous example, except that Raymond becomes a covered expatriate and is not considered domiciled in the U.S. at the time of his death. The receipt of the $54 million inheritance would be subject to the inheritance tax, and assuming a 40% tax rate, the grandson would owe $21.6 million of tax. The grandson would have a net bequest, after taxes, of $32.4 million, which is $22.194 million more than in the previous example. Because the transfer would not be subject to U.S. estate tax, the GST tax would not apply.

Transfers to Non-U.S. Persons

The inheritance tax is applied only to gifts or bequests from covered expatriates that are made to U.S. citizens or residents. As discussed above, non-resident aliens are generally subject to U.S. gift tax only on transfers of real property or tangible property located in the U.S. and U.S. estate tax on U.S. situs assets. If a wealthy individual does not intend to make gifts or leave inheritances to U.S. persons, then expatriating can result in substantial transfer tax savings.

Real Life: Expatriate bequest to non-U.S. person

Jacques, who is a long-time green card holder, recently sold his company for $200 million. None of Jacques' beneficiaries are U.S. citizens or residents. Assuming he has no meaningful appreciation in his assets, Jacques would not face an income tax under the new exit tax regime on expatriation because we are assuming his gains would be under the annual capital gains reduction amount; he would be considered a covered expatriate though. If Jacques expatriates and subsequently bequeaths $200 million to his heirs, no U.S. transfer tax would be imposed because his heirs are not U.S. people. Assuming a 40% tax rate, the estate tax savings would be nearly $80 million.

Also, the inheritance tax section of the code does not apply to transfers from covered expatriates to covered expatriates who are not U.S. residents, which can provide an excellent planning opportunity as well. Applying this to our example, assume one of the beneficiaries was also a covered expatriate; no inheritance tax would be applicable on the bequest left to this person either.

Real Life: Expatriate bequest planning

The facts are the same as in the previous example, except that Jacques has three wealthy children who are U.S. persons at the time of his expatriation. Ten years later, when Jacques is worth $400 million, he becomes very ill. His U.S. children could themselves become covered expatriates. If Jacques dies and leaves all his property to his covered expatriate children, no tax would be imposed under the inheritance tax rules because they would no longer be U.S. citizens or residents. Alternatively, prior to the expatriation of Jacques' children, he could also fund a foreign trust to hold the assets for their benefit until they become covered expatriates.

If they chose not to become covered expatriates, they would have to pay inheritance tax on the $400 Million bequest.

If a covered expatriate has beneficiaries that are U.S. citizens or residents, as well as beneficiaries that are non-U.S. persons, then estate planning can be done to minimize U.S. tax by having the covered expatriate leave the U.S. asset portion of the estate, which is subject to U.S. estate tax, to U.S. beneficiaries and leave the non-U.S. portion of the estate to non-U.S. persons, which would not be subject to U.S. tax.

This also allows for a tax-free inheritance to the U.S. recipients.

Planning Prior to Expatriation

A U.S. person is able to make lifetime gifts (i.e., gifts above the annual exclusion) of up to the gift and estate tax exclusion amount ($5.34 million in 2014) without being subject to tax. Applying this rule, prior to expatriating, a person should consider using up his or her full lifetime gifting amount to transfer assets to U.S. persons, free of gift tax. Once a person becomes a covered expatriate and is not a U.S. resident, the lifetime gift and estate tax exemption disappears. Using the lifetime gifting exclusion prior to expatriation for gifts to persons who are not U.S. citizens or residents is not very effective planning because, as previously mentioned, after expatriation a covered expatriate can make unlimited gifts of non-U.S. property to individuals who are not U.S. citizens or residents without tax implications.

Tax Basis Considerations

Generally, when a gift of appreciated property is made, the person receiving the gift (donee) inherits the same tax basis/cost it had in the hands of the donor. However, if the transfer is subject to U.S. gift tax, the donee's cost is increased by all or part of the gift tax paid on the gift. The basis increase is the gift tax attributable to the "net appreciation" of the gift, which is determined by multiplying the gift tax paid by the net appreciation in value of the gift, divided by the gift.

> ### Real Life: Basis calculation on appreciated gift subject to gift tax
>
> Jenny received Microsoft shares from her father in February 2014 that had a value of $36,000. Because the gift was over the $14,000 annual exclusion limit, Jenny's father paid $8,800 in gift tax ((36,000-14,000)*40%). Jenny's father paid $12,000 for the stocks when he originally purchased them but, because he had to pay gift tax on the transfer to Jenny, Jenny's basis in the stocks is $17,866.67 (i.e., this is her cost of the property). This is calculated as follows:
>
> | | |
> |---|---|
> | Appreciation in value (36,000-12,000) | $ 24,000.00 |
> | Gift tax on appreciated value ((24,000/36,000)*8,800) | $ 5,866.67 |
> | Jenny's adjusted basis of gift (12,000+5,866.67) | $ 17,866.67 |

The income tax provisions do not provide for such a basis increase for taxes paid by the donee under the inheritance tax rules which means that the inheritance tax will be an additional tax borne by the donee without an increase in basis for the tax paid. This means that if the person receiving the gift has to pay inheritance tax on the gift, they will not be able to add the amount of the inheritance tax to the cost of the property as they could with the gift tax paid. Often, the best tax planning involves a covered expatriate making gifts of high-basis property, or selling low-basis property and then gifting the proceeds.

Additional Planning by Covered Expatriates

There are some tax planning strategies that one can consider to try and reduce any potential inheritance tax that may be triggered on the gifts or bequests made by a covered expatriate. Planning around this is key because this is an additional tax imposed on covered expatriates which results in less money/assets available to the beneficiary for their use and enjoyment.

A covered expatriate should be able to make loans to a U.S. person, as well as to trusts or entities owned by U.S. persons, without triggering an inheritance tax as long as the loans bear an adequate interest rate (i.e., they are bona fide loans).

Also, avoiding or strategically planning around covered expatriates within one's family is an important part of a family's overall estate planning. For example, if a grandfather is a non-resident alien, who is also not domiciled in the U.S., instead of transferring property to his son who is a covered expatriate, which could create future inheritance tax issues, he could make the transfers to his grandchildren instead, who are not considered covered expatriates. By bypassing the covered expatriate with the transfer of assets that are ultimately intended for grandchildren or future generations anyway, the future inheritance taxes that could be imposed on the covered expatriate are potentially eliminated.

 Keep in mind that the above rules are applicable only to "covered expatriates"; meaning that if you are a U.S. expatriate who does not meet the tests under the code, you are therefore not considered a covered expatriate, inheritance tax will not apply to your gifts or bequests after expatriation.

US. Inheritances: What You Need to Know

Canadians receiving U.S. inheritances

- Inheriting money or property is not taxable no matter where it comes from.
- Inheriting income from a decedent is taxable to the recipient in the year received.
- The basis/cost of the property received is usually the same basis that the original owner had, unless gift tax is applicable or it is a bequest.
- The basis of property received as a bequest is the fair value used in the deceased's gross estate.

U.S. persons receiving inheritances

- Inheriting money or property is not taxable no matter where it comes from.
- Inheriting income from a decedent is taxable to the recipient in the year received.
- Inheriting anything from a U.S. covered expatriate can result in U.S. inheritance tax for the recipient.
- The basis of the property received is usually the same basis that the original owner had, unless gift tax is applicable or it is a bequest.
- The basis of property received as a bequest is the fair value used in the deceased's gross estate.

WHAT YOU NEED TO KNOW ABOUT UNCLE SAM:

When a U.S person passes away, the assets are valued at the fair value immediately prior to death and if the total estate is more than the lifetime estate tax exemption (i.e., $5,340,000 for 2014) then estate tax is payable at a 40% rate. The assets included in the deceased's estate receive a bump up in cost base equal to the fair value used in the estate valuation. Any beneficiary receiving assets from the estate receive them at the bumped up cost basis as well, which means that they will only pay capital gains tax on any appreciated value after the date of death.

Gifts, bequests and inheritances are generally not taxable in Canada or the U.S. as long as the property received is of cash or property and it is not from a U.S. covered expatriate. However, a gift, bequest or inheritance of income is taxable to the recipient.

Sometimes assets are left directly to a beneficiary and not first included in a deceased person's estate. If this occurs, there are instances when bequests of income can occur which makes the inheritance taxable to the recipient. For example, if a deceased person leaves an IRA to a direct beneficiary, the IRA distribution is fully taxable to the beneficiary as income in that year. This is because no tax has been paid on this money during the deceased's life or at death.

Covered expatriates have special rules applied to them when they leave property to U.S. persons. U.S. beneficiaries of gifts or bequests from covered expatriates are subject to U.S. inheritance tax if the gift or bequest is subject to regular U.S. gift tax. The difference between gift tax and inheritance tax is that gift tax is paid by the person making the gift and inheritance tax is paid by the person receiving the gift. There are planning strategies one can use to try and avoid potential inheritance tax on gifts or bequests from covered expatriates but it all depends on the expatriate's particular circumstances.

Everyone's situation can differ entirely, which is why a good understanding of all the facts is crucial, and proper planning is a must to ensure unnecessary taxes are eliminated during a person's life and on a person's death.

CHAPTER 10

Doing Business in the U.S.

Case Study 1:

Nathan is a Canadian citizen and resident, operating an online consulting business from his home. He has been approached by a large U.S. corporation to come down to their head office in Atlanta, Georgia, and assist them with some very big projects they have on the go, on a contract basis. Nathan would be required to stay in Georgia for 6 to 8 months but once his term is up he would head back to Canada. Nathan is married with 3 children but his family will stay back in Canada as he is only gone for a few months and he'll make frequent trips home to visit them.

Questions & Answers:

Does Nathan need a U.S. visa? What kind?
Yes, likely a TN visa is what he would apply for because he is a professional working on a contract basis.

Will Nathan be a U.S. resident while doing business in the U.S.?
No, because he plans to stay in the U.S. only on a temporary basis and his family will stay behind in Canada, which helps maintain his residential ties to Canada.

Case Study 2:

Jenna owns her own restaurant in Penticton, British Columbia, and is thinking about branching into the United States. She is planning to open up a new restaurant in Seattle, Washington, before the end of the year and is looking to transfer one of her top chefs down to that location to work and oversee the operations;

she plans to visit the restaurant frequently to check the progress and make sure it is operating to her standards.

Questions & Answers:

Does Jenna need to get a visa for the chef?
Yes, because he or she is going to be employed in the U.S.

What are Jenna's options for setting up her restaurant in the U.S.?
She can set up a separate U.S. corporation, she could set up a branch of her Canadian corporation, or she could use a U.S. LLC.

How will this new restaurant be taxed?
It depends on how the U.S. operations are set up, but the profits will be subject to regular income tax in the U.S. because it operates there (i.e., as a permanent establishment); however, it could also be subject to other taxes.

Many Canadians consider doing business in the United States, whether it is as an individual employee, sole proprietor or as a corporation. Depending on the context of how one plans to conduct business in the U.S., there are different procedures and rules that apply in each scenario and it is always good practice to know what is required before jumping into an endeavour such as this.

Entry into the United States

Foreign individuals wanting to enter the United States as non-immigrants are required to obtain a visa, which can be applied for at a U.S. Consular Office.

Basically, if you want to work in the U.S. and are not a U.S. person, you must apply for a work visa. A foreign individual is referred to as an "alien" and, for U.S. tax purposes, is classified as either a resident alien or a non-resident alien. In the year of entry or departure, an alien may be classified as both a resident and a non-resident, and will be required to file a "Dual Status" Return. The correct identification of the alien's status is critical to determine the proper tax liabilities for the year.

An alien is categorized as a non-resident alien unless he or she meets one of the two residency tests.

The first test, the green card test, automatically classifies an alien as a resident in the United States if the person is a "lawful permanent resident," a status obtained by holding a green card at any time during the year. Keep in mind that for tax purposes, an individual is considered to be a lawful permanent resident as soon as they apply for a green card; it does not have to first be issued for this test to be met. The second test that would give the alien resident status is the substantial presence test. In order to meet this test, the alien must be physically present in the United States for at least 31 days during the current year and 183 days over a three-year look-back period. The 183-days test considers all days present in the current year, one-third of the days present in the first preceding year and one-sixth of the days present in the second preceding year.

These defined rules do not override any treaty definitions of residency.

 Even if the alien meets the substantial presence test described above, not the green card test, he or she can still be taxed as a non-resident if he or she has closer ties to a treaty country, i.e., Canada.

Remaining a legal resident of Canada may be beneficial in some cases, especially if a deemed disposition would arise for an individual no longer being considered a Canadian resident (i.e., deemed capital gains tax on departure from Canada).

U.S. Visas

Your qualifications and purpose for entering the United States will dictate the type of business visa required to enter the U.S. legally. U.S. business visas are classified as follows (taken from the U.S. Department of State website):

Purpose of Travel to U.S. and Nonimmigrant Visas	Visa Type	Required Before Applying for Visa*
Athletes, amateur & professional (compete for prize money only)	B-1	(NA)
Business visitors	B-1	(NA)
Domestic employees or nanny -must be accompanying a foreign national employer	B-1	(NA)
Employees of a designated international organization, and NATO	G1-G5, NATO	(NA)
Foreign nationals with extraordinary ability in Sciences, Arts, Education, Business or Athletics	O	USCIS
Free Trade Agreement (FTA) Professionals: Chile, Singapore	H-1B1 - Chile H-1B1 - Singapore	DOL

Intra-company transferees	L	USCIS
Medical treatment, visitors for	B-2	(NA)
Media, journalists	I	(NA)
NAFTA professional workers: Mexico, Canada	TN/TD	(NA)
Performing athletes, artists, entertainers	P	USCIS
Physician	J , H-1B	SEVIS
Professor, scholar, teacher (exchange visitor)	J	SEVIS
Religious workers	R	USCIS
Specialty occupations in fields requiring highly specialized knowledge	H-1B	DOL then USCIS
Temporary agricultural workers	H-2A	DOL then USCIS
Temporary workers performing other services or labor of a temporary or seasonal nature.	H-2B	DOL then USCIS

Before applying for a visa at a U.S. Embassy abroad the following is required:

- **DOL** = The U.S. employer must obtain foreign labor certification from the U.S. Department of Labor, prior to filing a petition with USCIS.

- **USCIS** = DHS, U.S. Citizenship and Immigration Services (USCIS) approval of a petition or application (The required petition or application depends on the visa category you plan to apply for.)

- **SEVIS** = Program approval entered in the Student and Exchange Visitor Information System (SEVIS)

- **(NA)** = Not Applicable - Means that additional approval by other government agencies is not required prior to applying for a visa at the U.S. Embassy abroad.

Note: see Chapter 4 for another summary of U.S. visas and what each is used for (i.e., what you can and cannot do with that particular visa).

U.S. Employees

The Social Security Act provides retirement, disability and health benefits to U.S. employees. Self-employed individuals pay self-employment tax based on a tax rate of 12.4 percent (2013) on income up to $113,700 (2013) and a Medicare rate of 2.9 percent on all self-employed income.

Resident and non-resident aliens with U.S. source wages or salary compensation income are subject to these employment taxes.

For example, in the two case studies discussed at the beginning of the chapter, Nathan would be subjected to these taxes because he is earning U.S. self-employment income and Jenna's chef would also be subject to these taxes because he or she would be earning U.S. employment income.

Beginning January 1, 2013, Additional Medicare Tax applies to an individual's Medicare wages that exceed a threshold amount based on the taxpayer's filing status. Employers are responsible for withholding the 0.9% Additional Medicare Tax on an individual's wages in excess of $200,000 per calendar year. An employer is required to begin withholding Additional Medicare Tax in the pay period in which it pays wages in excess of $200,000 to an employee. There is no employer match for Additional Medicare Tax and this applies for self-employed individuals as well.

Totalization Agreements on Social Security

A number of bilateral Social Security agreements coordinate the U.S. Social Security program with comparable programs in other countries. The purpose of these "totalization agreements" is to eliminate dual Social Security taxation, which can arise when a worker from one country works in another country and is required to pay Social Security taxes to both countries on the same earnings. The agreements also help fill gaps in benefit protection for workers who divide their careers between the United States and another country.

In other words, if you work in another country (in this case, Canada), and pay social security tax there (CPP) but have to report and pay tax on that same income in the U.S., you will not be required to pay social security tax on that income for U.S. tax purposes because Canada and the U.S. have a totalization agreement and it works both ways.

In some cases, a signed form may be required to confirm that social security tax is paid in the source country.

Real Life: Canadian earning U.S. Social Security Benefits

Michael worked in the U.S. on a TN visa for 12 years before he moved back to Canada; he is not a U.S. citizen or long-term resident. While working in the U.S. he paid into U.S. social security (SS) and now qualifies to receive benefit payments. Michael will receive $5,400 from U.S. SS each year starting in 2014 and this will be his only U.S. source income.

For U.S. tax purposes, Michael would have to file a non-resident 1040NR return to report his U.S. SS income; however, it would be reported in a special section of the return which shows tax exempt income under treaty rules (i.e., this is on the last page of the return). A return is required because the value of the benefits received is over the personal exemption filing threshold but this income is not taxable in the U.S. therefore no tax would result.

For Canadian tax purposes, Michael would include these benefits as income on his T1 return but he would only be taxed on 85% of the SS amount received.

Real Life: Dual citizen living in Canada earning self-employment income

Daniel was born in North Carolina while his parents were on vacation but he has never lived in the U.S. and has been a Canadian resident and citizen his entire life.

Daniel runs his own business in Oakville, Ontario as a sole proprietorship and in 2013 he reported profits of $119,450. On his Canadian return he will be required to pay maximum CPP on this income; however, on his U.S. 1040 return he will be exempt from paying into U.S. social security on this same income because of the totalization agreement between Canada and the U.S. (i.e., CPP is payable in Canada because that is where the income originates, which means that the U.S. will not impose their Social Security tax on the same income).

Starting a Business in the U.S.

Accountingweb.com posts a booklet, written by PKF (previously known as Pannell Kerr Forster, A Global Network of Independent Accounting Firms), that outlines some of the things that are involved in doing business in the United States. In particular, it discusses the types of entities that can be set up in the U.S. and what is involved with each. Many people wonder if they can start a business or form a company in the U.S. if they are a non-resident of the U.S. and the short answer is yes.

To establish a company in the U.S., one does not need to be a U.S. resident or citizen; however, a U.S. non-resident must abide by the following guidelines:

- They are required to have a physical address;
- Any legal person can be a registered agent of entity;
- A P.O. Box is not acceptable;
- They must keep the company compliant which involves filing yearly annual reports;
- They must keep the company in good standing, which means they need to file and pay State Taxes if applicable, and Federal Taxes;
- As a U.S. non-resident, it will only be liable for State and federal taxes and it may not be required to pay U.S. Social Security and Medicare Taxes;
- They can form a C-Corporation or an LLC but not an S-Corporation. A person must be a U.S. resident or citizen to form an S-corporation;
- A C-Corporation can be converted to an S-Corporation once the individual obtains permanent residency status in the U.S.;
- There is no restriction to hire employees under their entity;
- A U.S. non-resident can open a foreign entity of their existing overseas company to conduct business in the U.S., or they can open a separate entity that would serve the same purpose.

Do You Need to Incorporate in the United States?

BizFilings.com discusses some factors to consider when incorporating in the U.S. A summary of the factors discussed are detailed below.

If you only plan to sell goods through the Internet or by wholesaling to U.S. companies it may not be necessary to form a U.S. company. Some other factors to consider in making your decision to incorporate in the U.S. include the differences in individual state tax laws, transportation costs, tariff/trade regulations, size and scope of your company and leases and employees.

Which Business Type Should You Choose?

Certain business structures limit whether non-U.S. citizens can be owners of a business incorporated in the United States. However, with Limited Liability Corporations (LLCs), there are no limitations on the number of investors who can own an interest in the business and no restriction on foreign citizens being owners.

Under U.S. tax law, a non-U.S. citizen may own shares in a C corporation, but may not be an owner in an S corporation. S corporations are treated as a pass-through entity in the U.S. which means that the owner pays tax on the net profits similar to a partnership. Keep in mind that an S Corporation, an LLC and a C corporation are all considered corporations under Canadian tax law.

 Remember, you want to ensure you match the tax treatment of the entity in both countries when possible to assist in eliminating the potential of double taxation.

In Which State Should You Choose to Incorporate Your Company?

This answer depends on whether your company has an actual presence in the United States. For instance, if your company has an office in Denver, you may wish to incorporate your business in Colorado. If your company does not plan to have a physical presence in the U.S. (i.e., it will not have a permanent establishment), then it may be preferable to form a corporation or LLC in Delaware or Nevada, which are the two most business-friendly states. If your foreign company operates in more than one U.S. state, you may incorporate in any of these states, but you must also register to do business in the other states.

Do You Need a U.S. Address to Incorporate a Business in the United States?

You will need to name a registered agent, who can be anyone involved with the business, in your state of incorporation, and the registered agent must have a physical address in that state. The registered agent is responsible for important legal and tax documents on behalf of incorporated companies, such as:

- Service of Process – sometimes called Notice of Litigation – which initiates a lawsuit;
- Important state mail, such as annual reports or statements; and
- Tax documents sent by the state's department of taxation.

The registered agent must also be available at that designated address during normal business hours.

 The registered agent address is only intended for receipt of official documents, which mean that the agent's address cannot be used as your corporation's legal address, the legal address of your company has to be your home or office in your country of residence.

Filing Requirements

A U.S. domestic corporation is required to file an 1120 corporate tax return each year to report its worldwide income and it is due by the 15th day of the third month after year-end.

 A foreign corporation is required to file an 1120-F non-resident corporate tax return each year to report its U.S. source income and the due date is the 15th day of the third month after year-end but only if it has an office or place of business in the U.S. If the foreign corporation does not have an office or place of business in the U.S. then the 1120-F return is due on the 15th day of the sixth month after year-end.

Form 7004 can be filed to request a 6-month extension if filed by the original due date of the required return. This form only extends the time to file, not the time to pay the tax.

 A corporation's taxes are always due by the 15th of the third month after year-end.

Partnerships in the U.S. file a 1065 tax return and prepare K-1 forms to report the partners' share of income or losses. Form 1065 is due on the 15th day of the fourth month following the tax year-end. If the books and records of the partnership are held outside the U.S., a 2-month extension to file and pay is granted if a statement is attached to the partnership return stating that the partnership qualifies for the extension; however, form 7004 may also be filed to request an additional 3-month extension if the additional 2 months is not long enough.

U.S. citizens and residents file a 1040 individual income tax return that is due on April 15th of the following tax year; however, form 4868 may be filed by the April 15th deadline to request an additional 6 months to file.

 There is no extension of payment; any tax owing is due on April 15th or interest is charged on the unpaid balance.

If the U.S. citizen lives outside the U.S. and does not have U.S. employment income, an automatic 2-month extension is granted to June 15th; however, if that still isn't enough time, form 4868 can be filed to request an additional 4 months.

Non-resident individuals file a 1040NR individual income tax return and have a due date of June 15th, unless they have U.S. employment income to report, which would make their return due on April 15th. If either date cannot be met, form 4868 can be filed to request a 6-month extension as well.

Keep in mind that state returns may also be required as well. Some states have their own due dates and extension requirements that are separate from the federal rule, which means you will need to comply with their extension requirements as well.

Forms of U.S. Business Organizations

U.S. Corporation

A corporation is a separate legal entity usually created under the laws of one of the states or the District of Columbia. When we talk about a corporation in the U.S. we are generally referring to what is called a C Corporation (discussed in more detail below). Each state enacts its own laws regarding the formation and operation of corporations and although the basic corporate laws are similar, there are differences that may argue for or against specific states when deciding in which to incorporate.

In any state, the documents necessary to create a corporation may be obtained from the secretary of state's office in the state's capital city. After incorporation, annual reports must be filed and a fee must be paid. A corporation doing business outside its state of incorporation may be required to register to do business in other states. Filing the appropriate documents and paying the filing fee with the secretary of that particular state is how to register. Generally, registration will automatically subject a corporation to taxation (including state, local income and franchise taxes) in that jurisdiction.

The U.S. has many entities that are organizes like corporations but can operate as pass-through entities, which means that the profits and losses within the entities pass through to the owners. Some of these entities, often referred to as eligible entities, have the ability to choose to be taxed as a corporation by electing corporate status. If no election is made, then the entity is treated a) as a partnership for tax purposes if it has two or more owners, or b) "disregarded" as an entity separate from its owner if it has a single owner. Typical examples of an eligible entity are limited liability companies (LLCs), partnerships or sole proprietorships. LLCs and partnerships are discussed below.

Distribution and Taxation of Corporate Profits

 U.S. corporate earnings are generally subject to double taxation: initially at the company level and then at the shareholder level when dividends are received (U.S. tax law does not integrate dividends the same way Canadian tax tries to).

A distribution from a U.S. corporation (i.e., C Corporation) to a shareholder will be treated as a dividend if it is paid out of current or accumulated earnings and profits, and dividends are not deductible by the corporation. If it is not paid out of accumulated earnings and profits, the dividend is considered a return of capital and if it is in excess of the shareholder's capital it is treated as a capital gain and taxed accordingly in the hands of the shareholder. Some relief rules exist for certain inter-company dividends. Dividends paid by a U.S. corporation to non-U.S. persons are subject to a 30% withholding tax, unless reduced treaty rates exists (i.e., Canada-U.S. treaty reduces the rate to 10%). U.S. C corporations are similar to Canadian corporations and are treated as regular corporations for Canadian tax purposes (i.e., Canada would ignore these companies for income tax purposes unless the company had Canadian sourced income or if income was paid out to a Canadian shareholder).

If a C corporation distributes profits to the shareholders in the form of dividends, as mentioned above, shareholders pay income tax on those distributions but because these dividends do not receive any form of dividend tax credits for tax already paid by the corporation, as is done in Canada, C corporations are often criticized for double taxation.

Branch of a Foreign Corporation

A branch is a part of a corporation and not a separate legal entity in the United States. A foreign corporation may establish a U.S. branch and launch a business at any time. Advice should be obtained from legal counsel before setting up a U.S. branch so one can obtain the knowledge one needs to properly set it up, manage the branch and fully understand how it will be taxed.

If a foreign corporation wants to establish a U.S. branch, use of an LLC should be considered. As a general rule, the U.S. branch of a foreign corporation is subject to regular U.S. income tax on net income that is effectively connected to the U.S. business. Investment income not effectively connected with a U.S. trade or business is taxed at 30% (or a lower treaty rate). The U.S. also maintains a Branch

Profits Tax (BPT) that is applied in addition to the regular corporate tax. The BPT is calculated as 30% of the "dividend equivalent amount," and can result in federal corporate tax liabilities as high as 54%. The BPT can be reduced or eliminated through tax treaties (i.e., the Canada-U.S. Tax Treaty exempts the first $500,000 of income from BPT; anything over that is taxed at a 5% rate).

A Canadian corporation may use a U.S. branch to introduce its business into the U.S. market place, especially if the branch is only operating limited business in the U.S. For example, if a company wants to set up a separate location in the U.S. to "sell their Canadian product" they may want to set up a branch; however, if they want to establish a location in the U.S. to manufacture and sell the U.S. manufactured product within the U.S., they may look at setting up a C corporation instead.

Partnership

 For legal purposes, a partnership is defined as an association of two or more persons formed for the purpose of carrying on a business for profit as co-owners.

Each state has its own laws governing the formation and operation of partnerships, as does the District of Columbia.

Limited partnerships are usually formed under the state's recognized *Limited Partnership Act*. Public partnerships are defined as those whose interests are traded on an established securities market and are taxed as corporations.

Partnerships are generally treated as conduits for U.S. income tax purposes, and each partner recognizes a proportionate share of income, loss and credit, whether or not it is distributed. Any partnership engaged in a trade or business in the United States that has foreign partners must withhold the highest rate of U.S. withholding tax applicable to that partner's share of business income. Similar rules may apply at the state level to non-resident partners. Partnerships are taxed the same in Canada as they are in the U.S.

Partnerships are also a common vehicle for individuals to use when purchasing U.S. rental properties, especially if they are purchased by unrelated individuals. Using a limited liability partnership in the U.S. allows the partners liability coverage similar to a corporation but also allows them to flow the income and losses through to themselves and deal with any tax at a personal level.

The one downside to partnerships in the U.S. is that the filing requirements and partnership rules can make things a bit more complicated than they need to be in some cases.

Limited Liability Company

 The limited liability company (LLC) is still a relatively new organizational structure. Its purpose is to provide limited liability for owners while maintaining a single level of tax by allowing the income to be passed through and taxed in the hands of the owner(s).

Properly structured, an LLC with more than one member is treated as a partnership for tax purposes, providing all of a partnership's flexibility with the limited liability protection of a corporation. The LLC also may have foreign persons as members. Because LLCs provide significant flexibility for U.S. tax planning, the use of these entities is very common. For example, single-member LLCs can serve as divisions of corporations, or as owners of sole proprietorships while enjoying limited liability protection. State tax planning needs to be considered with LLCs since the treatment varies throughout the nation.

 Proper tax planning needs to be considered from a Canadian perspective as well because an LLC is treated like a corporation for Canadian tax purposes, which means that it is not taxed the same in Canada as it is in the U.S. and this can cause double taxation for the owner.

For example, many individuals set up an LLC to purchase a U.S. rental property in order to get the limited liability protection but still have the income and losses flow through to themselves personally for tax purposes. The issue with this structure arises when the owner of the LLC is a dual citizen living in Canada or a Canadian resident and non-U.S. citizen. The issue is the mismatching of income because even though the U.S. may treat this entity as a flow-through, Canada treats an LLC as a corporation. The potential result is double taxation.

Taxation

There are a number of different taxing jurisdictions in the United States, including states, counties, cities, towns and villages. However, in this section we will highlight only federal taxation information that organizations should consider. The best way to understand your potential tax requirements is to discuss the issues with a tax professional because every situation can be slightly different, which can lead to varying results.

An entity is generally subject to U.S. tax if the individual or corporation is a resident in the U.S. or has income that is "effectively connected with the conduct of a trade or business in the U.S."

This is an ongoing test, which means that any trade or business that has income in the U.S. at any time during the year could be subject to U.S. tax for that particular tax year.

The federal government imposes income taxes on corporations, individuals, estates and trusts. It also imposes payroll taxes, the primary one being the Social Security tax levied on the employer and the employee. There are also estate and gift taxes and a number of excise taxes. No national sales or value-added tax is imposed though.

State and local taxes can significantly increase an individual's or business's tax liability but every state has its own rules so you need to do your research well in advance. The U.S. individual income tax system is a self-assessment method that requires withholding tax from employees' salaries and certain other payments. When a taxpayer, individual or corporate, is required to withhold taxes on payments to another person, the taxpayer, individual or corporate, is acting as an agent for the IRS and must remit those taxes to the government. Failure to withhold or failure to remit will generally subject the taxpayer, individual or corporate, to liability for the taxes and penalties. In addition, businesses and individuals can be required to make quarterly estimated payments during the year and penalties and interest can apply on any unpaid amounts (this is similar to Canadian rules as well).

After the end of the tax year, taxpayers, individual or corporate, must file a tax return that reports all taxable income and allowable deductions. The tax is computed on net taxable income and the difference between total taxes and what was withheld from income or paid as estimated installments of tax is the final tax payment by or refund due to the taxpayer. Businesses and individuals have different filing deadlines and payment deadlines.

Businesses, i.e., corporations, generally must file their tax returns by the 15th of the third month after their year-end. For individual filing deadlines see chapter 1.

Statute of Limitations (SOL)

Absent a material misstatement of income or fraud, the Statute of Limitations (SOL) on a tax return usually ends three years from the date the return is filed (or is required to be filed) or two years from the date of payment, whichever is later. If a return has not been filed, the SOL period will not begin, leaving the year open indefinitely.

This means that if you never file a tax return, it will never be "untouchable" by the IRS. If you file a tax return, the IRS has 3 years from the date the return was filed or 2 years from the date of the tax payment, whichever is the longest period of time, to audit and review that return unless it is determined that a material income item was missed being reported or the return is fraudulent. If a material misstatement or fraud occurs, the IRS has an unlimited time period to access that return.

Transfer Pricing

Whenever a Canadian company buys and or sells services or products to or from a U.S. related company or entity (i.e., it could be a U.S. subsidiary or a separate U.S. corporation with common ownership), it has to worry about transfer pricing issues because both Canada and the U.S. don't want an avoidance of tax to occur simply because the two entities are related and want to apply special rates to benefit each other.

Transfer pricing issues relate to the authority of the IRS to allocate income, deductions, credits and other items between or among related entities to prevent evasion of tax or to clearly reflect income.

The IRS increases its examination on transfer pricing when related United States and foreign group members are involved.

Regulations exist that reinforce the "arms-length" standard. Arms-length transactions are transactions between two unrelated companies, which means that transactions between a holding company and its wholly owned subsidiary are not considered at arms-length. If an individual or corporate taxpayer is dealing with an arms-length person or entity, the transaction is generally going to occur at current fair market values; however, if related parties transact with each other (i.e., non arms-length transactions), there may be an preference to complete the transaction at a vale below market because the two entities or persons have something to gain by not paying market rates. Transfer pricing exists to stop this from happening and is a separate form of taxation in addition to regular income tax.

Taxpayers must identify and document the best method to calculate a proper arms-length price for their particular circumstances. Failure to maintain simultaneous documentation of pricing determinations, including a written transfer price study, could result in substantial penalties – as much as 40% of the tax due related to the transfer pricing adjustment. In other words, if a transfer price adjustment is required because the transaction did not occur at fair values, each taxpayer may be on the hook for paying a 40% transfer pricing tax on the value of the adjustment made (i.e., product sold for $10,000 when it should have been sold at $20,000 could result in a transfer pricing tax of $4,000 (20,000-10,000=10,000x40%).

If a Canadian company owns 100% of the shares of a U.S. company and that U.S. company buys product from the Canadian company for use in the manufacturing of their final product, both companies will need to make sure the transactions are completed at fair value rates in order to avoid the application of the transfer pricing.

Taxation of a U.S. Resident Corporation

A U.S. resident corporation is a company incorporated under the laws of a state or the District of Columbia. It is also an entity treated as a corporation under "check-the-box" regulations; management control is irrelevant, which means that management could control the company from another country and that won't matter as long as the company physically exists in the U.S.

 A U.S. resident corporation is taxed by the United States on its worldwide income, including capital gains. Net taxable income is subject to a graduated rate structure ranging from 15 percent to 35 percent.

At certain income levels, higher marginal rates are applied to eliminate the benefit of the graduated rates for corporations. The highest effective rate is 35 percent. The U.S. tries to deter its owners from keeping excess cash and profits inside their corporations, which is the opposite of what Canada encourages. This is an important concept to be aware of because there may be a point in time where a

Canadian shareholder is required to draw monies out of the U.S. Corporation to avoid an excess profits tax; discussed below.

The U.S. tax laws also propose several penalty taxes that may be applied, such as accumulated earnings and personal holding company taxes. Those add-on taxes are imposed if the corporation retains excessive earnings over what it needs to operate efficiently or holds substantial passive assets such as rental properties or portfolio investments. These are further examples of the U.S. trying to deter its business owners from keeping excess cash and profits inside their corporations. The U.S. encourages monies to be paid out to the shareholders of the company so it can be taxed in their personal hands instead, which can mean that the IRS gets their tax earlier than if the excess monies were to stay in the company and not be paid out until a later date. Remember, double taxation can result when corporate monies are paid as dividends to the shareholders because there is no integration in the two tax structures in the U.S. (i.e., the corporation and the individual pay tax at whatever marginal rate applies and there are no tax breaks to the individual because the corporation already paid some tax on that same income).

 U.S. corporations are required to file income tax returns for each tax year and the returns are due on the 15th day of the third month following the close of the tax year.

Extensions of time to file may be obtained for up to 6 months as long as they are filed by the original due date. Estimated income taxes must be paid quarterly during the year or penalties are charged for failure to make adequate estimated payments; the same is true in Canada.

Affiliated Companies and Consolidated Returns

The U.S. allows affiliated companies to file one combined return, which is called a consolidated return, which can result in a reduced amount of tax being paid by the whole group if losses are available in one company to help offset profits in another.

Members of a group of U.S. corporations affiliated by 80 percent or more of direct ownership may elect to join in the filing of a consolidated U.S. income tax return.

 An affiliated group exists where one or more chains of included corporations are connected through share ownership with a common parent corporation.

The common parent files one return on behalf of the entire group. Non-includible corporations, including foreign corporations, are prohibited from joining such a group.

As mentioned, one advantage of filing a consolidated return is the ability to combine losses of some members with income of other members.

It can be a disadvantage to file as a consolidated group in some cases as well. This could occur in a year where both companies are earning taxable profits. The result would be that the combined income could result in higher taxes being paid than if both companies filed separately and paid lower marginal rates on their separate income. Once a group elects to file on the consolidated basis, it must continue to do so unless the ownership chain is broken or the IRS grants permission to discontinue filing on that basis (but this doesn't happen very often).

Real Life: U.S. Corporation owns 100% of another U.S. corporation

ABC Limited owns 100% of QRZ Limited and both have July 31st year-ends. ABC Limited has taxable profits of $275,000 in 2014 but QRZ Limited has a business loss of $124,000. If the companies elect to file a consolidated return, ABC Limited can utilize QRZ's losses to offset their profits and only pay tax on the net amount of $151,000.

However, if in 2015, QRZ Limited has taxable income of $96,000 and ABC Limited has taxable income of $300,000, filing a consolidated return would likely result in a higher rate of tax being paid on the $396,000 than if the $96,000 was taxed on its own (i.e., the $300,000 may be taxed at the highest marginal rate already). Because they filed a consolidate return in 2014, they would have to file on a consolidated basis in 2015 as well.

Real Life: Canada Co. owns 100% of U.S. Co.

Canada Co. operates out of British Columbia an U.S. Co. operates out of Texas but U.S. Co. is owned 100% by Canada Co. In 2014, Canada Co. had a taxable business profit of $497,000 and U.S. Co. had a business loss of $95,600 and is expecting to generate similar losses over the next couple of years due to tough markets.

Canada Co. cannot file a consolidated return with U.S. Co. to utilize that company's losses because it is prohibited from doing so under the consolidated return rules in the U.S. This is due to the fact that Canada Co. is not required to file a U.S. tax return and U.S. Co. is not required to file a Canadian tax return.

Computation of Taxable Income

Taxable income is defined as gross income minus all allowable deductions. Canada and the U.S. have similar rules regarding what is to be included as income and what can be deducted as a business expense. There is a partial to full exclusion for certain dividends received by one U.S. Corporation from another U.S. corporation.

A corporation may also be subject to the Alternative Minimum Tax (AMT), an amount calculated by adjusting regular taxable income to eliminate certain deductions that are allowable as deductions for regular tax purposes but not for alternative minimum tax purposes. One of the most common adjustments is depreciation because the amount is calculated differently for regular tax purposes than it is for AMT purposes. The AMT rate is 20% and is payable if it exceeds the regular tax liability. AMT is designed to accelerate the timing of income and AMT paid is available as a credit against regular tax in future years if regular tax exceeds current AMT. Canada also has AMT.

Real Life: U.S. Corporation subject to AMT

Let's assume that U.S. Co. has taxable income of $224,000 for regular tax purposes but for AMT purposes it has taxable income of $234,000. For ease of calculations, let's assume the regular corporate tax rate is 15% and the AMT rate is 20%, as mentioned above. Regular tax would be $33,600 and AMT would be $46,800, which means that a total of $46,800 would be payable by U.S. Co. in that year; $33,600 of regular tax and $3,200 of AMT. The $3,200 of AMT paid would be used as a credit for taxes due in the next year or future years.

Depreciation and Amortization

Since capital expenditures may not be written off in the year incurred, just like in Canada, the U.S. tax laws established a system of depreciation in order for taxpayers to recover the cost of property over its estimated useful life. The U.S. law sets up tables based on a Modified Accelerated Cost Recovery System (MACRS). Tangible personal property, such as furniture or office equipment, is depreciated over a 3, 5, 7, 10, 15 or 20-year period using an accelerated method.

Residential real property is depreciated on a straight line basis over 27½ years and non-residential real property is depreciated over 39 years. Organization costs, start-up costs, research and development expenses, and depletion of natural resources, are all recovered through amortization deductions. Goodwill and many other intangibles attained in connection with the acquisition of a trade or business, such as patents or customer lists, are amortized over a 15-year period beginning in the month of acquisition.

Foreign Source Income Rules and Foreign Tax Credit

A U.S. corporation is taxed on its worldwide income and gains. In addition, income of a foreign affiliate may be attributed, as a deemed dividend, to the U.S. corporation under what is referred to as Subpart F rules in the U.S. (this basically means that the income of a related foreign subsidiary corporation flows through to the parent company). For relief from double taxation, the U.S. business may claim a foreign tax credit or deduct foreign taxes paid or accrued to another country; however, only taxes based on net income or capital gains may be credited but taxes that cannot be claimed as a credit may be deducted. Any excess foreign tax credits may be carried back two years and forward five.

For example, U.S. Ltd. owns 100% of Canada Ltd. and Canada Ltd. has after tax profits of $125,000 after paying $15,000 in Canadian corporate income taxes. Under the foreign affiliate rules, U.S. Ltd. may have to report a taxable dividend of $140,000 in the U.S. but will be able to claim the $15,000 in corporate tax paid as a foreign tax credit on their return so they are not double taxed.

Taxation of Foreign Corporations

More and more Canadian companies are doing business in the U.S., whether it is through ownership of U.S. rental properties, corporate branch operations or actually transacting business from within the U.S.

A foreign corporation is any corporation that is not organized under the laws of a state or the District of Columbia and the income of a foreign corporation may be taxed under two separate tax regimes

1. Income from U.S. sources and certain types of foreign source income that are effectively connected with a U.S. trade or business are taxed at graduated U.S. corporation tax rates.

2. Certain types of U.S. source interest, dividends, royalties, rents and annuity income are taxed at a flat rate of 30% of gross income, unless a lower treaty rate exists.

Effectively connected U.S. income is taxable in the U.S. only if the foreign corporation is actually engaged in a U.S. trade or business; however, if the taxpayer can demonstrate that a "permanent establishment" has not been created, then the U.S. taxation can generally be avoided if the taxpayer claims the benefits of the treaty. Keep in mind that U.S. rental income can be treated as effectively connected income in the U.S. within a corporation as well if an election is made to opt out of withholding tax treatment by completing form W-8ECI (see chapter 5 for more details).

Permanent Establishment Rule and Business Income

A foreign corporation resident in a treaty country (in this case, Canada) conducting business in the United States is normally subject to U.S. income tax on its business income but only if it has a permanent establishment in the United States; however, only income that is attributed to that permanent establishment is taxable (i.e., income that is earned from a permanent place of business within the U.S. is taxable in the U.S.). In general, a foreign corporation's U.S. agent's office location is not considered a permanent establishment unless the agent regularly exercises power to negotiate and conclude contracts, or has inventory which he or she regularly sells on behalf of the foreign company.

 To the extent the income is attributable to a permanent establishment, a foreign corporation's U.S. source business income and gains are taxed on the same basis and at the same rates as a U.S. corporation.

Real Life: Canadian Corporation with no permanent establishment in the U.S.

XYZ Company manufactures and sells log furniture in Alberta, Canada; however, they maintain a warehouse in Colorado for distribution of its products to its U.S. buyers. Because all contracts and sales are completed from within Canada and the U.S. warehouse is simply used to store goods until delivery to the U.S. buyers, XYZ Company is not considered to have a permanent establishment in the U.S., which means that none of its business income is taxable in the U.S.

Real Life: Canadian Corporation with a permanent establishment in the U.S.

Assume the same facts as in the previous example except now XYZ Company contracts with an agent in the U.S. who sells XYZ product to U.S. buyers. The agent maintains the warehouse in Colorado and arranges for distribution of the products to the U.S. buyers once it has been received from the Canadian manufacturing plant. Because the agent has the power to sell directly to U.S. buyers on behalf of the Canadian company, XYZ Company is considered to have a permanent establishment in the U.S., which means that any business income generated by the permanent establishment (i.e., all U.S. Sales) will be taxable in the U.S. as well as Canada. XYZ will receive a foreign tax credit for any tax paid in the U.S.

Non-Business Income and FIRPTA

As previously stated, certain types of fixed, determinable, annual, periodic (FDAP) income are taxed at a flat rate of 30% unless a lower treaty rate exists. FDAP income is income not effectively connected with the conduct of a U.S. trade or business and includes interest, dividends, rents, royalties, annuities and gains from the sale of certain property. Gains from the sale of U.S. real property are subject to tax under the Foreign Investment in Real Property Tax Act (FIRPTA), see chapter 5 for more details on this topic.

 A foreign person's gain or loss on the sale or other disposition of a U.S. real property is taxed under FIRPTA as if the sale were effectively connected with the conduct of a U.S. trade or business.

 A withholding tax of 10% of the gross sales proceeds is usually required on the disposition of a U.S. real property interest by foreign persons; U.S. partnerships must withhold up to 35% of the gain reported on the disposition to corporate foreign partners and 39.6% to individual foreign partners.

It is possible to obtain a withholding certificate from the IRS that reduces or eliminates the required withholding tax. If an application for a withholding certificate is submitted to the IRS before or on the date of a transfer and the application is still pending on the date of transfer, the correct withholding tax must be withheld, but does not have to be reported and paid immediately. The amount withheld (or lesser amount as determined by the IRS) must be reported and paid within 20 days after the day a copy of the withholding certificate or notice of denial is mailed by the IRS.

Capital Gains Tax

Capital gains are taxable in Canada as well as the U.S.; however, Canada only taxes 50% of the capital gain whereas the U.S. taxes 100% of the capital gain.

For corporations, the excess capital gains from the sale of capital assets over net losses or net capital gains is taxed at the same rates applicable to ordinary income (i.e., no flat capital gains rate exists for corporations as it does for individual taxpayers).

Capital losses may only be used against capital gains and any excess losses may be carried back three years or forward five.

Note: Losses must be applied to the earliest carry-back year before any carry forwards may be used.

This is an important matter to consider when deciding how to own a U.S. rental property because even though holding it within a corporation will shelter that property from U.S. estate tax, the tax paid on the disposition of the property may be more than it would be had it been owned personally by an individual and taxed at the flat long-term capital gains rate of 15% or 20%.

Branch Operations and the Branch Profits Tax (BPT)

Income from the operation of a branch in the United States will generally be considered effectively connected with the conduct of a U.S. trade or business. The branch would then be taxed at graduated rates; however, additional taxes may apply, such as: branch profits tax (BPT), branch interest tax (BIT) and second level withholding. As previously mentioned, BPT is a 30% tax on the branch's income that is not reinvested in the U.S. operations; however, Canada-U.S. tax treaty reduces the rate to 5% (see Branch of a Foreign Corporation above). Gross income is computed from the branch's separate records and expenses are allocated between the branch and the head office based on specific allocation rules.

In addition to the BPT, a BIT is levied at a 30% statutory rate on interest paid by or attributed to a U.S. branch with respect to a foreign corporation unless the treaty reduces this rate as well.

Doing Business in the U.S.: What You Need to Know

Non-residents of the U.S. (i.e., Canadians)

- Need a U.S. visa in order to legally live and work in the U.S.
- Can be working temporarily in the U.S. and still deemed a resident of Canada for tax purposes.
- If earning U.S. employment or self-employment income you will be subject to regular employment taxes such as U.S. social security tax but will not be subject to the equivalent tax in Canada if that is your resident country.

- Can be an owner of any U.S. entity (i.e., C corporation, LLC, LLP, etc.), except an S corporation.

U.S. residents and citizens living abroad

- If earning U.S. employment or self-employment income you will be subject to regular employment taxes such as U.S. social security tax but will not be subject to the equivalent tax in Canada if that is your resident country.

- Can set up and be a shareholder of any type of U.S. entity (i.e., C corporation, S corporation, LLC, etc.).

- Income earned through a U.S. entity may not be taxed in the same manner in Canada or may not be taxed at all if there isn't income matching in both countries.

WHAT YOU NEED TO KNOW ABOUT UNCLE SAM:

U.S. citizens and residents are allowed to live and work in the U.S. without restrictions; however, non-residents and non-U.S. citizens must obtain a working visa or apply for a U.S. green card in order to live and work there.

If you work in the U.S. as a self-employed individual or as an employee, your earnings will be subject to the U.S. payroll tax regime (i.e., social security, etc.). However, Canada and the U.S. have a Social Security totalization agreement which exempts a person from paying the equivalent social security tax on the same income in the individual's country of residence if the tax is paid on income earned in the non-resident country. The Canada-U.S. tax treaty exempts social security income from being taxed in the individual's non-resident country, which means that if a U.S. resident works in Canada and then eventually receives CPP benefits; those benefits will only be taxable in the U.S. as long as the individual still lives there and vice versa.

Canadians have the ability to set up a business in the U.S. and there are many U.S. business structures available to them; however, choosing the right structure can be the tricky part. The most beneficial structure depends on the particular circumstances that exists at the time and everyone's situation can be different so what works for one person may not be the best alternative for another. Consulting a tax advisor with knowledge in both Canadian and U.S. tax law is the best option when making these kinds of decisions. Not all entities are taxed the same on both sides of the border so one needs to examine all aspects of the varying structures before making a decision.

CHAPTER 11

I'm a Canadian but
Could I be an American too?

Case Study:

Kathy was born in Cincinnati, Ohio, in 1957 but moved to Canada with her parents in 1969 and has lived in Saskatchewan ever since. She married her husband, George, a Canadian citizen and resident, in 1982 and they had their first child in 1985. They now have 3 children, 2 that were born in Canada and one that was born in Cincinnati when Kathy and her family were visiting family one Christmas and she unexpectedly went into labour 5 weeks early.

Kathy's brother, Henry, was 17 when they moved to Canada and he now lives in Ontario with his wife. They have 2 children, all of whom were born and raised in Canada, and who are currently attending university in Toronto. Henry's first child was born in 1980 and his second child was born in 1983.

Questions & Answers:

Is Kathy a U.S. citizen?
Yes, because she was born in the U.S.

Are Kathy's children U.S. citizens?
No, because Kathy did not live in the U.S. after the age of 14 for the required period of time.

Is Henry a U.S. citizen?
Yes, because he was born in the U.S.

Are Henry's children U.S. citizens?

Yes, because Henry lived in the U.S. after the age of 14 for the required amount of time to meet the naturalization tests, which automatically transfers his U.S. citizenship status onto his children.

What does this mean for them for tax purposes?

This means that Kathy, Henry and Henry's children must abide by U.S. tax laws for as long as they maintain their U.S. citizenship status.

Basic Rules Recap

U.S. tax is based on citizenship and residency. U.S. citizens are subject to U.S. federal tax no matter where they live in the world; however, U.S. state tax is applicable only if you are a resident of a particular state in the U.S. or if you earn income from a particular state and are subject to their non-resident state tax rules.

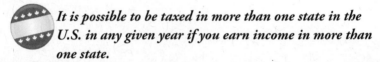 *It is possible to be taxed in more than one state in the U.S. in any given year if you earn income in more than one state.*

U.S. citizens pay tax on worldwide income in U.S. dollars; however, if income is earned in a country that has a tax treaty with the U.S.; tax relief may be available to assist the taxpayer in eliminating double taxation. For example, an individual can be a dual citizen and potentially subject to tax in both Canada and the U.S. Luckily, Canada does have a tax treaty with the U.S., so it is possible to avoid being taxed by both countries on the same income while living in only one.

Who is a U.S. Citizen?

The Fourteenth Amendment to the United States Constitution states that all people born or naturalized in the United States are citizens of the United States and of the state where they live. This means that if you were born in the U.S., you are automatically a U.S. citizen.

In the case of *United States v. Wong Kim Ark*, 169 U.S. 649 (1898), the Supreme Court ruled that a person becomes a citizen of the United States at the time of birth if that person meets one of the following tests:

- Is born in the United States;
- Has parents that are subjects of a foreign power, but not in any diplomatic or official capacity of that foreign power;
- Has parents that have permanent domicile and residence in the United States; or
- Has parents that are in the United States for business

Through Birth Abroad to U.S. Citizens

Birth abroad to two U.S. citizens

A child is automatically granted U.S. citizenship if *all* of the following are true:

1. Born to two U.S. citizen parents;
2. The parents are married; and
3. At least one parent lived in the United States before the child was born and one of whom has had a U.S. residence.

The FAM (Foreign Affairs Manual) states "no amount of time specified."

Birth Abroad to One United States Citizen

A person born on or after November 14, 1986, is a U.S. citizen if all of the following are true (different rules apply if the child was born out of wedlock).

1. The person's parents were married at the time of the child's birth;
2. One of the person's parents was a U.S. citizen when the person in question was born;
3. The citizen parent lived at least five years in the United States before the child's birth; and
4. A minimum of two of these five years in the United States were after the citizen parent's 14th birthday.

Different rules apply for persons born abroad to one U.S. citizen before November 14, 1986. United States law on this subject changed multiple times throughout the twentieth century, and the law applies to those individuals as it existed at the time of their birth.

For people born between December 24, 1952, and November 14, 1986, a person is a U.S. citizen if *all* of the following are true (except if born out of wedlock):

1. The person's parents were married at the time of birth;
2. One of the person's parents was a U.S. citizen when the person was born;
3. The citizen parent lived at least ten years in the United States before the child's birth; and
4. A minimum of 5 of these 10 years in the United States were after the citizen parent's 14th birthday.

Persons born abroad out of wedlock to a U.S.-citizen mother are considered U.S. citizens if all the following apply:

1. The mother was a U.S. citizen at the time of the person's birth; and

2. The mother was physically present in the United States or one of its outlying possessions for a continuous period of one year prior to the person's birth.

A person born abroad out of wedlock to a U.S.-citizen father may acquire U.S. citizenship as well, if all of the following are true:

1. A blood relationship between the person and the father is established by clear and convincing evidence;

2. The father was a U.S. citizens at the time of the person's birth;

3. The father was physically present in the United States or its outlying possessions prior to the child's birth for five years, at least two of which were after reaching the age of 14;

4. The father (unless deceased) has agreed in writing to provide financial support for the person until the person reaches the age of 18 years; and

5. While the person is under the age of 18:

    a. the person becomes a citizen or permanent resident in the country of his/her residence or domicile;

    b. the father acknowledges paternity of the person in writing under oath; or

    c. the paternity of the person is established by adjudication of a competent court.

Real Life: U.S. citizenship status with one U.S. citizen parent

Janice was born in the U.S. but immigrated with her parents to Canada when she was 11 years old and has lived in Canada ever since. She married a Canadian citizen and they now have 3 children, all born in Canada and all born between 1977 and 1986.

Janice's kids would not automatically be U.S. citizens because, even though she lived in the U.S. for 10 years prior to their birth, she did not live there for 5 years after attaining the age of 14.

Real Life: U.S. citizenship status with two U.S. citizen parents

Murray was born in Canada but his parents were both born in the U.S. and immigrated to Canada when they were 22 years old and have lived in Canada ever since. He married a Canadian citizen and they now have 4 children, all born in Canada and all born between 1967 and 1976.

Murray would automatically be a U.S. citizen because his parents are U.S. citizens, they both lived in the U.S. and one of them would have likely had a residence (i.e., owned or rented a home). It is also safe to assume they were married when Murray was born. Murray's kids would not automatically be U.S. citizens because he never lived in the U.S.

Adoption

The Child Citizenship Act of 2000 (CCA), amends the Immigration and Nationality Act (INA) to offer U.S. citizenship to certain foreign-born children (including adopted children) of U.S. citizens. Prior to this changed, adopted children could not obtain U.S. citizenship through their adopted parents, only naturally born children could.

Unregistered Citizens

All of the individuals described above are U.S. citizens under U.S. immigration law, whether they obtain that status outright or by naturalization. This means that even though they may not be registered with the U.S. Social Security Administration (i.e., they do not have a U.S. social security number), they are still U.S. citizens and are required to abide by all U.S. tax and immigration laws applicable to such citizens. Delinquent U.S. persons are simply considered unregistered U.S. citizens in the eyes of the U.S. government.

Real Life: Unregistered U.S. citizen

Bert has lived in Manitoba Canada his entire life but because his parents lived in a "border town" when he was born in 1956, he was born in a U.S. hospital as it was the closest hospital available to them for birthing babies and Manitoba medical covered the birth.

Bert's parents never applied for a U.S. social security number (SSN) for his and also never applied for his official U.S. citizenship papers; however, because he was physically born in the U.S., Bert is a U.S. citizen. He is considered an unregistered U.S. citizen because he doesn't yet have a SSN; however, because he is a citizen he must abide by all the U.S. tax laws no matter where he lives or how long he has lived there.

Dual Citizenship

Based on the U.S. Department of State regulation on dual citizenship, the Supreme Court of the United States has stated that dual citizenship is a "status long recognized in the law" and that "a person may have and exercise rights of nationality in two countries and be subject to the responsibilities of both. The mere fact he asserts the rights of one citizenship does not without more mean that he renounces the other," (*Kawakita v. U.S.*, 343 U.S. 717) (1952). In *Schneider v. Rusk* 377 U.S. 163 (1964), the U.S. Supreme Court ruled that "a naturalized U.S. citizen has the right to return to his native country and to resume his former citizenship, and also to remain a U.S. citizen even if he never returns to the United States." This means that a person can have dual citizenship and live elsewhere in the world but can still return to the U.S. at any time. This also means that no matter where else in the world this dual citizen lives, including in the country of his birth, he remains subject to U.S. tax law and can face stiff penalties for non-compliance.

Green Cards

Applying for a green card means applying for permanent residence status in the U.S. For tax purposes you are considered a U.S. resident as soon as you apply for a green card. The green card serves as proof that its holder, a lawful permanent resident (LPR), has been officially granted immigration benefits, which include permission to live and work in the United States.

A person may have technically abandoned their status if he or she moves to another country to live there permanently, stays outside the U.S. for more than 365 days (without getting a re-entry permit before leaving), or does not file an income tax return; however, until you officially surrender your green card, you could still be considered a permanent resident for U.S. tax purposes. Failure to renew the green card does not result in the loss of status because you have the ability to renew it at any time.

A green card does not provide the holder with U.S. citizenship but it is one of the first steps in gaining U.S. citizenship.

Real Life: U.S. green card holder still deemed resident for tax purposes

Tanner was born in Canada but lived in the U.S. for 15 years after taking a job offer at a major brokerage firm in New York. 3 years ago he moved back to Canada to work in Vancouver. He kept his green card upon returning to Canada because it didn't expire for another year so he thought he would just hold on to it until it expired, in case he needed it. He still has the expired green card but doesn't plan to ever use it again.

Unfortunately he didn't realize he would still be treated as a U.S. person as long as he holds his green card, so now he is delinquent on a number of his U.S. tax returns and foreign reporting requirements.

In order to "stop the clock" on the U.S. side, Tanner will need to physically relinquish his green card and make sure he follows the required relinquishing process under the new exit tax rules.

1040 Filing Requirements

U.S. citizens and residents are required to file a U.S. 1040 income tax return each year and report their worldwide income on that return. The difference between U.S. residents and citizens is that if an individual is a U.S. citizen or green card holder, he must file a U.S. 1040 income tax return each year no matter where he lives in the world; however, if he is merely a U.S. resident because he physically lives in the U.S., once he moves away from the U.S., unless he has U.S.-source income, his filing requirements would end. For example, if you are a U.S. citizen or green card holder, you could live in Australia, China, Canada or Europe and you would still be required to file a U.S. 1040 return and report your worldwide income on that return and potentially pay tax in the U.S. on that worldwide income (joint returns may be filed for married taxpayers). However, if you were simply physically residing in the U.S. and working with a temporary U.S. visa, you would be required to file a U.S. 1040 return only while you are considered a U.S. resident, and would no longer have to file once you moved away and took up residency in another country.

A U.S. 1040 personal income tax return is due by April 15th of the following calendar year; however, you can get an automatic 6-month extension if you file form 4868, request for extension of time to file, no later than April 15th, the original due date of the return.

Any taxes payable are due by April 15th of the following calendar year and any extension of time to file does not extend the tax payment deadline.

This means that if you pay any balance due after the April 15th deadline, you will likely be charged a late payment penalty and interest on the balance owing as well.

If you are a U.S. citizen or resident alien you may qualify for an automatic 2-month extension of time to file without filing form 4868; in this case your return would be due by June 15th. You qualify for this automatic extension if the following conditions apply:

- You live outside the U.S. and Puerto Rico and your main place of business is outside the U.S. and Puerto Rico (i.e., you live outside the U.S. and do not have U.S employment income).
- You are in military or naval service on duty outside the U.S. and Puerto Rico.

If you are still unable to file by the June 15th deadline, you can file form 4868 no later than June 15th to get an additional 4-month extension. *Remember, this extension of time to file does not extend the due date of the taxes owing.*

The 1040 return is only part of your annual filing requirements, depending on your situation, see chapter 3 for other potential forms you may need to file.

Foreign Earned Income Exclusion

Qualifying U.S. citizens and resident aliens who live and work abroad may be able to exclude from their U.S. taxable income all or part of their foreign salary or wages, or amounts received as compensation for their personal services.

A common misunderstanding is that this potentially excludable foreign earned income is exempt income not reportable on a U.S. tax return; however, you may elect to exclude foreign earned income only if you meet certain criteria (see below), and this exclusion applies only if a tax return is filed and the income is reported. The bottom line is **you still need to file.**

To qualify for the foreign earned income exclusion, a U.S. citizen or resident alien must:

- Have foreign earned income (income received for working in a foreign country);
- Have a tax home in a foreign country; and
- Meet either the *bona fide* residence test or the physical presence test.

To meet the *bona fide* residence test, you must have established a *bona fide* residence in a foreign country (in this case, Canada). The *bona fide* residence test applies to both U.S. citizens and resident aliens.

You meet the physical presence test if you are physically present in a foreign country (in this case, Canada) or countries 330 full days during a period of 12 consecutive months. The 330 qualifying days do not have to be consecutive. The physical presence test applies to both U.S. citizens and resident aliens.

The foreign earned income exclusion amount is adjusted annually for inflation; the maximum foreign earned income exclusion is up to $99,200 per qualifying person in 2014 ($97,600 for 2013). If you are married and both individuals work abroad, and both meet either the bona fide residence test or the physical presence test, each one can choose to claim the foreign earned income exclusion.

Since the foreign earned income exclusion is voluntary, qualifying individuals must choose to claim the exclusion. The foreign earned income exclusion is claimed and calculated using Form 2555, which must be attached to Form 1040.

Once the choice is made to exclude foreign earned income, that choice remains in effect for the year the election is made and all later years, unless revoked.

 A qualifying individual may claim the foreign earned income exclusion on foreign earned self-employment income as well.

 Once the foreign earned income exclusion is chosen, a foreign tax credit, or deduction for taxes, cannot be claimed on the income that can be excluded.

If a foreign tax credit or tax deduction is claimed for any of the foreign taxes on the excluded income, the foreign earned income exclusion may be considered revoked (i.e., you can only claim a foreign tax credit for taxes paid on any of the earned income that is over the exclusion amount and potentially subject to U.S. income tax).

Real Life: Foreign Earned Income Exclusion

Angela is a dual citizen who lives and works in London, Ontario. She earns an annual salary of $86,000 from her job as an accountant but she also earned $28,000 in self-employment income in 2013 from a business she operates on the side. When she files her U.S. 1040 return, she must claim the full $114,000 in income; however, she will be eligible to exclude $97,600 of this income from taxable income in the U.S. because she would qualify for the foreign earned income exclusion. This would leave $16,400 still potentially taxable in the U.S. But Angela may not have to pay tax in the U.S. on this income if she has enough taxes paid in Canada on the same income (i.e., she can claim a foreign tax credit against this income as it is over and above the amount of income eligible under the foreign earned income exclusion but the total tax attributable to the $114,000 must be enough to cover the U.S. tax applicable on the $16,400; 16,400/114,000=14% multiplied by the taxes paid on the full $114,000 are available as a foreign tax credit).

Delinquent Filers

The regular IRS policy for personal income tax returns is to go back 6 years for delinquent filers; however, there is a new Voluntary Disclosure Program (more commonly referred to as the Streamline Program) in place that requires 3 years of 1040 tax returns and 6 years of FBAR filings and any other foreign reporting that may be required (effective September 2012); penalties for late filing are dramatically reduced if reasonable cause exists. Some examples of a reasonable cause are death, illness or natural disaster. Ignorance or not knowing what is required is generally not accepted as a reasonable cause; however, when millions of individuals are in the same boat because they had no idea what was required of them, ignorance is a reasonable cause.

The VDP was put into place in order to encourage compliance by providing a reduced penalty regime for those "hiding" assets offshore, even if they weren't trying to "hide" their assets but simply didn't know they had to report anything.

A lot of individuals are also becoming compliant by using what is called a "quiet disclosure" approach. This involves basically the same filing requirements as the streamline process except the additional forms required under the streamline process are not submitted here, reasonable cause letters are filed with each return and the returns are sent directly to the regular IRS offices rather than the criminal investigation division office.

Renouncing/Relinquishing U.S. Citizenship

Renouncing one's U.S. citizenship wasn't something that was commonly thought of in past years; however, now with the dramatic increase in U.S. compliance issues and the huge financial burden it is placing on a number of people, this concept is being tossed around more frequently these days. If you never plan to live or work in the U.S. at any time in your future, maintaining your U.S. citizenship may not be important to you anymore.

Renouncing your U.S. citizenship or long-term residency will get you out of the annual compliance requirements in the U.S. but depending on your particular situation, can cause some future issues for you or your heirs so proper planning is key before making this decision.

The Expatriation Process

To renounce U.S. citizenship or long-term residency, you must go in person to a U.S. embassy or consulate outside the U.S. and sign before a consular officer an oath or affirmation that you intend to renounce your citizenship.

In most cases, the process for renouncing one's citizenship or permanent residency status can be broken down into 5 steps:

Step 1: Choose a diplomatic post

Step 2: Appointment / submission of documents

Step 3: First visit to the diplomatic post: review documents and initial interview

Step 4: Second visit to the diplomatic post: final interview and signing of documents

Step 5: The renunciation "ceremony" and next steps

Note: The Department of State usually charges $450 for "documentation of formal renunciation of U.S. Citizenship." There previously was no charge and the process was free, but the Department of State began imposing the $450 fee for all renunciations after July 13, 2010.

Step 1: Choose a Diplomatic Post

The law says that you have to renounce in person outside the United States before a diplomatic or consular officer. This means that you have to go personally to a U.S. embassy or consulate.

The embassy or consulate (i.e., "diplomatic posts") will handle all the paperwork. The actual renunciation will be examined and approved by the Department of State in Washington, D.C., but the diplomatic post you choose will control all other aspects of the renunciation process.

Step 2: Make an Appointment / Submit Documents

Next you must follow that diplomatic post's procedures before the renunciation. Depending on which post you choose, you might have to make an appointment and complete some forms.

Step 3: First Visit to the Diplomatic Post: Review Documents and Interview

On the day of your appointment you must present your U.S. passport to the diplomatic post and if you don't have a U.S. passport, then you'll need to provide some form of identification (e.g., your current non-U.S. passport). If you don't have a U.S. passport, it would help to have some proof that you are a U.S. citizen, such as a birth certificate, naturalization papers, military documents, etc.; however, it is not a legal requirement.

Documents

The requested information is fairly basic: name, date of birth, previous U.S. address, last U.S. passport number/issue date, how you became a U.S. citizen (born in the U.S., born outside the U.S. to U.S. parent(s), naturalized), and when and where you have lived outside the U.S. You will also have to sign either an oath or affirmation that you understand the consequences of renunciation (i.e., you cannot live or work in the U.S. without special permission, you may be subject to exit tax, you may be restricted in the amount of time you are allowed to spend in the U.S., etc.)

Interview

The interview itself is generally brief and professional. The officer will ask why you want to renounce your U.S. citizenship as their task is to make sure your renunciation is voluntary and intentional.

The officer will then explain to you the consequences and ramifications of renunciation, and ask if you understand and have any questions. The list of consequences will be similar to the document, Statement of Understanding Concerning the Consequences and Ramifications of Relinquishment or Renunciation of U.S. Citizenship. On several occasions, the consular officer simply reads the full text of this document out loud.

Step 4: Second Visit to the Diplomatic Post: Final Interview and Signing of Documents

In the second interview, the consular officer will confirm that you have considered the seriousness of expatriation and that you are still certain you want to renounce. He or she will confirm that you are renouncing voluntarily and if the consular officer is different than in your first interview, or if some time has passed since the first interview, the officer may ask you to explain again why you want to renounce.

You can renounce for tax reasons; however, it is not recommended that you state this as a reason for renouncing because you could be subject to unfavourable treatment in the U.S. after renouncing.

A more acceptable reason for renouncing one's citizenship is that your home, life and family are here in Canada and you never plan to live or work in the U.S. at any time in your future so you don't see the benefit or need to keep your U.S. citizenship.

Step 5: After the Renunciation "Ceremony"

The diplomatic post that conducted your renunciation ceremony will forward all documents to Washington, D.C., where the Department of State will decide whether to accept your expatriation application. Approval generally takes 1-2 months but could be longer if they have a large number of applications to process.

After your renunciation, your name will be flagged in the Department of State's consular lookout computer system so that passport officers will know not to issue you a U.S. passport in the future.

After issuing the Certificate of Loss of Nationality, the Department of State will forward your name to the IRS and, by law; the IRS must publish quarterly in the Federal Register a list of all renunciants. Information from the Department of State is used to create this list.

Although the process of renouncing your U.S. citizenship or long-term residency is relatively simple, the decision should not be taken lightly. There can be consequences to renouncing your U.S. citizenship or long-term residency, some of which may benefit you but some may negatively impact you as well. The consequences all depend on what category of expatriate you fall into and which renunciation rules apply to you.

There are slightly different rules for renouncing one's citizenship or long-term resident status depending on the date that a person renounces.

 Although the renouncing process is the same for everyone, the tax rules relating to an individual giving up citizenship or terminating long-term residency before June 17, 2008, are different than the tax rules applicable to an individual giving up citizenship or terminating long-term residency after June 16, 2008.

The U.S. has enforced an alternative expatriation tax regime for those individuals who wish to renounce their U.S. citizenship or long-term residency status; however, the tax will not apply to all expatriates. Depending on the year in which you expatriate and if you meet the expatriation tests applicable to your year of renunciation will determine if you are subject to the U.S. exit tax rules.

What is 'Exit Tax'

 The alternative expatriation tax rules (i.e., exit tax) impose what is called a mark-to-market regime, which means that all property of a covered expatriate is deemed sold for its fair market value on the day before the expatriation date (i.e., same idea as Canadian departure tax) and tax is due on any capital gains resulting from the deemed disposition (i.e., exit tax).

Any gain arising from the deemed sale is taken into income in the year of the deemed sale. Any loss from the deemed sale is taken into income in the year of the deemed sale as well; however, wash sale rules do not apply (i.e., if you sell a security at a loss and then buy the same stock back within 30 days of the sale, the loss is denied and subtracted from the new cost so it isn't realized until the new stock is sold).

Special exemptions available to other individuals will not apply under this regime as well, which means, as an example, the $250,000 personal residence exemption does not exist, etc.

Due to the above rules, it may be a good idea to actually sell one's principal residence prior to renouncing in order to receive the exempt income treatment, especially if this helps reduce their net worth below the $2,000,000 threshold or their total capital gains will be over the exclusion amount available (discussed below).

Under the exit tax rules, the capital gain that would otherwise be included in gross income as a result of the deemed sale rule is reduced (but not to below zero) by $680,000 in 2014 ($663,000 in 2013 and $651,000 for 2012).

If the property is subsequently sold, the amount of any gain or loss later realized on the sale of the property will be adjusted for gains and losses taken into account under the exit tax mark-to-market regime, ignoring the exclusion amount. A taxpayer may elect to defer payment of the tax attributed to the property deemed to be sold.

Real Life: Exit tax calculation

Jason was granted renunciation on June 14, 2012, and at that time he had property worth a FMV of $2,275,000 which he was deemed to dispose of immediately before his date of expatriation. The cost on this property was $1,895,000, which resulted in a gain of $380,000; however, because Jason can reduce his gain by up to $651,000 in 2012, no gains were taxable to him on expatriation.

A cost base adjustment is applied to all property subject to the deemed disposition rule to ensure double taxation does not result on a future sale of the same property. This means that the market value used in the deemed disposition becomes the new cost base for the property.

One of the technical requirements for renouncing one's citizenship in the U.S. is to file the last 5 years of income tax returns. The rules state that individuals who renounced their U.S. citizenship or terminated their long-term resident status for tax purposes after June 3, 2004, are required to certify to the IRS that they have satisfied all federal tax requirements for the 5 years prior to expatriation.

If all federal tax requirements have not been satisfied for the 5 years prior to expatriation, even if the individual does not meet the monetary thresholds, the individual will be subject to the expatriation tax provisions.

Individuals that have expatriated should file all tax returns that are due, regardless of whether or not full payment can be made with the return; payment plans are possible.

Renouncing Before June 17, 2008

The exit tax is applied to any individual with an average income tax liability of $124,000 for tax year 2004, $127,000 for tax year 2005, $131,000 for 2006, $136,000 for 2007, or $139,000 for 2008 over the 5 years prior to the year or expatriation, or a net worth of $2,000,000 on the date of expatriation. In addition, it requires individuals to certify, under penalties of perjury, that they have satisfied all federal tax filing requirements for the 5 years prior to expatriation and it requires that annual information reporting be made for each taxable year that an individual is subject to the exit tax rules.

 Expatriated individuals will also be subject to U.S. tax on their worldwide income for any of the 10 years following expatriation if they are present in the U.S. for more than 30 days in a particular year, or 60 days in the case of individuals working in the U.S. for an unrelated employer (this is no longer applicable for renunciations occurring after June 16, 2008).

Finally, even if you don't meet the monetary thresholds stated above, individuals will continue to be treated as U.S. citizens or long-term residents for U.S. tax purposes until they have notified both the Internal Revenue Service (via Form 8854) and the Secretary of the Department of State (for former U.S. citizens) or the Department of Homeland Security (for long-term permanent residents) of their expatriation or termination of residency; therefore, **it is important to file form 8854 as soon as possible.**

Also, for individuals who expatriated after June 3, 2004, and before June 16, 2008, annual information reporting is required for each taxable year during which the individual is subject to the expatriation rules (i.e., foreign reporting rules, such as FBARs, are still applicable).

Form 8854 is due on the date that the individual's U.S. income tax return is due or would be due in that year if such a return were required to be filed.

Renouncing after June 16, 2008

A citizen will be treated as renouncing U.S. citizenship on the earliest of four dates: (1) the date the individual renounces his or her U.S. nationality before a diplomatic or consular officer of the U.S., provided the renunciation is subsequently approved by the U.S. Department of State; (2) the date the individual furnishes to the U.S. Department of State a signed form 8854 confirming the act of expatriation, provided the voluntary relinquishment is subsequently approved by the U.S. Department of State; (3) the date the U.S. Department of State issues to the individual a certificate of loss of nationality; or (4) the date a U.S. court cancels a naturalized citizen's certificate of naturalization.

For long-term residents, a long-term resident ceases to be a lawful permanent resident of the U.S. if (A) the individual's U.S. residency status as an immigrant has been revoked or determined to have been abandoned, or if (B) the individual (1) commences to be treated as a resident of a foreign country under the provisions of a tax treaty between the United States and the foreign country, (2) does not waive the benefits of the treaty applicable to residents of the foreign country, and (3) notifies the IRS of such treatment on Forms 8833 and 8854.

A long-term permanent resident is generally any individual who was a lawful permanent resident (i.e., green card holder) for any part of at least 8 of the last 15 years.

The expatriation tax applies if:

1. The individual's average annual net income tax for the 5 tax years prior to renunciation is greater than $155,000 for 2013 ($151,000 for 2012), adjusted for inflation;

2. The individual's net worth as of the expatriation date is $2,000,000 or more; or

3. The individual fails to certify on form 8854, under penalties of perjury, that he or she is up-to-date with the last 5 years of tax filings.

There are exceptions to the alternative expatriation tax so if you meet one of the tests above it applies to you, if not then it doesn't apply. If it applies, you are considered a 'covered expatriate.'

 Dual citizens are exempt from the alternative expatriation tax if that individual became a U.S. citizen at birth and a citizen of another country (i.e., Canada) and continues to be a citizen of the other country (i.e., Canada), and the individual has had no substantial contacts with the U.S.

No substantial contact with the U.S. is met if, and only if:

4. The individual was never a resident of the U.S.;

5. The individual has never held a U.S. passport; and

6. The individual was not present in the U.S. for more than 30 days during any calendar year, which is within the 10 calendar years before the individual's loss of U.S. citizenship.

 Certain minors are also exempt from the alternative expatriation tax; however, this is only if the individual became a U.S. citizen at birth, neither parent was a U.S. citizen at the time of the child's birth, the individual's loss of U.S. citizenship occurs before such an individual reaches the age of 18 1/2, and the individual was not present in the U.S. more than 30 days during any calendar year which is within the 10 calendar years before the individual's loss of U.S. citizenship.

Implications of Not Filing Expatriation Form

 Anyone who has expatriated or terminated his or her U.S. residency status must file Form 8854, Initial and Annual Expatriation Information Statement.

Form 8854 must also be filed to comply with the annual information reporting requirements, if the person is subject to the expatriation tax.

A $10,000 penalty may be imposed for failure to file Form 8854 when required.

IRS is sending notices to expatriates who have not complied with the Form 8854 requirements, and are imposing the $10,000 penalty.

Technically this form cannot be filed until the end of the calendar year of the expatriation because the IRS issues new forms each year in December. If you file before the new version of the forms is released for that year, you run the risk that your filing will be rejected, which can result in a required resubmission when the new forms are available. The issue here is that they suggest you file the form as soon as possible because you are technically still treated as a U.S. person until this form is filed. Having to resubmit the form isn't the end of the world as long as they considered your date of filing as being that of your original submission.

Special Rules Applicable to Gifts from Covered Expatriates

U.S. citizens and long-term residents who relinquished their U.S. citizenship or ceased to be U.S. lawful permanent residents (green card holders) on or after June 17, 2008, and who meet specific average tax or net worth thresholds on the day prior to their expatriation are considered "covered expatriates" (i.e., an individual is considered a covered expatriate if he or she is subject to the alternative expatriation tax).

If you take the steps to renounce your U.S. citizenship and are considered a cover expatriate, any U.S. citizens or residents who receive gifts or bequests from covered expatriates may be subject to tax under a new inheritance tax section, which imposes a transfer tax on U.S. persons who receive gifts or bequests on or after June 17, 2008, from former U.S. citizens or former U.S. lawful permanent residents who are considered covered expatriates (see chapter 9 for more details).

Another complication exists as well because covered expatriates are not considered U.S. expatriates for purposes of Form 706NA, United States Estate (and Generation-Skipping) Tax Return, Estate of a non-resident not a citizen of the United States. This means that when a covered expatriate dies, their bequests will be subject to the new U.S. inheritance tax in addition to non-resident U.S. estate tax rules.

For lifetime gifts, the total value of the gift is reduced by the available annual exclusion of $14,000 (2014), and tax is then assessed at the highest applicable gift tax rate in the year of the gift (40% in 2014).

Real Life: Death of U.S. covered expatriate

A man worth $55 Million renounces his citizenship and becomes a citizen of Canada. If he leaves each of his three U.S. grandchildren $10 Million when he dies, each one will owe $4.0 Million of federal gift tax on the bequest, as a substitute for estate taxes the man did not pay.

Not Yet Law

Rumor has it that the U.S. government is thinking about making it difficult for expatriates to re-enter the U.S. after they have renounced their citizenship. You could be denied entry into the U.S. as an expatriate unless you have a visitor's visa. Once in the U.S., it may be hard for you to spend as much time as you want in the U.S., and you must not appear to be using your visitor visa status to live in the U.S. The granting of the visitor's visa is at the discretion of the State Department and can be denied without due process.

No law prohibits renouncing citizenship for tax reasons; however, under the "Reed amendment," U.S. officials may bar entry to any person who has renounced their citizenship for tax reasons. In practice, this provision is rarely called upon but you should be aware of it nonetheless.

 There is a law that states a covered expatriate may not spend more than 30 days in the U.S. on an annual basis or he will be treated as a U.S. resident and taxed on his worldwide income.

I'm a Canadian But Could I be an American Too: What You Need to Know:

Canadians born to U.S. citizen parent(s)

- Depending on the year you were born, and even if you were born in Canada, if your U.S. citizen parent(s) meet specific tests, you could be a naturalized U.S. citizen.

- If you are a U.S. citizen you must file a 1040 return each year and potentially various other foreign reporting forms as well. If you do not file annually, you will be in non-compliance and could face stiff tax penalties in the U.S.

  - You can earn up to $99,200 of earned income annually in Canada and have it exempt from tax in the U.S.

  - You can renounce your U.S. citizenship if you want to, but make sure you aren't considered a "covered expatriate" or you may still have some tax issues after renunciation.

  - Depending on your situation, if you are a dual citizen you may be exempt from exit tax no matter what your net worth value is; however, you must still meet the 5 year filing test

WHAT YOU NEED TO KNOW ABOUT UNCLE SAM:

Uncle Sam has a long reach when it comes to taxation of U.S. citizens. You can be considered a naturalized U.S. citizen from birth if you are born outside of the U.S. to a U.S. citizen parent(s) who meet certain tests. A naturalized citizen of the U.S. is subject to all the same rules as a regular U.S. citizen, which means that all the same filing requirements exist. All citizens of the U.S., no matter where they live, are entitled to the same tax exemptions and credits as well, so just because you have to file in the U.S. doesn't mean you will have to pay tax.

Renouncing your U.S. citizenship is an option to get out of the many filing requirements and taxation rules that are applicable each year, but before you do so you need to make sure you have all your ducks in a row to determine if there will be any ramifications for you after you renounce. An individual who renounces their citizenship may be subject to "exit tax" if certain tests are met immediately prior to renunciation. If you are subject to exit tax, then you will be considered a covered expatriate and there are some U.S. tax rules that will follow you after you renounce. Trying to make sure you are not considered a covered expatriate is your best approach before renouncing.

CHAPTER 12

U.S. Gift & Estate Tax for a Non-Resident

Case Study:

Anthony is a Canadian citizen and resident living in Canmore, Alberta. Anthony loves to vacation in Scottsdale, Arizona, so last year he decided to purchase a property there. He bought a 1,600-square-foot home jointly with his wife, Anna, for $210,000 in November 2012; he spent 6 weeks vacationing there in 2013.

Anthony's Canadian estate value is $2,750,000 and Anna's is approximately $1,078,000. They plan to spend at least 6 weeks every year in their vacation home and don't plan to sell it anytime soon. Thinking about the future, Anna and Anthony are considering making their children part owners in the Arizona property by adding their names to the title document.

Questions & Answers:

Will Anna & Anthony be subject to U.S. estate tax?
No, because each of their worldwide net worth values are under the $5,250,000 current estate tax exemption amount.

Can they give their children an interest in their vacation home without any tax issues?
No, because it is U.S. situs property (i.e., property that is physically located in the U.S.) and they are subject to the U.S. gift tax rules on all U.S. situs property.

Are there any tax implications for them while they own the property (i.e., do they need to file and pay income tax in the U.S.)?
No, because it doesn't appear that they plan to use it for anything other than personal purposes. They would file and potentially pay tax in the U.S. only in the year they sell the property.

When people hear the terms U.S. gift tax or U.S. estate tax, they often think that this is something they will never have to worry about because they are not U.S. citizens; however, this is not true.

 U.S. gift and estate tax is generally applicable to U.S. citizens and residents; however, non-residents and non-citizens of the U.S. can be caught by the U.S. gift and estate tax rules on U.S. situs property owned at any given time.

The rules are slightly different when dealing with non-residents and non-citizens as well as in situations where a U.S. citizen is married to a non-U.S. citizen. In order to understand how U.S. gift and estate tax may affect you as a non-resident and non-citizen of the U.S., you first need to understand how each tax works and to do that we need to discuss how it applies to U.S. citizens and U.S. residents.

Estate Tax of a U.S. Citizen/Resident

The U.S. estate tax is a tax on a person's right to transfer property at his or her death. For a U.S. person, it consists of an accounting of everything he or she owns or holds certain interests in at the date of death. The fair market value of these items is used to calculate U.S. estate tax, not necessarily what was paid for them or what the value was when they were acquired. The total of all of such items is called the "gross estate." The includible property can consist of cash and securities, real estate, insurance, trusts, annuities, business interests and other assets.

Once you have calculated the gross estate, certain deductions are allowed in arriving at the "taxable estate." These can include mortgages and other debts, estate administration expenses, and property that passes to a surviving spouse and qualified charities. Applying these deductions reduces the amount of the gross estate by the total amount of the allowable deductions.

After the net amount is computed, the value of lifetime taxable gifts (beginning with gifts made in 1977) is added to this number and the tax is computed. The tax is then reduced by the available unified credit. The unified credit is the tax applicable on the lifetime exemption amount.

Lifetime taxable gifts are gifts that were made by an individual in any year after 1977 that were above the annual exclusion, which means that they would have otherwise been taxable, had the individual not used a portion of the lifetime gift tax exemption.

Real Life: U.S. *citizen decedent with lifetime taxable gifts*

Bernice died in March 2014 and at that time had a gross estate worth $4,300,000. For the past 6 years she filed a gift tax return to claim a portion of her lifetime gift exemption amount to eliminate the gift tax on various gifts she made in those years. Her total lifetime taxable gifts are $375,000 and she had no other taxable gifts prior to this. Bernice still had a $30,000 mortgage on her house but no other debts existed.

Bernice's taxable estate would be $4,270,000 ($4,300,000-30,000) before adding lifetime taxable gifts of $375,000, which would produce a net taxable estate of $4,645,000. Estate tax would then be calculated on the $4,645,000; however, because the net taxable estate is under the $5,340,000 exemption amount, Bernice will have enough of her unified credit available to reduce the estate tax to zero.

Most relatively simple estates (consisting of cash, publicly traded securities, small amounts of other easily valued assets, and no special deductions or elections, or jointly held property) do not require the filing of an estate tax return. A filing is required for estates with combined gross assets and prior taxable gifts exceeding:

Year of Death:	File Return if Estate's Value is More Than:
2002 and 2003	1,000,000
2004 and 2005	1,500,000
2006, 2007, and 2008	2,000,000
2009	3,500,000
2010 and 2011	5,000,000
2012	5,120,000
2013	5,250,000
2014	5,340,000

The estate tax rate for estate values over the exemption amount is 40% for 2013 and 2014 (35% in 2012).

 Beginning January 1, 2011, estates of decedents may elect to pass any of the decedent's unused exemption (DSUE) to the U.S. surviving spouse, if there is one. This election is made on an estate tax return that is filed on time.

The ability to transfer the unused exemption amount to a surviving spouse can be very beneficial, especially if the estate value for the surviving spouse is over their own estate tax exemption.

Real Life: U.S. citizen decedent with DSUE

Margaret's husband, Jerry, passed away in October of 2013 and at that time his estate was valued at $3,245,000. Jerry's estate was under the exemption amount so a return was not required; however, because Margaret wanted Jerry's DSUE to transfer to her, she made sure the form 709 estate tax return was filed and the election made to transfer Jerry's DSUE.

Margaret made the election to transfer the DSUE because her estate was already worth $4,275,000 prior to Jerry's death, which means that her revised estate value after jerry's death would be over her own estate exemption amount of $5,340,000 so she needs more to cover any potential tax that could result.

Margaret's new estate tax exemption amount would be $7,345,000 ($5,340,000 + (5,250,000 - 3,245,000)).

Gross Estate

The gross estate includes the value of all property that the decedent owned at the time of death; including the following:

- Life insurance proceeds payable to the estate or, if the decedent owned the policy, to the heirs;
- The value of certain annuities payable to the estate or the decedent's heirs; and
- The value of certain property gifted within 3 years before the decedent's death.

Generally, the gross estate does not include property owned solely by the decedent's spouse or other individuals. Lifetime gifts that are complete (no powers or other control over the gifts are retained) are not included in the gross estate (but taxable gifts are used in the computation of the estate tax).

Taxable Estate

Allowable deductions permitted in determining the taxable estate include:

- Funeral expenses paid out of the estate;
- Debts owed at the time of death;
- The marital deduction (generally, the value of the property that passes from the estate to the decedent's surviving spouse);
- The charitable deduction (generally, the value of the property that passes from the estate to the United States, any state, a political subdivision of a state, the District of Columbia, or to a qualifying charity for exclusively charitable purposes); and
- The state death tax deduction (generally any estate, inheritance, legacy, or succession taxes paid as the result of the decedent's death to any state or the District of Columbia).

Applying the Unified Credit to Estate Tax

Basically, any unified credit not used to eliminate gift tax can be used to eliminate or reduce estate tax. To determine the unified credit available for use against the estate tax you must complete Form 706.

Filing an Estate Tax Return

 An estate tax return must be filed if the gross estate, plus any adjusted taxable gifts and specific gift tax exemption, is more than the basic exclusion amount.

The applicable exclusion amount is the total amount exempted from gift and/or estate tax. For decedents dying after December 31, 2010, the applicable exclusion amount equals the basic exclusion amount plus any Deceased Spousal Unused Exclusion (DSUE) amount. The DSUE is the unused lifetime exclusion amount from the estate of a predeceased spouse who died after December 31, 2010. The DSUE is available only where an election has been made on the Form 706 filed by the deceased spouse's estate.

 Form 706 is generally due within 9 months after the date of death of the decedent; however, if you are unable to file form 706 by the due date, you may receive an extension of time to file by filing Form 4768, Application for Extension of Time to File a Return and/or Pay U.S. Estate (and Generation-Skipping Transfer) Taxes, to apply for an automatic 6-month extension of time to file.

U.S. Estate Tax for Non-Resident Aliens

The taxable estate of a U.S. non-resident alien includes the following assets located in the U.S.:

- Real estate and tangible personal property;
- Stock in a U.S. corporation;
- Debt issued by, or enforceable against, a U.S. entity (but most corporate debt instruments issued after 1984 are exempt from U.S. estate tax); and
- An interest in a partnership, if the partnership's principal place of business is in the U.S.

The U.S. estate tax is based on the fair market value of each such asset on the date of death. There is no recognition of a capital gain or loss arising from a deemed disposition on the date of death for U.S. tax purposes. Non-resident aliens cannot claim foreign tax credits on a U.S. estate tax return for deemed-disposition capital gains income taxes paid to Canada; however, U.S. citizens can.

Article XXIX B:2 of the Canada-U.S Tax Convention allows non-resident aliens of the U.S. a prorated share of the U.S. estate exemption.

For the transfer of a decedent's U.S. assets, the IRS requires Form 706NA, *United States Estate (and Generation-Skipping Transfer) Tax Return*, if the value of the U.S. assets exceeds $60,000 on the date of death. In other words, even if the decedent will not be subject to U.S. estate tax, if the value of their U.S. estate is over $60,000, he or she must file a U.S. estate return, whereas a U.S. citizen is only required to file a return if their estate value is over the gross exemption amount for the applicable year (i.e., $5,250,000 for 2013).

U.S. Estate Tax for Non-Resident Aliens

The taxable estate of a U.S. non-resident alien includes the following assets located in the U.S.:

- Real estate and tangible personal property;
- Stock in a U.S. corporation;
- Debt issued by, or enforceable against, a U.S. entity (but most corporate debt instruments issued after 1984 are exempt from U.S. estate tax); and
- An interest in a partnership, if the partnership's principal place of business is in the U.S.

The U.S. estate tax is based on the fair market value of each such asset on the date of death.

There is no recognition of a capital gain or loss arising from a deemed disposition on the date of death for U.S. tax purposes.

Non-resident aliens cannot claim foreign tax credits on a U.S. estate tax return for deemed-disposition capital gains income taxes paid to Canada; however, U.S. citizens can.

The Canada-U.S Tax Convention allows non-resident aliens of the U.S. a pro-rated share of the U.S. estate exemption and it is calculated by taking the fair value of the U.S. situs assets over the fair value of worldwide assets.

A non-resident of the U.S. must file Form 706NA, United States Estate (and Generation-Skipping Transfer) Tax Return, if the value of the U.S. assets exceeds $60,000 on the date of death.

In other words, even if the decedent will not be subject to U.S. estate tax, if the value of their U.S. estate is over $60,000, he or she must file a U.S. estate return, whereas a U.S. citizen is only required to file a return if their estate value is over the gross exemption amount for the applicable year.

Real Life: U.S. non-resident subject to U.S. estate tax

Hanna is a 65-year-old Canadian citizen and resident who recently bought a vacation property in Miami, Florida. She is the sole owner of the property and its current value is $385,000. Her current estate value is $3,475,000, including the U.S. property; however, her elderly mother is on her death bed and, as an only child, Hanna stands to inherit her mother's estate which is currently valued at $2,325,000.

If Hanna's estate remains at $5,800,000 and she were to die in 2013, she would be subject to U.S. estate tax of $14,603 ((385,000/5,800,000)*5,250,000 = $348,491; (385,000-348,491) *40% = $14,603).

Real Life: *Joint U.S. non-residents not subject to U.S. estate tax*

Donald and his wife, Gina, are Canadian citizens and residents who jointly own a rental property in Phoenix, Arizona, and have owned this property for the past 2 years. They purchased this property for $145,000 but it is now worth $185,000 and in another 5 years they are expecting that it will be worth $215,000.

If Donald and Gina currently have a joint estate worth $3.5 Million and they both unexpectedly die in December 2014 and their U.S. property is worth $215,000 at that time, neither one of them would be subject to U.S. estate tax on their U.S. rental property because they would receive a large enough portion of the estate tax exemption amount to fully cover the value of their U.S. property; $215,000*50%=$107,500 & $3,500,000*50%=$1,750,000; (107,500/1,750,000)*5,340,000=$328,028; $328,028 is the pro-rated portion of the exemption and it is greater than $107,500; therefore, full exemption for each (i.e., this calculation is the same for each person). However, they would be required to file IRS FORM 706NA, United States Estate (and Generation-Skipping Transfer) Tax Return to access the increased estate tax exemption permitted under the Treaty.

Real Life: *Joint U.S. non-residents partially subject to U.S. estate tax*

Gerald and his son, Jordan, bought a vacation property in Southern California which the whole family enjoys. The property is a beach-side property and has an approximate fair market value of $550,000 at the present time, although they bought it for much less.

If Gerald's estate is currently worth $5,100,000, plus his share of the U.S. property, and Jordan's current estate value is $1,000,000, plus his share of the U.S. property, and they were both to unexpectedly die in 2013, Gerald would be subject to U.S. estate tax but Jordan would not.

Note: $550,000*50%=$275,000 (50% share of property value)

Gerald's estate = $5,100,000+275,000=$5,375,000

Jordan's estate = $1,000,000+275,000=$1,275,000

Gerald: (275,000/5,375,000)*5,250,000=$268,605; $275,000-268,605=$6,395*40%=$2,558 of U.S. estate tax

Jordon: (275,000/1,275,000)*5,250,000=$1,132,353; $1,132,353 is greater than $275,000; therefore, no estate tax because a full exemption applies; however, estate returns would be required to be filed for both Gerald and Jordan because their U.S. estate values are over $60,000 each.

U.S. Gift Tax

U.S. gift tax is basically U.S. estate tax while a person is still alive. The U.S. doesn't want taxpayers to be able to give their estate away during their lifetime just so they can reduce their estate value below the exemption amount to avoid paying estate tax when they die. For this reason, the gift tax regime was created.

 Gift tax is a tax on the transfer of property by one individual to another while receiving nothing, or less than full value, in return. The tax applies whether the transfer is intended to be a gift or not.

Gift tax applies to the transfer by gift of any property when the total taxable gifts are more than the annual exclusion amount of $14,000 per person or more than $5,340,000 (the value of the lifetime gift exemption amount in 2014); claiming any amount over the annual exemption requires the filing of a gift tax return. You make a gift if you give property (including money), or the use of income from property, without expecting to receive something of at least equal value in return. If you sell something at less than its full value or if you make an interest-free or reduced-interest loan, you may also be making a gift under U.S. tax laws.

Gifting rules are a bit different in Canada than in the U.S. because in Canada a gift is not taxable; however, depending on the situation, a gift could result in income attribution rules being applied in Canada (i.e., income on the gifted property reverts back to the person who gave the gift in some circumstances). Changing title on certain assets may trigger a taxable event in Canada but it will not generate a gift tax but in the U.S. gift tax can result so proper planning is key when U.S. gift tax may be involved.

The following gifts *are not* considered taxable gifts:

- Gifts, excluding gifts of future interests (see below), that are not more than the annual exclusion for the calendar year;
- Tuition or medical expenses paid directly to an educational or medical institution for someone else;
- Gifts to your spouse (U.S. citizen/resident spouse only);
- Gifts to a political organization for its use; and
- Gifts to charities.

Exclusions

A separate annual exclusion applies to each person to whom you make a gift (i.e., you are allowed to gift up to $14,000 per year per person). The gift tax annual exclusion is subject to cost-of-living increases.

- The annual exclusion for gifts is $11,000 (2004-2005), $12,000 (2006-2008), $13,000 (2009- 2012) and $14,000 (2013 and 2014).
- The applicable lifetime exclusion amount for gifts is $1,000,000 (2010), $5,000,000 (2011), $5,120,000 (2012), $5,250,000 (2013) and $5,340,000 (2014).

Currently, you can give gifts valued up to $14,000 per person to any number of people and none of the gifts will be taxable and are not included in calculating taxable gifts for estate tax purposes; however, you can give an unlimited gift to a spouse if that spouse is a U.S. citizen/resident spouse. When the recipient spouse is a non-U.S. citizen or non-resident of the U.S., an annual exemption of $145,000 (2014) ($143,000-2013) is allowed.

 Gifts of future interests do not qualify under the annual exclusion regime.

A gift of a future interest is a gift that is limited so that its use or enjoyment will begin at some point in the future.

 If you are married, both you and your spouse can separately give gifts valued up to $14,000 to the same person without making a taxable gift.

If one of you gives more than the $14,000 exclusion, the gift splitting rules may apply, see below.

Gift Splitting

f you or your spouse makes a gift to a third party, the gift can be considered as made one-half by you and one-half by your spouse. This is known as gift splitting. Both of you must agree to split the gift and if you do, each spouse can take the annual exclusion for that part of the gift. Therefore, gift splitting permits married couples to give up to $28,000 to a person without making a taxable gift.

If you split a gift you made, you must file a gift tax return to show that you and your spouse agree to the use of the gift splitting rules. You must file a Form 709 even if half of the split gift is less than the annual exclusion.

Real Life: Gift splitting

Harold and his wife, Helen, agree to split the gifts that they made during 2014. Harold gives his nephew, George, $21,000, and Helen gives her niece, Gina, $18,000. Although each gift is more than the annual exclusion amount ($14,000 to each person), by gift splitting they can make these gifts without making a taxable gift.

Harold's gift to George is treated as one-half ($10,500) from Harold and one-half ($10,500) from Helen. Helen's gift to Gina is also treated as one-half ($9,000) from Helen and one-half ($9,000) from Harold. In each case, because one-half of the split gifts are not more than the annual exclusion, it is not a taxable gift. However, each of them must file a separate gift tax return.

Applying the Unified Credit to Gift Tax

After determining which gifts are taxable, you must calculate the amount of gift tax on the total taxable gifts and apply your unified credit for the year.

 The unified credit applies to both the gift tax and the estate tax and it equals the tax on the applicable exclusion amount.

Real Life: Unified credit application for gift tax

In 2013, you give your niece, Mary, a cash gift of $8,000. It is your only gift to her this year. You pay the $15,000 college tuition for your friend, David. You give your 25-year-old daughter, Lisa, $25,000. You also give your 27-year-old son, Ken, $25,000. You have never given a taxable gift before. You apply the exceptions to the gift tax and the unified credit as follows:

Apply the educational exclusion; payment of tuition expenses is not subject to the gift tax. Therefore, the gift to David is not a taxable gift (i.e., assuming it is paid directly to the school).

Apply the annual exclusion; the first $14,000 you give someone is not a taxable gift. Therefore, your $8,000 gift to Mary, the first $14,000 of your gift to Lisa, and the first $14,000 of your gift to Ken are not taxable gifts.

Apply the unified credit; the gift tax on $22,000 ($11,000 remaining from your gift to Lisa plus $11,000 remaining from your gift to Ken) is $8,800 ($22,000*40%). Subtract the $8,800 from your unified credit of $2,045,800 for 2013. The unified credit that you can use against the gift or estate tax in a later year is $2,037,000.

> You do not have to pay any gift tax for 2013 because you have enough unified credit to reduce the tax to zero; however, you do have to file Form 709.

You must subtract the unified credit from any gift or estate tax that you owe. Any unified credit you use against gift tax in one year reduces the amount of credit that you can use against gift or estate taxes in a later year.

Beginning in 2011, the amount of unified credit available to a person will equal the tax on the basic exclusion amount plus the tax on any Deceased Spousal Unused Exclusion (DSUE) amount. The DSUE is only available if an election was made on the deceased spouse's Form 706 estate return.

The following table shows the unified credit (recalculated at current rates) for the calendar years in which a gift is made or a decedent dies after 1976.

Table of Unified Credits (Recalculated at Current Rates)

Period	Recalculated Unified Credit
1977 (Quarters 1 and 2)	$6,000
1977 (Quarters 3 and 4)	$30,000
1978	$34,000
1979	$38,000
1980	$42,500
1981	$47,000
1982	$62,800
1983	$79,300
1984	$96,300
1985	$121,800
1986	$155,800
1987 through 1997	$190,800
1998	$199,500
1999	$208,300
2000 and 2001	$217,050
2002 through 2010	$330,800
2011	$1,730,800
2012	$1,772,800
2013	$2,045,800
2014	$2,081,800

Gift Tax for Non-Residents/Non-Citizens

Non-citizens and non-residents of the U.S. still need to be aware of U.S. gift and generation-skipping tax if they own U.S. situs assets.

 Just like estate tax, gift tax and generation-skipping tax can apply to U.S. situs property held by a non-resident.

The difference is that there is no pro-ration of the annual exclusion amounts, but there is still a pro-ration of the lifetime gift exemption amount (i.e., you cannot pro-rate the $14,000 annual exclusion but you can pro-rate the $5,340,000 exemption.

Filing a Gift Tax Return

Generally, an individual must file a gift tax return if any of the following apply:

- An individual gave gifts to at least one person (other than your spouse) that are more than the annual exclusion for the year;
- An individual and his or her spouse are splitting a gift;
- An individual gave someone (other than your spouse) a gift of a future interest that he or she cannot actually possess, enjoy, or receive income from until sometime in the future; or
- An individual gave his or her spouse an interest in property that will be terminated by some future event.

You do not have to file a gift tax return to report gifts to (or for the use of) political organizations and gifts made by paying someone's tuition or medical expenses (i.e., gifts exempt from gift tax). You also don't need to report gifts to charities.

 Form 709 must be filed no earlier than January 1, but not later than April 15, of the year after the gift was made.

If the donor died during the year, the executor must file the donor's Form 709 not later than the earlier of:

- the due date (with extensions) for filing the donor's estate tax return; or
- April 15th of the year after the gift was made, or the extended due date granted for filing the donor's gift tax return.

Extension of Time to File

There are two methods of extending the time to file the gift tax return; however, the time to pay the gift or GST tax is not extended, although you can request that separately.

By extending the time to file your income tax return: Any extension of time to file your federal income tax return will also automatically extend the time to file your federal gift tax return. Income tax extensions are made by filing Form 4868, Application for Automatic Extension of Time to File U.S. Individual Income Tax Return, or Form 2350, Application for Extension of Time to File U.S. Income Tax Return. You may only use these forms to extend the time for filing your gift tax return if you are also requesting an extension of time to file your income tax return.

By filing Form 8892: If you do not request an extension for your income tax return, use Form 8892, Application for Automatic Extension of Time To File Form 709 and/or Payment of Gift/Generation-Skipping Transfer Tax, to request an automatic 6-month extension of time to file your federal gift tax return. Form 8892 is also used as a payment voucher (Form 8892-V) for a balance due on federal gift taxes.

Generation-Skipping Transfer Tax

 The GST tax may apply to gifts during your life or bequests at your death, made to skip persons.

A skip person is a person who belongs to a generation that is two or more generations below the generation of the donor. For instance, a grandchild will generally be a skip person to grandparents; however, if the parents of the grandchild were deceased, the grandchild would not be considered a skip person.

 The GST tax is calculated on the amount of the gift or bequest transferred to a skip person, after subtracting any GST exemption allocated to the gift or bequest at the maximum gift and estate tax rates.

Each individual has a GST exemption equal to the basic exclusion amount for the year involved which is the same exemption amount available for regular gift and estate taxes (i.e., $5,340,000 in 2014).

GSTs have three forms: direct skip, taxable distribution, and taxable termination..

• A direct skip is a transfer made during life or at death that is:
   1. subject to the gift or estate tax;
   2. of an interest in property, and
   3. made to a skip person.

- A taxable distribution is any distribution from a trust to a skip person which is not a direct skip or a taxable termination.

- A taxable termination is the end of a trust's interest in property where the property interest will be transferred to a skip person (i.e., asset held in trust for a minor/grandchild that transfers automatically when the beneficiary reaches 18 years of age).

 Transfers that are not subject to gift tax because of the gift tax annual exclusion and unlimited exclusion for direct payment of medical and tuition expenses are not subject to GST tax either.

Real Life: Gift tax and Generation-Skipping Tax (GST)

Assume that you give your adult sister a gift of $12,000 to help get her out of debt and your daughter receives a gift from her grandfather in the amount of $16,000 so she can buy a car. All donors are U.S. citizens.

The gift to your sister is not subject to gift tax because it is under the $14,000 exemption amount; however, the gift the grandfather gives to his granddaughter would be subject to both gift tax and generation-skipping tax. Generation-skipping tax does not apply to gifts where gift tax does not apply (i.e., certain categories of gifts that are not considered taxable gifts or the gift is under the annual exclusion amount); however, because the grandfather's gift is considered a taxable gift and it is over the $14,000 exclusion amount, gift tax would apply. Generation-skipping tax also applies because the granddaughter is a second-generation person (i.e., a skip person).

In this scenario, the grandfather would have to pay gift tax of $800 and generation-skipping tax of $800 for a total tax of $1,600. The tax is calculated as follows:

Gift tax = $16,000-14,000 = $2,000*40% = $800

GST = $16,000-14,000 = $2,000*40% = $800

U.S. Gift & Estate Tax for a Non-resident: What You Need to Know

U.S. Citizen/Resident

- Annual gift exclusion is $14,000 per person per year, except to spouse.
- Gift splitting is available to keep gifts under the annual exemption amount.
- Unlimited gifts to U.S.-citizen spouse; $145,000 per year to non-U.S. citizen spouse.
- Lifetime gift, GST and estate tax exemption of $5,340,000.
- Gift, estate and generation-skipping tax rate is 40% on amounts over the exemptions.
- Estate tax return is not required unless estate value is over the exemption amount.
- Can elect to transfer deceased spouse's unused exemption amounts (DSUE).

U.S. non-residents

- U.S. gift, estate and GST are applicable on U.S. situs property.
- The lifetime exemption amount is pro-rated based on percentage U.S. assets over worldwide assets.
- Estate tax return must be filed if U.S. estate value is over $60,000.
- Gift splitting is available to non-residents as well.
- Annual exemptions are not prorated.

WHAT YOU NEED TO KNOW ABOUT UNCLE SAM:

U.S. gift, estate and GST can apply to non-residents of the U.S. as well; these taxes apply not only to U.S. residents and citizens. U.S. situs assets are subject to these taxes as long as you own them and if the situation exists to trigger the tax.

Gifting rules are different in Canada so you need to be careful with any strategies involving your U.S. situs assets. Transferring title on a U.S. property may not be an issue in Canada but is considered a gift for U.S. purposes, which can trigger a large amount of tax, depending on the value of the property, so be careful.

Effective tax planning can be done to maximize one's use of the lifetime exemptions available in the U.S., which can simplify and minimize one's taxes going forward. Consult a U.S. tax advisor prior to owning U.S. assets so you know what issues may arise now and in the future.

CHAPTER 13

Summary

Chapter 1 – Tax Filing Requirements

The Canadian tax system is based on residency, which means, unless you are living outside of Canada and have Canadian source income of some kind, you will be subject to income tax in Canada only if you are a Canadian resident. The U.S. bases their tax system on citizenship, which means that no matter where a person lives in the world, if they are a U.S. citizen or treated like a U.S. citizen because of their situation, they must abide by the U.S. tax laws and could possibly be subject to tax in the United States of America. This is also the case if you are a U.S. resident but not a citizen.

Residency

Residency can be determined by many factors but it is mainly determined by the following:

- Physical presence (i.e., number of days in a country);
- Residential ties to a country; and
- A person's intentions.

An individual taxpayer is ordinarily considered a resident in the place where he or she regularly lives and maintains the routine of his or her business and social life (a factual resident). Residency can mean the difference between a person being subject to income tax on worldwide income versus being taxed only on the income sourced in that particular country or state. For example, Canadian residents are taxed on their worldwide income; whereas non-residents are taxed only on their Canadian sourced income. The same is true for U.S. residents and non-residents; however, U.S. citizens are taxed on worldwide income no matter where they are actually physically resident.

Keep in mind an individual can be a U.S. citizen even though he or she is not born in the U.S. U.S. citizenship can transfer automatically from parent(s) to child if the U.S. citizen parent(s) meet certain requirements under U.S. immigration law. The tests require the U.S. citizen parent(s) to have lived in the U.S. for a certain period of time prior to the child's birth; the age of the child dictates which test must be met.

Chapter 2 – Reporting Income & Assets

Taxation of Income

There are many different types of income that an individual can be taxed on; however, this book focuses only on some of the more common sources that are treated differently in Canada and the U.S. The following income types/concepts are taxed differently on both sides of the border:

- Gambling/lottery winnings
- Rental income
- Capital dividends
- Taxable capital gains
- Lifetime capital gains exemption
- Employment income
- Corporate and individual taxpayers

Chapter 3 – Reporting Foreign Holdings

Filing Requirements

Canada requires an individual to file his or her personal tax return by April 30th of the following tax year, unless you are self-employed, in which case the filing deadline is June 15th of the following tax year. In the U.S. you are required to file your individual income tax return by April 15th of the following tax year. However, if you are a U.S. citizen living abroad and do not have U.S. employment income, you receive an automatic 2-month filing extension to June 15th of the following tax year. If you cannot file by the applicable due date in the U.S., an individual can file for a 6-month extension. Filing extensions are not available in Canada. All taxes owing in Canada must be paid by April 30th to avoid interest and by April 15th in the U.S. to avoid interest.

There are many other reports/returns that a U.S. person may be required to file depending on his or her personal situation and each separate report has its own due date and potential late filing penalty attached to it. Canada has several other returns or forms (i.e., T1135, T1134B) that may need to be filed if you meet certain tests, but they are not nearly as numerous or onerous as potential filing requirements in the U.S.

Chapter 4 – Snowbirds and Uncle Sam

The term *"snowbird"* refers to a person who is ordinarily resident in Canada but spends part of the year in the U.S. The name was given to this category of individuals because they are usually individuals who travel outside Canada during the winter months to a warmer climate down south.

Residency

In the United States, the substantial presence test determines residency; in order to be considered a resident you must pass both the 31-day and 183-day tests.

The 31-day test is simple:

Were you present in United States 31 days during the current year?

The 183-day test operates as follows:

   A. Current year days in United States x 1 =_____days

   B. First preceding year days in United States x 1/3 =_____days

   C. Second preceding year days in United States x 1/6 =_____days

   D. Total Days in United States =_____days (add lines A, B, and C)

   If line D equals or exceeds 183 days, you have passed the183-day test.

Where this is the case, you will be deemed to be resident in the U.S. for tax purposes. There are some exceptions to the substantial presence test that are of high importance when making the calculation (see chapter material). Even if a person is technically considered a U.S. resident by meeting the substantial presence test, if the taxpayer has closer ties to Canada (i.e., a treaty country), the taxpayer can file form 8840 Closer Connection Exception or an 8833 Treaty election to be taxed only as a non-resident of the U.S. This is the preferred result because if one is deemed to be a U.S. resident, the individual must abide by all the U.S. tax laws that are applicable to U.S. citizens, making their Canadian income subject to tax in the U.S.

Visitors to the U.S. are generally allowed to stay in the country for only 6 months over a one-year period without obtaining a visitor's visa. Most Canadian provinces will allow a person to be absent for only a 6-month period and still be covered by the provincial health plan. There are many types of U.S. visas that a person can obtain for entry into the U.S. The appropriate visa depends on each particular situation or circumstance (see chapter material for visa list).

Chapter 5 – Non-Residents Owning U.S. Real Estate

An interest in U.S. real property is considered to be any interest in real property (including a mine, well, or other natural deposit) located in the U.S. Real property includes land and unsevered timber, crops and minerals. A non-resident's interest can be any interest, such as direct ownership, fee-ownership, or co-ownership of the property, as well as any leasehold or option to acquire the property.

Individual Taxpayer Identification Number (ITIN)

Generally, a Canadian taxpayer need not apply to obtain a U.S. ITIN when purchasing a U.S. property interest. If the property is being sold by a non-resident of the U.S., the buyer must withhold tax equal to 10% of the gross proceeds unless certain exceptions exist. The seller can apply for a reduced amount of withholding tax if the actual tax liability on the sale will be less than the regular withholding tax; however, both the buyer and the seller need ITINs to have the application approved. To obtain an Individual Taxpayer Identification Number (ITIN), an individual must meet one of the options available to apply for an ITIN and you must complete the W-7 application form.

Once the application has been processed, an ITIN will be issued and a copy of the assigned number will be mailed to you. This is the number that the individual will use for any and all U.S. forms going forward; however, this number is only for tax filing purposes and does not allow the individual to work in the U.S. If the property is owned in joint title, both owners will need to apply for ITINs and file separate 1040NR returns.

Gift Tax

U.S. gift tax is a tax on the transfer of property from one individual to another while receiving nothing, or less than full value, in return. The tax applies whether the donor intends the transfer to be a gift or not. Gift tax is basically estate tax applied while a person is alive. Trusts and corporations are not subject to gift tax.

Even though gift tax is a U.S. tax, it is applicable to all U.S. property. For example, if a non-resident owns U.S. property, he or she must be aware of the potential for U.S. gift tax on that property. The annual gift tax exemption amount is $14,000 per person; however, an exemption of $145,000 ($143,000 in 2013) is allowed by a donor to a spouse who is not a U.S. citizen. Gift tax is combined with estate tax when a person dies.

Gift tax rates are graduated and range from 18% to 40% for 2014 (40% maximum in 2013).

Estate Tax

Estate tax is a tax on your right to transfer property at your death. An individual's gross estate consists of everything that person owned or held an interest in, on the date of death. Estate tax is generally calculated using fair market value (FMV) on the date of death; however, an alternative valuation date may be used if the value of the estate would be less than on the date of death. The alternative valuation day is any day between the date of death and 6 months after the date of death.

Every U.S. citizen and resident has access to the estate tax exemption amount of $5,340,000 (2014), which means that a person's estate is not taxable unless it is over this exemption amount. Any amount over the estate exemption is taxed at a rate of 40% (2014).

All U.S. situs assets, i.e., assets located in the U.S., held by an individual can trigger U.S. gift and/or estate tax. For a U.S. person, gift and estate tax can apply on worldwide assets but for a Canadian who is a non-resident of the U.S., these taxes are only applicable on U.S. property. Thankfully the Canada/U.S. Tax Convention allows some relief from these taxes for a Canadian resident by giving the Canadian the ability to apply a prorated portion of the U.S. estate tax exemption amount against the fair value of the U.S. property which results in a reduction in the potential U.S. gift and/or estate tax that might otherwise be owing (i.e., the $5,340,000 exemption is multiplied by the ratio of U.S. situs assets over worldwide assets).

The *gross estate* includes the value of all property that the decedent owned partially or outright at the time of death and it also includes life insurance proceeds payable to the estate or to the decedent's heirs, the value of certain annuities payable to the estate or the decedent's heirs, and the value of certain property transferred by the decedent within 3 years before death.

Rental Income

Generally, a 30% withholding tax applies to the gross amount of rent paid to a non-resident of the U.S. on real estate located in the U.S. However, to avoid this withholding tax deduction, a Canadian taxpayer can make an election to opt out of the withholding tax requirements by promising to file a U.S. tax return and pay tax on their net rental income by completing form W-8ECI (elect to treat the income as effectively connected with a trade or business in the U.S.). This results in keeping more money in your jeans during the year instead of having to file a tax return at the end of the year to claim back a refund.

In Canada, you are allowed to deduct depreciation only up to the amount of profit reported before depreciation is taken; you cannot create a loss for income tax purposes using depreciation (i.e., you can deduct depreciation simply to NIL out income). In the U.S., depreciation is mandatory on all property/assets used for income-producing purposes, which means that even if the deduction of depreciation creates a loss for income tax purposes in the U.S. you must take the full deduction. For example, if someone has a U.S. rental property that has net profits before depreciation of $2,450 but for U.S. tax purposes the maximum depreciation that exists for the year is $3,000, it must be deducted to produce a loss of $550; however, if the same situation exists for Canadian tax, only $2,450 would be allowed as a deduction to bring the profits down to zero (i.e., you cannot create a loss in Canada by deducting depreciation).

If the property in the U.S. is used for non-active business purposes (i.e., rental property) and the *cost* of the property is over $100,000, a separate foreign property reporting form is required in Canada, a T1135. This form has been revised to include more detail for 2013 going forward.

FIRPTA

The disposition of U.S. real property by a foreign person is subject to the Foreign Investment in Real Property Tax Act (FIRPTA) of 1980 income tax withholding. The FIRPTA withholding tax amount is 10% of the gross proceeds for an individual disposing of the property. In most cases, the buyer is the withholding agent. If you are the buyer you must find out if the seller is a foreign person. If the seller is a foreign person and you fail to withhold, you will be held liable for the tax.

Ownership Structures

There are a few options for Canadians when it comes to purchasing a U.S. property interest. The U.S. property can be purchased in a Canadian holding company if it is used for rental purposes, it can be purchased by a trust or it can be purchased directly by the individual(s). Tax consequences will vary for each type of ownership structure. See chapter 5 for further details.

Chapter 6 – Investing in the U.S. & U.S. Source Income

Canadian Pension Plans

RRSPs and RRIFs are Canadian deferred pension plans; however, for U.S. purposes, these are foreign pension plans, which means that a tax deduction is not available for contributions made to the plan and they are not automatically treated as tax-deferred plans in the U.S. either. This means that if a U.S. citizen living in Canada makes an RRSP contribution during the year to help reduce the

Canadian tax liability, a similar deduction will not be allowed on the U.S. tax return, which results in more income potentially being subject to income tax in the U.S. The Canada-U.S. Tax Convention does allow an election to be made in the U.S. to have these plans treated as tax deferred retirement plans in the U.S. in the same manner that they are treated in Canada (i.e., only taxable as income when the money is drawn from the plan). The election is made using form 8891. This is beneficial for U.S. citizens living in Canada as well as for Canadians who may be living in the U.S. who have these kinds of plans.

U.S. Pension Plans

A U.S. 401(k) plan, 403(b) plan and IRAs are qualified tax-deferred compensation plans. Distributions received before age 59 1/2 are subject to an early distribution penalty of 10% additional tax unless an exception applies. This additional tax is in addition to regular income tax and is calculated and due when your income tax payment is due (i.e., April 15th of the following year).

Tax-Free Rollover

Canada's *Income Tax Act* (ITA) allows resident taxpayers in Canada to transfer benefits of some U.S. retirement arrangements (401(k)/403(b) plans) or individual retirement accounts (IRAs) to Canada on a tax-deferred basis. Depending on age and the rules governing the U.S. plan, a Canadian resident taxpayer can collapse his or her U.S. plan and transfer lump-sum superannuation or pension benefits on plan assets that are individual contributions on a tax-deferred basis in Canada without using RRSP contribution room. However, if you want to transfer contributions made by an employer or government entity on the individual's behalf, you must have sufficient RRSP contribution room.

Under Canadian and U.S. tax rules, funds withdrawn from a foreign retirement plan such as a 401(k) or IRA are taxable as income in the year the plan is collapsed in the U.S. The withdrawal amount must be included as income in the Canadian tax return, but a deduction for the amount transferred to an RRSP can offset the income inclusion (if contributed within 60 days after the end of the year). Upon collapse of the U.S. plan, the U.S. administrator will withhold 15% tax for non-resident aliens or non-U.S. citizens. Normally the withholding tax is 20% for U.S. residents, but the Canada-U.S. tax treaty reduces this rate to 15%.

In the U.S., the rollover of a 401(K), 403(b) or IRA withdrawal will be subject to the 10% penalty tax mentioned above if you are under the age limit; it will also be taxable. The tax treaty limits the tax to 15% for non-residents of the U.S. which means you would have 85% of the withdrawal to put into the RRSP instead of the usual 80%, unless you make up the 15% out of your own pocket. This means, however, that the 15% is now subject to income tax in Canada. Your RRSP contribution limits do not apply if you are only transferring individual contributions; however, if you are transferring employer contributions as well, unused RRSP contribution room can be used to offset the required income inclusion.

RESPs & TFSAs

RESPs and TFSAs are two forms of Canadian savings plans that defer taxes; however, they are both considered foreign trusts for U.S. tax purposes and under the U.S. tax rules, foreign trusts are subject to separate reporting requirements and taxation rules. For example, U.S. citizens and residents who have these types of accounts are required to include the accrued income within the accounts in their taxable income on their U.S. tax returns in the applicable years, as well as complete a 3520 and 3520-A Foreign Trust reporting form to report contributions to and deemed distributions from these accounts in any given year. The compliance fees related to these foreign trust forms can be substantial and can far outweigh the benefits of having these types of accounts.

Mutual Funds

Canadian mutual funds are considered Passive Foreign Investment Companies (PFICs) for U.S. tax purposes, which means that separate reporting requirements and tax treatment exist for these types of investments. For example, any distributions from these types of investments are to be treated as dividend income for U.S. tax purposes, no matter if the distribution is actually in the form of a capital gain or interest or dividend. The dividend income is reported on the individual's 1040 return plus a separate 8621 form is required which can result in further income being taxable in the year. ETFs and REITs are treated the same for U.S. tax purposes.

Capital Gains

The Canada-U.S. Tax Convention treats gains from the sale of portfolio investments as taxable only in the taxpayer's country of residence (i.e., capital gains from non-registered portfolio investments are earned outside a country's tax system when you don't physically reside in that country). This basically means that gains on these types of investments are considered "sourced" in the taxpayer's country of residence for income tax purposes; however, this isn't necessarily true for U.S. citizens. In order for U.S. portfolio investments to be treated as "sourced" in Canada for U.S. citizens living in Canada, the taxpayer needs to have paid a minimum of 10% in income tax on these same gains in Canada.

U.S. securities are considered U.S. situs assets for U.S. estate tax purposes, which means that a non-resident holding U.S. securities can potentially be subject to U.S. estate tax on those assets upon his or her death. However, U.S. securities held inside a Canadian mutual fund or within a privately-owned Canadian corporation are not seen as U.S. situs assets and are therefore not subject to U.S. estate tax.

Withholding taxes may be applicable on U.S. or Canadian investment income being earned by a non-resident.

Chapter 7 – Married to a U.S. Citizen & Moving Between Countries

Marrying a Canadian or U.S. citizen does not automatically give you Canadian or U.S. citizenship. A person must apply for permanent residency and then once residency is granted, he or she can apply for citizenship within the applicable country. However, there are some conditions that must first be met (see chapter for details).

Leaving the U.S.

There aren't many tax implications when a U.S. person wants to leave the U.S. and move to Canada, but wants to maintain his or her U.S. citizenship or long-term residency status. The U.S. does not have deemed disposition rules like Canada; however, Canada will give the emigrant a bump-up in cost base for all his assets owned at the time of the move (i.e., effectively declaring the cost of the asset to equal its fair value upon deemed disposition, showing no taxable gains).

The cost bump is part of Canada's deemed disposition rules. Canada considers an emigrant to have sold each property for its fair market value immediately before emigrating and then immediately buying it back for the same fair market value. The cost bump, however, does not apply to taxable Canadian property already owned by the emigrant. The cost bump is important because this means that Canada will tax only the gains that are accrued after moving to Canada.

Renouncing U.S. Citizenship/Long-Term Residency

Some individuals who immigrate to Canada may want to renounce their U.S. citizenship or relinquish their long-term residency status in order to stop the U.S. tax clock from ticking. If U.S. citizenship or long-term residency status is maintained, the person will still be subject to the IRS regime and potentially on the hook for more tax that if the person was considered to be a non-resident of the U.S. All expatriates must determine whether or not they will be subject to the alternative expatriation tax.

Under a mark-to-market deemed sale rule, property of certain U.S. citizens who relinquish their U.S. citizenship and certain long-term residents who terminate their U.S. residency after June 16, 2008, would be treated as sold on the day before the expatriation date at its fair market value (FMV).

Any net gain realized on the deemed sale is recognized to the extent that it exceeds an inflation adjusted amount. That amount is $636,000 for 2011, $651,000 for 2012, $663,000 for 2013 and $680,000 for 2014. Gains or losses that are realized on the actual disposition of the properties would be adjusted for the gains and losses taken into account under the deemed sale rules, without regard to the exemption. This means that if someone realized gains of $45,000 on expatriation but then realized a gain of $60,000 when the assets were physically sold, the actual gain realized for tax purposes when the physical disposition took place would only be $15,000 (60,000 - 45,000).

The alternative expatriate income tax applies to U.S. citizens and long-term residents who relinquish their citizenship or terminate residency and meet the average annual net income tax test, net worth test, or failure to certify test described below:

1. The individual's average annual net income tax for the period of five tax years ending before the date of residency termination is greater than an inflation adjusted amount that is $155,000 for 2013 ($151,000 for 2012; $147,000 for 2011);

2. The individual's net worth as of the date in (1) is $2,000,000 or more; or

3. The individual fails to certify under penalty of perjury that he has met the requirements of the Code for the five preceding tax years, or fails to submit evidence of his compliance as IRS may require.

The certification is made on Form 8854.

Applying for a green card means applying for U.S. permanent residency status, which means you are treated as a U.S. resident for tax purposes as soon as you apply. A person may technically abandon their green card; however, until a person physically surrenders it, that person will be treated as a U.S. resident for tax purposes.

Leaving Canada

If you are leaving Canada, you become a deemed non-resident of Canada when your residential ties in the other country are such that, under the tax treaty between Canada and that country, you are considered to be a resident of that country.

In the year you leave Canada, you must file a Canadian tax return if you owe tax or want to receive a refund because you paid too much tax in the tax year.

For the part of the tax year that you are a resident of Canada, you must report your worldwide income (income from all sources, both inside and outside Canada) on your Canadian tax return.

For the part of the tax year that you are not a resident of Canada, you pay Canadian income tax only on your Canadian source income, if any.

You are considered to have disposed of almost all your property at its fair market value on the day you emigrate from Canada and immediately reacquire it for the same fair market value. This generally results in the realization of capital gains and losses on the disposition of certain investments (e.g. non-registered securities, etc.) and taxes paid on the net gains realized after capital losses have been subtracted from the capital gains.

After you leave Canada, if you continue to receive Canadian source income, withholding taxes will generally apply but the rate of withholding depends on the type of income being received. If you are a non-resident of Canada and you have no Canadian source income or your income has had the applicable withholding taxes taken, you are not required to file a Canadian tax return; however, you can elect to file in some situations but you would only do so if the result was less tax owing in Canada (i.e., withholding tax taken on gross rents would result in a refund for tax purposes because actual tax is only owed on the net profits after expenses are deducted from the gross income).

Chapter 8 – Going to School or Working Temporarily in the U.S.

A citizen of a foreign country who wishes to enter the United States must first obtain a visa, either a non-immigrant visa for temporary stay, or an immigrant visa for permanent residence. You must have a student visa to study in the United States. Your course of study and the type of school you plan to attend determines whether you need an F-1 visa or an M-1 visa.

Studying in the U.S.

Foreign Students in F-1 or J-1 status are usually allowed to be employed for no more than 20 hours per week during the academic year, but are allowed to work 40 hours per week during the summer and other vacations. Certain students may be allowed to work off campus with permission from USCIS (United States Citizenship and Immigration Services) or from the Designated School Official (usually the foreign student advisor).

The U.S. substantial presence test dictates who may be deemed to be a U.S.

resident taxpayer in any given year based on the number of days spent in the U.S.; however, some individuals receive special exemptions regarding the days to include in this calculation.

The definition of Exempt Individual under the substantial presence test includes students:

- Students on an F, J, M or Q visa:
  - They must wait 5 calendar years before counting 183 days;
  - The 5 calendar years need not be consecutive; and once a cumulative total of 5 calendar years is reached during the student's lifetime after 1984 he may never be an exempt individual as a student ever again during his lifetime;
  - The classification of Exempt Individual applies also to a spouse and children on F-2, J-2, M-2, or Q-3 visas.

Once the 5-year period has passed, the student could technically be considered a deemed resident for U.S. tax purposes; however, even if you are deemed a resident of the United States because you meet the substantial presence test, there are some exceptions that allow you not to be treated as a U.S. resident for income tax purposes.

To claim the exception for students on an income tax return, a student should attach Form 8843, Statement for Exempt Individuals and Individuals with a Medical Condition to his or her form 1040NR or 1040NR-EZ.

Form 8843 is filed to explain an individual's basis of claim that he or she is allowed to exclude days of presence in the United States for purposes of the substantial presence test. If the individual is not required to file a 1040NR return in a particular year, form 8843 should be filed on its own by the due date of the 1040NR return. Failure to file form 8843 could result in the individual being denied the exclusion of days and being considered a U.S. resident under the substantial presence test.

The Canada-U.S. Tax Convention exempts remuneration earned by a non-resident if it is under $10,000 and the recipient is in the other country for less than 183 days in any 12-month period commencing or ending in the fiscal year concerned, and the remuneration is not paid by, or on behalf of, a person who is a resident of the other country and is not due to a permanent establishment in that other country. The exemption is per employer or income source.

Scholarships in Canada are non-taxable no matter what the dollar amount if the individual is eligible for the tuition/education tax credits; however, in the U.S. only the amount of the scholarship that is used to pay for tuition and eligible education expenses is exempt from tax. Any remaining scholarship amounts are brought into income in the year received.

Working in the U.S. Temporarily

A non-resident individual who wishes to work in the U.S. on a temporary basis first needs a temporary U.S. work visa before this can occur. Working temporarily in the U.S. may require the individual to be physically present in the U.S. for more than 183 days which would deem him to be a U.S. resident for tax purposes; however, circumstances can still exist that give him closer ties to Canada, allowing him to be treated as a non-resident of the U.S. and a resident of Canada for tax purposes. This may be an important factor when dealing with Canadian deemed disposition rules.

Chapter 9 – U.S. Inheritances

Tax-free bequests, devises and inheritances are defined as "money and any property that passes on the death of a person by his will or under intestacy, including amounts received in settlement of a will contest." Property you receive as a gift, bequest, or inheritance is not included in your income. However, if property you receive this way later produces income such as interest, dividends, or rents, that income is taxable to you. If property is given to a trust and the income from it is paid, credited, or distributed to you, that income also is taxable to you. If the gift, bequest, or inheritance is the income from property, that income is taxable to you.

Estate Value

When a U.S. individual dies, his or her estate is either valued at the fair market value on the date of death or at the alternative valuation date. The basis or cost base of property acquired from a decedent through a bequest, inheritance, etc. is generally equal to the fair market value of the property on the date of the decedent's death if the property hasn't been sold, exchanged, or otherwise disposed of before then.

Income

Income in respect of a decedent (IRD) is income that is received by a beneficiary and includes income that the decedent had a right to receive but didn't actually receive prior to death.IRD can include insurance renewal commissions, a monthly pension paid to a deceased employee's widow, taxable distributions from an IRA or qualified employee plan, a death benefit under a deferred annuity contract, partnership income of a deceased partner and S corporation income of a deceased shareholder.

The income that was due to the decedent but not received prior to death must be included in income in the tax year when received, by:

- The decedent's estate, if it has the right to receive the income from the decedent;

- The person who, by reason of the decedent's death, acquires the right to the income whenever this right isn't acquired by the decedent's estate from the decedent; or

- The person who is bequeathed the income, if the amount is received as a distribution by the decedent's estate.

The character of the income is the same as it would have been had the decedent received the income himself, had he not passed away; in other words, a dividend is still a dividend.

Filing Requirements

If you are a U.S. person receiving a bequest or inheritance from a non-U.S. person, you may have to report this information to the IRS using form 3520 - Annual Return to Report Transactions with Foreign Trusts and Receipt of Certain Foreign Gifts.

In general, Form 3520 is due on the date that your income tax return is due, including extensions. In the case of a Form 3520 filed with respect to a U.S. decedent, Form 3520 is due on the date that Form 706, United States Estate (and Generation-Skipping Transfer) Tax Return, is due (including extensions), or would be due if the estate were required to file a return.

Covered Expatriate Rules

The rules change if the gift, bequest or inheritance is from a "covered expatriate" (i.e., an expatriate subject to the U.S. exit tax) and the one receiving the gift, bequest or inheritance is a U.S. person. Inheritance tax is imposed on the receipt of a gift or bequest from a covered expatriate by a U.S. citizen or resident. This inheritance tax contrasts with traditional U.S. estate and gift tax because this tax is imposed on the gift recipient, not the gift donor and is only applicable when a covered expatriate is making the gift or bequest.

The inheritance tax applies to indirect gifts to U.S. persons, unless they are "taxable gifts." The inheritance tax applies when a covered expatriate pays for the education or medical expenses of a U.S. person. Unlike under the regular gift tax rules that would exempt gifts paid directly to an educational institution or medical facility; under the new inheritance tax rules these gifts have no exemption.

A U.S. citizen is not required to file an estate tax return unless the gross estate is over the estate exemption amount, which is $5,340,000 for 2014. A non-resident, non-citizen normally has a minimum $60,000 estate tax exemption for bequests of U.S. situs property, but under the Canada-U.S. Tax Convention, also has access to a larger percentage of the $5.34 million estate tax exemption available to regular U.S. citizens and residents. However, these rules change for a covered expatriate. A covered expatriate, who is now a non-resident and non-citizen of the U.S., will automatically trigger tax on the gift or bequest of property to a U.S. person, regardless of where the property is located. Moreover, they will receive only a $14,000 (2014) per beneficiary exception. The IRS, in a sense, is penalizing the expatriate for giving up U.S. status.

If the covered expatriate wants to make gifts of U.S. property, he or she should make sure the gift is subjected to U.S. estate and gift tax and not the inheritance tax. Gift and estate tax is borne by the person leaving the gift (i.e., tax exclusive), whereas inheritance tax is borne by the person receiving the gift (i.e., tax inclusive), which means that if the expatriate wants to leave or give a certain amount to a certain person the tax consequences will need to be considered so the desired outcome can occur.. For example, if Jake wants to make sure that Holly receives $55,000 net of taxes, he would need to gift her money while he was alive and pay the 40% gift tax himself or leave her more money so she can pay the inheritance tax and still keep $55,000 in her pocket.

Chapter 10 – Doing Business in the U.S.

Foreign individuals wanting to enter the United States as non-immigrants are required to have Visas that can be applied for at a U.S. Consular Office. A foreign individual is referred to as an "alien" and, for U.S. tax purposes, is classified as either a resident or a non-resident alien. An alien is categorized as a non-resident alien unless he meets one of the two residency tests; the Green Card test or the substantial presence test (i.e., 183 day test).

Visas

Various business visas are available to non-residents but the type of visa required depends on the individual's qualifications and purpose for being in the U.S. Resident and non-resident aliens with U.S. source wages or salary compensation income are subject to social security tax and Medicare tax; therefore, the employer must deduct these amounts from wages.

Social Security

Canada and the U.S. have a social security totalization agreement to eliminate double taxation of social security income, occurring when a worker from one country works in the other country and is required to pay Social Security taxes to both countries on the same earnings. Because of this, social security income is taxable only in the country of residence.

Business Structures

To establish a company in the U.S., there is no requirement for the incorporating person to be a resident or citizen of the U.S.; however, a U.S. non-resident has to follow some guidelines (see chapter material for details). There are various forms of business organization that an individual can use to do business in the U.S.; they are:

- U.S. corporation (C Corp);
- Branch of a foreign corporation;
- Partnership; and
- Limited Liability Company (LLC).

An entity is generally subject to U.S. tax if the individual or corporation is a resident in the U.S. or has income that is "effectively connected with the conduct of a trade or business within the United States."

If you only plan to sell goods (perhaps through the Internet or wholesaling to U.S. companies) it may not be necessary to form a U.S. company. Other variables to take into account in making your decision to incorporate in the United States include: differences in individual state tax laws, transportation costs, tariff/trade regulations, size and scope of your company, leases, employees and much more.

Chapter 11 – I'm a Canadian But Could I be an American Too?

U.S. Citizenship

In the case of *United States v. Wong Kim Ark*, 169 U.S. 649 (1898), the Supreme Court ruled that a person becomes a citizen of the United States at the time of birth, by virtue of the first clause of the 14th Amendment, if that person:

- Is born in the United States;
- Has parents that are subjects of a foreign power, but not in any diplomatic or official capacity of that foreign power;
- Has parents that have permanent domicile and residence in the United States; or
- Has parents that are in the United States for business

Birth Abroad to Two U.S. Citizens

A child is automatically granted citizenship in the following cases:

1. Both parents were U.S. citizens at the time of the child's birth;
2. The parents are married; and
3. At least one parent lived in the United States prior to the child's birth. INA 301(c) and INA 301(a) (3) state, "and one of whom has had a residence."

The FAM (Foreign Affairs Manual) states "no amount of time specified."

Birth Abroad to One United States Citizen

A person born on or after November 14, 1986, is a U.S. citizen if all of the following are true (different rules apply if child was born out of wedlock).

1. The person's parents were married at time of birth;
2. One of the person's parents was a U.S. citizen when the person in question was born;
3. The citizen parent lived at least 5 years in the United States before the child's birth; and
4. A minimum of 2 of these 5 years in the United States were after the citizen parent's 14th birthday.

For persons born between December 24, 1952 and November 14, 1986, a person is a U.S. citizen if *all* of the following are true (except if born out of wedlock):

1. The person's parents were married at the time of birth;
2. One of the person's parents was a U.S. citizen when the person was born;
3. The citizen parent lived at least 10 years in the United States before the child's birth; and
4. A minimum of 5 of these 10 years in the United States were after the citizen parent's 14th birthday.

Filing Requirements

U.S. citizens and residents are required to file a U.S. 1040 income tax return each year and report their worldwide income on that return. The difference between U.S. residents and citizens is that citizens must file a U.S. 1040 income tax return each year no matter where they live in the world.

The IRS policy for personal income tax returns is to go back 6 years for delinquent filers; however, there is a new Voluntary Disclosure Program in place that requires 3 years of 1040 tax returns and 6 years of FBAR filings (effective September 2012). Penalties for late filing are dramatically reduced if reasonable cause exists.

Renouncing Citizenship/Long-term Residency

There are slightly different rules for renouncing one's U.S. citizenship or permanent resident status depending on the date that person renounces. Although the renouncing process is the same for everyone, the tax rules relating to an individual giving up citizenship or terminating long-term residency before June 17, 2008, are different than the tax rules applicable to an individual giving up citizenship or terminating long-term residency after June 16, 2008.

Before June 17, 2008, the alternative expatriation tax is imposed on individuals with an average income tax liability for the 5 prior years of $124,000 for tax year 2004, $127,000 for tax year 2005, $131,000 for 2006, $136,000 for 2007, or $139,000 for 2008, or a net worth of $2,000,000 on the date of expatriation. In addition, it requires individuals to certify to the IRS that they have satisfied all federal tax requirements for the 5 years prior to expatriation and requires annual information reporting for each taxable year during which an individual is subject to the alternative expatriation tax.

Expatriated individuals who have renounced prior to June 17, 2008, will be subject to U.S. tax on their worldwide income for any of the 10 years following expatriation in which they are present in the U.S. for more than 30 days, or 60 days in the case of individuals working in the U.S. for an unrelated employer.

If an individual renounces after June 17, 2008, the expatriation rules apply if:

1. The individual's average annual net income tax for the period of 5 tax years ending before the date of the loss of U.S. citizenship is greater than an inflation adjusted amount that is $155,000 for 2013 ($151,000 for 2012);

2. The individual's net worth as of the date in (1) is $2,000,000 or more; or

3. The individual: (i) fails to certify under penalty of perjury that he has met the requirements of the Code for the five preceding tax years, or (ii) fails to submit evidence of his compliance as IRS may require. The certification is made on Form 8854.

A $10,000 penalty may be imposed for failure to file Form 8854 when required. In most cases, the process for renouncing one's citizenship or permanent residency status can be broken down into 5 steps:

> Step 1: Choose a diplomatic post
>
> Step 2: Appointment / submission of documents
>
> Step 3: First visit to the diplomatic post: documents and initial interview
>
> Step 4: Second visit to the diplomatic post: final Interview and signing of documents

Step 5: After the renunciation "ceremony"

"Note that the Department of State charges $450 for 'documentation of formal renunciation of U.S. Citizenship.' In the past, there was no charge and the whole process was free, but the Department of State began imposing the $450 fee effective on all renunciations after July 13, 2010."

U.S. citizens and residents who receive gifts or bequests from covered expatriates may be subject to tax under the new inheritance tax rules, which imposes a transfer tax on U.S. persons who receive gifts or bequests on or after June 17, 2008, from such former U.S. citizens or former U.S. lawful permanent residents.

For lifetime gifts, the total value of the gift is reduced by the available annual exclusion of $14,000 (2014), and tax is then assessed at the highest applicable gift tax rate in the year of the gift (40% in 2013).

Chapter 12 – U.S. Gift & Estate Tax for a Non-Resident

Estate Tax

The Estate Tax is a tax on your right to transfer property at your death. For a U.S. person, it consists of an accounting of everything you own or have certain interests in at the date of death. The fair market value of these items is used, not necessarily what you paid for them or what their values were when you acquired them. The total of all of these items is your "gross estate." The includible property may consist of cash and securities, real estate, insurance, trusts, annuities, business interests and other assets.

Once your gross estate has been calculated, certain deductions are allowed to arrive at your taxable estate. Once the net amount is computed, the value of lifetime taxable gifts (beginning with gifts made in 1977) is added to this number and the tax is computed. The tax is then reduced by the available unified credit (i.e., the tax credit applicable to the lifetime gift and estate tax exemption amount).

A filing is required for estates with combined gross assets and prior taxable gifts exceeding $1,500,000 in 2004 - 2005; $2,000,000 in 2006 - 2008; $3,500,000 for decedents dying in 2009; and $5,000,000 or more for decedents dying in 2010 and 2011 (note: there are special rules for decedents dying in 2010); $5,120,000 in 2012; $5,250,000 in 2013; and $5,350,000 in 2014. The estate tax rate for estate values over the exemption amount is 40% for 2014 (40% in 2013).

Beginning January 1, 2011, estates of decedents survived by a spouse may elect to pass any of the decedent's unused exemption to the surviving spouse. This election is made on a timely filed estate tax return for the decedent with a surviving spouse.

Any Canadians who are not resident in the U.S. but hold any of the following assets, which are located in the U.S., could find that this portion of their estate is taxable in the U.S.:

- Real estate and tangible personal property;

- Stock in a U.S. corporation;

- Debt issued by, or enforceable against, a U.S. entity (but most corporate debt instruments issued after 1984 are exempt from U.S. estate tax); and

- Interest in a partnership, if the partnership's principal place of business is in the U.S.

The U.S. estate tax is based on the fair market value of the asset on the date of death, so there is no impact from a profit or loss because of a deemed disposition on the date of death. Non-resident aliens cannot claim foreign tax credits on a U.S. estate tax return for deemed-disposition capital gains income taxes paid to Canada.

The Canada-U.S Tax Convention allows non-resident aliens of the U.S. a pro-rated share of the U.S. estate exemption.

If the value of the U.S. assets exceeds $60,000 on the date of death, he or she must file a U.S. estate return, whereas a U.S. citizen is only required to file if their estate value is over the gross exemption amount for the applicable year (i.e., $5,340,000 for 2014).

Gift Tax

U.S. gift tax is basically U.S. estate tax while a person is still alive. According to U.S. Publication 950, "the gift tax is a tax on the transfer of property by one individual to another while receiving nothing, or less than full value, in return. The tax applies whether the donor intends the transfer to be a gift or not."

The gift tax applies to the transfer by gift of any property when the total taxable gifts are more than $5,340,000 over the donor's lifetime (lifetime gift exemption amount in 2014). You make a gift if you give property (including money), or the use of or income from property, without expecting to receive something of at least equal value in return. If you sell something at less than its full value or if you make an interest-free or reduced-interest loan, you may be making a gift.

The following gifts are not considered taxable gifts:

- Gifts, excluding gifts of future interests, that are not more than the annual exclusion for the calendar year;

- Tuition or medical expenses paid directly to an educational or medical institution for someone else;
- Gifts to your spouse (U.S. citizen/resident spouse only);
- Gifts to a political organization; and
- Gifts to charities.

Currently, you can give gifts valued up to $14,000 per person, to any number of people, and none of the gifts will be taxable; however, you can give an unlimited gift to a spouse if that spouse is a U.S. citizen/resident spouse. When the recipient spouse is a non-U.S. citizen or resident an annual exemption of $145,000 ($143,000 in 2013) is allowed.

Summary Notes

When entering into any kind of transaction or other cross-border situation, nothing is usually as simple as it seems, whether it relates to business ventures or personal transactions; however, your best defense is the knowledge of what, if anything, can arise from a tax perspective in your particular situation.

Seeking advice from an expert can save you a substantial amount of time, money and frustration. The tax considerations can complicate matters. Therefore identifying the implications of your transaction up front is always better than finding out what is wrong after the fact.

APPENDICES

Appendix 1. Definitions

Arm's Length Transactions – transactions with individuals and other entities that are unrelated to each other (i.e., all parties in the transaction are unrelated to each other).

Alternative expatriation tax – also called exit tax, it is a capital gains tax applied to an expatriate's capital gains resulting from the fair value deemed disposition of all assets immediately before the expatriate renounces his or her citizenship or long-term residency status.

Branch of a Foreign Corporation – A part of a foreign corporation and not a separate legal entity in the United States.

Contracting State – Another state or country in which you are not a resident

Controlled Foreign Corporation (CFC) – A foreign corporation in which a U.S. person owns more than 50% of the value of the company.

Controlled Group of Corporations – uslegal.com states that a "Controlled group of corporations means any group of--

(1) Parent-subsidiary controlled group. One or more chains of corporations connected through stock ownership with a common parent corporation if--

   (a) stock possessing at least 80 percent of the total combined voting power of all classes of stock entitled to vote or at least 80 percent of the total value of shares of all classes of stock of each of the corporations, except the common parent corporation, is owned (within the meaning of subsection (d)(1)) by one or more of the other corporations; and

   (b) the common parent corporation owns (within the meaning of subsection (d)(1)) stock possessing at least 80 percent of the total combined voting power of all classes of stock entitled to vote or at least 80 percent of the total value of shares of all classes of stock of at least one of the other corporations, excluding, in computing such voting power or value, stock owned directly by such other corporations.

(2) Brother-sister controlled group. Two or more corporations if 5 or fewer persons who are individuals, estates, or trusts own (within the meaning of subsection (d)(2)) stock possessing more than 50 percent of the total combined voting

power of all classes of stock entitled to vote or more than 50 percent of the total value of shares of all classes of stock of each corporation, taking into account the stock ownership of each such person only to the extent such stock ownership is identical with respect to each such corporation.

(3) Combined group. Three or more corporations each of which is a member of a group of corporations described in paragraph (1) or (2), and one of which--

    a) is a common parent corporation included in a group of corporations described in paragraph (1), and also

    (b) is included in a group of corporations described in paragraph (2).

(4) Certain insurance companies."

Delinquent Filers – Refers to anyone who has an income tax filing requirement in a particular country but fails to abide by that country's tax rules and file the necessary returns.

Dual Citizenship – Occurs when an individual has more than one citizenship (i.e., an individual can be both a citizen of Canada and a citizen of the United States).

Dual Residency – being a resident of two countries in the same year (i.e., this can occur when you move between countries part way through a year).

Earned Income – Income from business/professional or employment sources.

Gift – transfer of property from one individual to another while receiving nothing, or less than full value, in return.

Income in Respect of a Decedent – (IRD) includes income that the decedent had a right to receive but:

(1) wasn't actually or constructively received by a cash basis decedent, or

(2) wasn't accrued by an accrual basis decedent.

Inheritance tax – 40% tax that is automatically applied to a gift or bequest received by a U.S. person from a covered expatriate.

Partnership – a partnership is defined as an association of two or more persons formed to carry on a business for profit as co-owners.

Passive Income – Income from any other source besides business/professional or employment (i.e., pension, interest, dividends, gains, etc.).

PFIC – A Passive Foreign Investment Company (PFIC) is "any foreign (i.e., non-U.S.) corporation meeting either the income test or the asset test with respect to each shareholder when the test is met. PFIC status applies separately for each U.S. person owning shares, and also separately with respect to shares acquired at different times. PFIC status does not, itself, have any impact on the foreign corporation or foreign shareholders.

The *income test* is met if 75% or more of the foreign corporation's gross income is passive income, defined as foreign personal holding company income with modifications.

The *asset test* is met if 50% or more of the foreign corporation's average assets produce, or could produce passive income, or are assets (such as cash and bare land) that produce no income. The test is applied based on the foreign corporation's adjusted basis, for U.S. tax purposes, of the assets, or at the election of the particular shareholder, fair market values of the assets.

Look-thru of 25% subsidiaries: Interests in 25% or more owned foreign corporations are treated similarly to partnership interests (i.e., looked through) for the income test and the asset test.

Principal Residence – The place where a taxpayer usually lives and calls home (i.e., main home in which the taxpayer lives).

Residency – An individual's status in a place that he or she considers "home" and can be determined by many factors but it is mainly determined by the following:

- Physical presence (i.e., number of days in a country);
- Residential ties to a country; and
- A person's intentions.

Residential Ties – factors that can connect a person to one country or another for tax purposes; can include the following:

- a home;
- a spouse or common-law partner (see the definition in the General Income Tax and Benefit Guide) or dependants;
- personal property, such as a car or furniture;
- social ties;
- economic ties
- a driver's licence;
- bank accounts or credit cards; and
- health insurance with a province, territory or state.

Snowbird - a person who is ordinarily resident in Canada but spends part of the year in the U.S.

Unified Credit – The income tax equivalent of the U.S. estate and gift tax exemption (i.e., take the exemption amount and multiply it by the tax rate and you will get the approximate unified credit amount which is deducted from tax on the applicable gift or estate tax return).

U.S. C Corporation – refers to any corporation that, under United States federal income tax law, is taxed separately from its owners.

U.S. S Corporation – corporations that elect to pass corporate income, losses, deductions, and credit through to their shareholders for federal tax purposes; therefore, an S corporation is not itself subject to income tax.

U.S. Citizen – An individual who is born in the United States, a naturalized individual, or an individual born outside the United States whose parent(s) meet the specific residency/citizenship tests (see chapter for full details).

U.S. Covered Expatriate – A former U.S. citizen or long-term resident who has relinquished or renounced his or her citizenship or long-term residency status and was subject to the U.S. exit tax on expatriation.

U.S. Estate Tax – Tax applied to deceased taxpayer's estates if their taxable estate value is over the estate exemption amount.

U.S. Expatriation – The act of relinquishing or renouncing a person's U.S. citizenship or long-term residency status.

U.S. Gift Tax – Tax applied to "gifts" made by U.S. citizens and residents and gifts of U.S. citus property that are over the annual exclusion amounts or in excess of the lifetime gift exemption amount.

U.S. Grantor – A taxpayer who is the original creator of a trust and owner of trust assets.

U.S. LLC – A Limited Liability Company is a flexible form of enterprise that blends elements of partnership and corporate structures. An LLC is not a corporation; it is a legal form of company that provides limited liability to its owners in the vast majority of United States jurisdictions. LLCs do not need to be organized for profit.

U.S. LLP – A Limited Liability Partnership is a partnership in which some or all partners (depending on the jurisdiction) have limited liabilities. It therefore exhibits elements of partnerships and corporations. In an LLP, one partner is not responsible or liable for another partner's misconduct or negligence.

U.S. Situs Property – U.S. property physically located in the United States (i.e., U.S. real property, shares in U.S. corporations, etc.).

Withholding Tax – prepayment of taxes to the country making the income payment to the non-resident.

Appendix 2. Filing Deadlines

Type of Return	Filing Deadline
Canadian Individual T1 return (regular individual)	April 30th of the following year
Canadian Individual T1 return (sole proprietor)	June 15th of the following year
Canadian T1135 Foreign Income Verification Statement	April 30th of the following year
Canadian individual income tax payment deadline	April 30th of the following year
U.S. 1040 individual income tax return (citizens & long-term residents with U.S. employment income)	April 15th of the following year
U.S. 1040NR individual non-resident income tax return (with U.S. employment income)	April 15th of the following year
U.S. 1040 individual income tax return (citizen & long-term residents living outside the U.S. without U.S. employment income)	June 15th of the following year
U.S. 1040NR individual non-resident income tax return (without U.S. employment income)	June 15th of the following year
U.S. individual income tax payment deadline	April 15th of the following year
U.S. Form 3520 & 3520-A	Same as applicable U.S. 1040 deadline
U.S. Form 5471	Same as applicable U.S. 1040 deadline
U.S. Form 8938	Same as applicable U.S. 1040 deadline
U.S. Form TDF 90-22.1	June 30th of following year
U.S. form 8621	Same as applicable U.S. 1040 deadline
U.S. State returns	Every State has their own filing deadline

INDEX

KNOWLEDGE BUREAU NEWSBOOKS

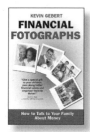

Financial Fotographs
How to Talk to Your Family About Money
By Kevin Gebert

"I wish my parents had talked to me about money." If this resonates with you, you are not alone. Millions of families have a difficult time embracing financial conversations so crucial to the ongoing health of family income and capital. This is especially true in times of transition: changes in health, career or retirement.

If you are raising a young family and challenged with how to teach principles for healthy money management, this book's for you! But if you are in your mid-thirties and wondering how to broach the subject of your role in the financial future of your ailing parents, you'll love this read, too.

Empower Your Presence
How to Build True Wealth With Your Personal Brand and Image
By Catherine Bell

"Presence" has always held a certain mystique that is empowering and attractive – it can improve relationships, transform situations, and influence success.

Whether starting out in your career, asking for venture capital, meeting potential clients, or advancing into a new social environment – including retirement – you will want to stride forward with confidence and ease. EMPOWER YOUR PRESENCE is about developing that distinctive quality that can create opportunities and propel you to new heights.

This is a must-read book for ALL generations – Gen Y (18 to 33), Gen X (34-48) and Boomers (49+) – who want to invest in their best attributes, passions, and skills and market their unique promise of value as an important part of their ongoing personal success.

Jacks on Tax
Your Do-It-Yourself Guide to Filing Taxes Online
By Evelyn Jacks

"Do-it-yourself" is back in vogue and that applies to your tax preparation as well. More Canadians are looking for ways to save money and this year, you can save time and money understanding your own return and take better control of your financial affairs too, with Canada's most trusted, best-selling tax author, Evelyn Jacks. Do you know what you don't know? When to talk to a pro? This book will help guide you, line-by-line. It's a book for everyone because its premise is simple: a more informed taxpayer, working with a collaborative professional community, will get more out of the tax system now and in the future.

Financial Books to Help You Grow and Preserve Your Wealth
At leading bookstores or order online at www.knowledgebureau.com

Knowledge Bureau®
Excellence in Financial Education

Start today with a free trial
Take Certificate Courses leading to a Diploma or Designation
www.knowledgebureau.com

Advanced Tax-Efficient
Retirement Income
Planning

Basic Bookkeeping for
Small Businesses

Cross Border
Taxation

Debt and Cash Flow
Management

Elements of Real
Wealth Management

Tax Strategies for
Financial Advisors

T1 Professional Tax
Preparation – Advanced

T1 Professional Tax
Preparation – Basic

For a free trial or confidential personal consultation:
1-866-953-4769